INVITATION
TO
BIBLICAL
CHRISTIANITY
FOR THE WELL-EDUCATED

INVITATION

TO

BIBLICAL

CHRISTIANITY

FOR THE WELL-EDUCATED

Henry J. Kohoutek

Pentland Press, Inc.
www.pentlandpressusa.com

The use of the masculine word "man" and masculine pronouns, to represent the whole mankind throughout the book, is convenient for brevity of statements and consistent with its biblical use and meaning. Such usage is also traditional, because "man" is a direct translation of the Latin scientific term *Homo* used to describe our species. Its use does not violate the general character of English as a strongly context-oriented language. When some distinctive message of the Bible or this study relates directly to either male or female—their nature, problems, role, etc.—it will be so stated clearly.

PUBLISHED BY PENTLAND PRESS, INC.
5122 Bur Oak Circle, Raleigh, North Carolina 27612
United States of America
919-782-0281

ISBN 1-57197-258-7
Library of Congress Control Number: 00-135721

Printed in the United States of America

This book is dedicated to readers who will seriously consider the presented invitation and accept God's offer of forgiveness, love, and eternal life.

"Come to me, all you who are weary and burdened, and I will give you rest. Take my yoke upon you and learn from me, for I am gentle and humble in heart, and you will find rest for your souls. For my yoke is easy and my burden is light."

—Jesus' invitation in Matt. 11:28–30

PREFACE

"Come now, let us reason together" was God's invitation to the rebellious nation of Israel conveyed by the prophet Isaiah twenty-seven centuries ago. The objective of this invitation had been to bring the Israelites to an understanding of the serious adverse consequences of their rebellion, and of the ways to get the best out of life and the best of their land. In our times, this invitation is extended to all humanity with unchanged authenticity, seriousness, and personal urgency. In addition, it has been supplemented by the best offer ever made: free, true resolution of life's problems through trust in the Lord God.

This book represents one possible approach to such reasoning. The concepts herein are hopefully attractive to intelligent and well-educated people needing or longing for solid answers to fundamental questions about the meaning of their own being, society, and the world: questions encountered at certain points in life by everybody. The book outlines all the very impressive relevant main bodies of man-created and accumulated knowledge, including their incompleteness, contradictions, and inability to provide definite answers, as detected not by the author but by qualified domain-experts. The Bible is then introduced as the most suitable source of knowledge needed for the stated purpose, with sketches of its dominant topics. The Bible provides the sought-after answers, answers that are clear, solid, and time- and situation-independent. Strict reliance on truths revealed there by the omniscient God minimizes influences of man's distorted perspective, human tradition–introduced ambiguities, and unnecessary complications due to the historical church's denominational diversity. The Bible also counsels what is to be done to achieve a secure, meaningful, peaceful, and joyful life. Foundations for answers to all critical questions are not in some well-articulated, intellectual systematization of biblical knowledge into a world improvement program, but in man's proper personal relationship with the initiator of this invitation: God, who revealed Himself in the Bible and in Jesus Christ.

Readers who have already selected their views of man and his world will benefit from the review of other perspectives. Readers placing a high value on diversity of beliefs will have their horizon enhanced by the introduction to biblical Christianity. Those who are still searching may find described biblical answers appealing and worthy of further investigation. Therefore, please subdue your intellectual prejudices and doubts and accept, in love and respect offered, God's invitation. You will not be disappointed because the ultimate gift obtainable through a positive response to His call is eternal life through Jesus Christ. May the Lord God help you to make the right decision and richly bless you afterwards.

ACKNOWLEDGEMENTS

My first and most important gratitude must go to my Lord and Savior Jesus Christ who accepted me into His family and led me through my life of faith. He gave me the opportunity to live in different cultural and political environments—twice as a refugee—to interface with a wide variety of people from illiterates to heads of advanced research institutions; to have jobs from physical work in a coal mine to managing state-of-the-art engineering work in the high-tech industry; to run the gamut from sleeping unprotected on the ground to relaxing in presidential suites of well-known hotels; and helped me to receive a reasonable academic background in theology and electrical engineering and become multilingual. I would also like to acknowledge the influence of the thousands of people I have met personally or in their literary works, too many to recognize by name, but all important.

But one person must be acknowledged openly and with many thanks: Mrs. Rebecca T. Paulson of the Loveland Language Institute, for her valuable linguistic and editorial help. Similar thanks must be extended to the professionals of Edit Ink (Cheektowaga, New York) for their valuable review of the manuscript and its constructive critique.

The Bible makes it clear that God rewards all good deeds even when done in secret (Matt. 6:4); therefore, my prayers are that He will richly reward all who positively influenced my life and work on this book.

TABLE OF CONTENTS

INTRODUCTION

Perceptive and reflective people who have spent a major part of their lives in the twentieth century, and were lucky to survive its upheavals, wonder about the irony of the obviously dichotomous development in major areas of human endeavor. The practical ways of creating and distributing wealth, improving quality of life, and achieving new levels in freedom of movement, helped Western society to reach a standard of living subject to envy by the rest of the world. On the other hand, developments in set theory, the theory of relativity, and quantum physics led to the loss of certainty in both mathematics and physics; the observed ever-increasing complexity complicates formulation of general laws in biology; intrusion of ideologies into social sciences compromised their original claim to objectivity; and rejection of metaphysics degraded philosophy into a methodological aid for dealing with contemporary political issues and confirmed the old Marxist assessment of its poverty. This confusion in conceptual and theoretical thinking is intensified by continuing streams of impressive statements by scholars, philosophers, politicians, scientists, religious leaders, and others from the best and brightest, about progress, increased knowledge of proper methods of governing the society leading toward social justice, peace, freedom, and respect for all human beings and their rights. There is no lack of ideas; quite the opposite, there are too many ideas. What is lacking is their credibility and a value system according to which they can be sorted out and ordered as per their importance to the individual's and society's well-being.

This uncertainty in the world of ideas makes even more important and valuable the well-known characteristics of intelligent people visible in their desire and search for better understanding of the principles and fundamentals behind the mysterious dynamics of the world we live in, the society we interface with, and the forces that shape our own personal lives. It is well documented that the best minds of all ages—the philosophers, scientists, and sages—made this search a lifetime occupation. Some of them were driven by the joy of learning and discovery, some by the urge for recognition, some by the lust for power associated with knowledge, while others were overpowered by fear of unknown. But they all asked fundamental questions, such as:

- Who am I? What is the nature of my identity?
- Where did I come from?
- Do I have free will?
- Am I of any value?
- Why was I born and what is the purpose or mission of my life?
- Who is the final arbiter about the success or failure in this mission?
- Must my knowledge and understanding stay within some fixed limits?
- How can I find real inner peace in this turbulent world?
- Whom can I trust and rely upon?
- What are the right criteria for life's important decisions?
- Are there any objective ethical truths?
- Why is there affliction in this world?
- Why is there something rather than nothing?
- What about death?
- What comes after death?

These and other similar questions arise from a natural concern with our value, significance, importance, and esteem as individuals. Like the previous generations, we want to love and be loved, to talk about trust, to dream about justice, and to make the world a better place in which to live. We abhor violence and other evil acts; we are afraid of sickness or injury damaging our physical and mental capacities; and, obviously, we are apprehensive about everything related to death and dying. Because of their fundamental importance in a person's life and direct impact on one's peace of mind, answers to these questions are pushing other questions, including those related to general success and happiness in some particular aspects of life, to lower levels of importance. If our lives cannot have meaning, if we are nothing more than puppets of some objective causes or forces, if our efforts and knowledge are foredoomed to failure, if we have no worth that others ought to respect, then we are devoid of value. But such a negative conclusion, regardless of being supported by some supposedly scientific theories, is in conflict with our intuition, conscience, and common sense. Even those claiming that such questions are meaningless are unintentionally admitting that they themselves addressed them and have found their own answers.

Currently, the number of visible and well-identified problems human society is facing seems to be increasing. Situational complexity is made worse by the new means of communication, namely television and worldwide information networks, allowing often uninformed opinions to contribute to this cacophony of external voices reaching people's minds. To complete the situation assessment of a contemporary member of our society, it is necessary to add to this chaos of unsorted ideas the growing set of personal problems and worries created by the confusing and sometimes dangerous physical, economic, and social environments, still even more complicated by issues of personal health, responsibility for well-being of one's own family, concerns about happiness of friends, satisfaction of demands of the job, desire to contribute to the welfare of others, and so on.

In spite of the significantly improved quality of material life and access to valuable conveniences, these developments have brought the contemporary knowledgeable man into a serious predicament reflecting the perception that in our current age there is no complete and comprehensive understanding of reality, no widely accepted vision of the future, nor a solid basis for recommendation how to properly conduct the affairs of individuals and society. We are witnessing the collapse of dreams of the Enlightenment and beginning to appreciate the validity and wisdom of observations such as that of Dante in his *Divine Comedy:*[1]

In the midway of this our mortal life,
I found me in gloomy wood, astray
Gone from the path direct.

or of Wagner in Goethe's *Faust:*[2]

How hard the scholars' means are to array
With which one works up to the source;
Before we have transversed but half the course,
We wretched devils pass away.

In reality, contemporary man's situation is not hopeless because it is not too different from the challenges people faced in the past, especially when considering their era's demands of time and resources needed for assuring subsistence, limits of available medical care, restricted mobility, elementary education, often oppressive employers and governments, no safety nets outside the family, and frequently unfavorable characteristics of the locally dominant culture. There is, therefore, wisdom in taking a look back in time, in search of life's important learning experiences.

The objective of this book is to suggest a serious and rational consideration of the best life strategy available to anyone, verified by many in both past and contemporary worlds. This strategy is based on proper personal relation and closeness to the most knowledgeable, most powerful, richest, just, and loving person known to man: the God revealed in the Bible.

The first part of this book (chapters 1 through 7) reviews the chaotic conditions of the current status of human knowledge that has been accumulated throughout history, with its careful evaluations by top experts from the reviewed domains. The nature of these evaluations is important to remember because it has become routine to assume that critiques of sciences and philosophies are coming only from uninformed parts of religious communities, not from their own midst. The second part (chapters 8 through 12) then turns to the Bible as the primary source of our knowledge about God, His plans for individuals and all mankind, and His promises and warnings. Finally, biblical answers to the posed questions are given, followed by a description of the few simple actions, necessary and sufficient, to establish the proper relationship with the Lord God who is their author. Besides answers, He also offers to everyone a stabilized and joyful spiritual life and attainment of the desired peace of mind through faith in His Son Jesus Christ.

The second part of the book contains many, sometimes repetitive, biblical quotations. They are not Christian substitutes for fashionable "one-liners" of the modern world of politics, but starting points in the search for a deeper meaning of the problem under consideration. Focus on individual quotes taken out of context carries a risk of getting caught in a simple-minded "bumper-sticker Christianity" that is easily contradicted by other biblical quotes.

Part One: Man's Confusion

Chapter 1 contains a tour across the domain of philosophy, with special attention paid to metaphysics and ideologies with their influence on the meaning of history.

Chapter 2 introduces fundamentals of exact sciences and reviews major influential theories with their inherent weaknesses and controversies.

Chapter 3 looks at the social sciences and their current deficient status caused by infiltration by ideologies.

Chapter 4 addresses the principal studies of man and presents the wide variety of opinions created by them.

Chapter 5 discusses problems of contemporary ethics and morality, and of legal systems as tools to control man's social behavior.

Chapter 6 turns attention to dominant elites through a review of related fundamental concepts of power and authority.

Chapter 7 summarizes the findings of previous chapters and concludes with acknowledgment that the man-created knowledge does not provide a solid enough basis for answering the questions posed in this Introduction and calls for turning attention to the Bible.

Part Two: God's Truth

Chapter 8 deals with the origins and contents of the Bible, as well as issues associated with its interpretation.

Chapter 9 is dedicated to the Lord God as the Creator, Judge, and Savior of the universe and man.

Chapter 10 is a tour through the created world as the stage for demonstration of God's holiness, power, and love.

Chapter 11 focuses on man and God's dealing with mankind in history in the framework of His plan.

Chapter 12 provides the answers and extends an invitation to breakthrough in an individual's life by acceptance of the biblical Gospel.

While planning the overall structure and format of this book, it was impossible not to consider as an example one of the most significant works of Czech literature, *The Labyrinth of the World and the Paradise of the Heart*[3] by John Amos Comenius (1592–1670),[4] written also for well-educated and knowledgeable readers, but those living in the chaotic times of the Thirty Years War and later suffering the consequences of the Peace of Westphalia. Violent episodes caused by rampaging armies and suppression and often forced emigration of Protestant groups out of their native lands were the upheavals of their times. Comenius's primary hero is a pilgrim investigating the variety of the world's occupations, professions, callings, endeavors, social classes, societal rulers, and estates as potential environments in his search for a peaceful and satisfying life. The final result of this pilgrimage is a sad confirmation that his world did not offer any worthy solution to his quest, and a grateful recognition that the biblical God revealed in the person of Jesus Christ and in the Bible is the only source of real peace, joy, and wisdom.

This book is an invitation to a similar search which, after assessing the trustworthiness and credibility of available human knowledge-based resources, will bring the reader to the situation demanding serious and open-minded consideration of biblical Christianity as the best solution, the best offer still available. An intelligent reader searching for assured certainties to guide his or her life will ask questions about the evidence supporting the presented benefits of biblical Christianity, yet the truth and power of gifts offered by God are not based on statements or arguments presented in this book, nor in any theological systems, or religious organization or ritual. It is found only in a respectful and loving personal relationship with the living Jesus Christ, as witnessed by the Bible when read and studied under the guidance of the Holy Spirit, and as reflected in the lives of true believers. The key players are the Lord God granting His invitation and you, the reader, facing the decision with its consequences. The author's role is secondary. In the first seven chapters he minimizes the temptation to editorialize and lets the voice of given knowledge-domain experts be loud and clear. In the second part of the book comes a serious promotion and selling of the benefits of biblical Christianity to help with the acceptance of God's invitation.

What should then be the final results of the eventual acceptance of the suggested strategy of life in closeness to God? First and most important is God's gift of forgiveness and spiritual birth into His own family that will turn this book's secondhand information into certainty of conscious personal fellowship with Jesus Christ. The second result is a better and growing understanding of the purpose and meaning of life. The third outcome is humble acceptance of the fact of man's limited capability to comprehend and influence the complete dynamics of the natural world and human society.[5] All that will lead to a new life, a life worth living.

PART ONE:

MAN'S CONFUSION

For with much wisdom comes much sorrow; the more knowledge, the more grief.

Eccl. 1:18

PHILOSOPHY

1

Observations of repetitive events and processes in nature, society, and the lives of individuals stimulate intuitive belief in some general laws or rules behind them. This belief is justified by discovery of the cause-effect relationship between events originally assumed as simply sequential. From such a recognition it takes only a small step to consider that there may be some more general laws and causes, even some ultimate and primary ones. Curiosity about such ultimates, and search for knowledge about them, are the starting points of philosophy—the love of wisdom—and the exercise of intelligence in attempts to satisfy the desire to find out. Understanding and application of ultimates has been considered the best assurance of a righteous and satisfying life. This focus on ultimates, or on most general principles and causes of things and events, separates philosophy from other bodies of knowledge interested more in their description or control.[1] Some philosophers, namely logical positivists and their successors, have expended major effort to show that this whole project is a mistaken one.

Another distinction used to support philosophy's claim to a special status has been based on assumption about unique particularities of philosophical methods, especially those of argumentation and dialectics. But this position is weak because methods actually used by philosophers overlap with those used for problem solving in other disciplines.

Throughout the history of philosophy the final aims of it were frequently narrowed, so we can encounter philosophy as the theory of value, as the science of man, as the science of sciences, as speculative cosmogony, as the theory of language, as the theory of critical discussion, and so on. This indicates there is room for a high diversity of topics of investigation[2] but also enormous difficulty in securing agreement among philosophers. All philosophies, both past and present, have been challenged and contradicted.

The questions crucial in our search are, for example, how to assess the instructiveness of the errors made and how to avoid repeating the mistakes of our predecessors. Does the variety of schools of thought that have emerged over time contain any sign of progress or ascent? Are the goals and beliefs associated with philosophy reasonable and achievable? Let us try to find out what the philosophers themselves concluded.

METAPHYSICS

The philosophical discipline dedicated to the investigation of the world and what really exists, which applies means of rational argument instead of direct intuition, is called metaphysics.[3] One frequently used definition comes from A. N. Whitehead:[4] *Metaphysics* is the endeavor to frame a coherent, logical, necessary system of general ideas in terms of which every element of our experience can be interpreted.

The primary section of metaphysics is ontology, which confirms or denies the existence of three major classes of things: concrete occupants of space and time, minds and their states, and abstract entities, i.e., universals.

Almost everything in metaphysics is controversial, as is apparent in the wide variety of different schools of metaphysical thought. Some of the schools carry the name of their primary originators (e.g., Platonism, Aristotelianism, Thomism, Hegelianism, Marxism, etc.), while others are identified by the character of their dominant ideas or principles. Examples of such schools follow.[5]

The life of mankind is a continuum in time, as is the history of philosophy. However, the limits and desires of the human mind call for some subdivisions of historical time in spite of all known dangers of arbitrariness and related irrational biases. For the purposes of our inquiry, the simplest division of the documented schools into two categories is adequate: views proposed before our generation that may be called "traditional views," and those that have emerged during our lifetime, the "contemporary views." Hopefully, this distinction will avoid conjecture about assigning preferences to any one of the examples.

Traditional Views

Transcendentalism holds that what really exists lies beyond the reach of ordinary experience. Emanuel Kant and the logical positivists both denied the legitimacy of this approach.

Immanentism takes reality as consisting only of the objects of experiences susceptible to empirical verification.

Monism is a group of views stressing unity of reality, unity of things in time (freedom from change), in space (indivisibility), or in quality (undifferentiatedness). To many people, a monistic theory is always the most attractive because it strives for unity in a world description for the sake of ease of comprehension and simplicity, responding to one of the perennial urges in human thought.

Dualism is a position pointing to some radical and irreducible differences between two realms of being, e.g., natural and supernatural, temporal and eternal, material and mental, particular and universal.

Pluralism assumes there are more than two kinds of identifiable existence seen, for example, in multiplicity of arrangements of political power, cultures, ethnic groups, social classes, habits, rituals, traditions, etc.

Idealism is the philosophical theory that insists that the only things that really exist are minds or mental states or both. Subjective idealism holds that the world consists of a multiplicity of separate minds and ideas possessed by them. Objective idealism holds that there is only one true mind (spirit) of which finite minds are dependent fragments. Plato's philosophy claiming only ideas as objects of knowledge represents a third type of idealism.

Materialism is a family of doctrines that gives the primary position in the nature of the world to matter, while the mind's position is secondary or, in the case of extreme materialism, even none at all. Materialists have traditionally been determinists claiming a cause for every event. The long-lasting appeal of materialism stems from its alliance with natural sciences, which have contributed most to understanding of the world we live in. The most critical unresolved problems facing contemporary materialism require providing an account of the mind and answering an argument of the need for both physical and mental categories to achieve a full understanding of human knowledge.

Empiricism is based on the thesis that all human knowledge derives ultimately from sensory experience. The only propositions we can know a priori are uninformative tautologies.

Rationalism stresses the role of reason in the acquisition of knowledge. It claims that certain important and substantive truths about reality, about the nature of the universe and the human mind, can be gained directly by the light of reason, independently of experience.

Pragmatism is a version of empiricism that interprets the meaning and justification of our beliefs in terms of their practical value, impact, or content. Therefore, pragmatism perceives knowledge as an instrument for action rather than an object of disinterested contemplation. Now, pragmatism connotes theorizing and conceptualization of experience.

Process philosophy rejected the concept of nature as having timeless, unchanging substance and behaving as a machine, a concept that originated with Galileo and Newton. It perceives all reality as permeated by process, stresses "becoming" over "being," and takes seriously the notions of time and development. It also assumes the outcome of this process as unknown (no guarantee that good will triumph), sees everything as a cosmic experiment, and accepts radical openness of the future with associated unknowns as the source of unrest in the world.

Phenomenalism is a theory that material objects are not directly perceived, that they are "permanent possibilities of sensations" at best, and illusions only at worst. The key argument for this view rests with the indubitable fact that our perceptions are fallible.

Existentialism is a body of philosophical doctrine that emphasizes the paradoxical contrast between the existence of humans, endowed with will and consciousness, and that of natural objects. It came to existence as a revolt against Hegelian romantic optimism, and as a reaction to the worship of science stimulated by liberal utopian optimism, tendencies that treat individuals as cases or instances, but never as individual humans. Real people are overwhelmed by the recognition of their insignificance, as well as of the natural world and all human values, up to the point of nausea. Some of the key themes addressed are the individual and systems, the nature and significance of choice, the nature of communication, and the role of extreme experiences.

Structuralism is founded on two fundamental concepts, namely "structure" and "system," and views structures as structures of systems. But systems function because they have the structure to do so; therefore, systems' structure seems to be more fundamental characteristics to be studied. Structuralism displays an extraordinary range of opinions of its practitioners, as well as its critics. It has been hailed as a fundamental and irreversible development in the pattern of human thought, and also dismissed as a mere fashion. It has been accused of borrowing its fundamental concept of "structure" from Marx and Engels. Its preoccupations are three sociophilosophical problems: the place of the individual in the collective, the relationship between the collective and the natural world, and the role of the ethnographer with respect to two cultures, the one he studies and his own. Linguistics is the master discipline of structuralism, closely followed by anthropology. Clear descriptions of its logic and metaphysics have not been developed yet.

Logical positivism asserts that metaphysics is essentially meaningless because it consists of propositions that are neither verifiable by empirical observations nor demonstrable as analytic.

Linguistic philosophy, the historical successor of logical positivism, is also hostile to metaphysics, but for a different reason. It views metaphysical propositions as incompatible with the commonsense view of the world. It is generally also suspicious of formal logic because it does not describe the actual ways people think or express their reasoning.

The last two examples, logical positivism and linguistic philosophy, represent contemporary sharp rebukes of metaphysics and, by that, of traditional philosophy in general. Currently, metaphysics is virtually dead. The only signs of some continuing interest are misguided efforts of scientists speculating about their mathematical models extended over total space of the universe and eons of time, and some trends in anthropology.[6] Modern philosophy is profoundly antimetaphysical in spirit, accepting that there may be no deep structure, no ultimates, no primary causes behind the observable reality.

Contemporary Views

This crisis of metaphysics is only one aspect of the much broader crisis in philosophy, which is visible in doubts about what its proper subject matter is. Philosophy has been found unable to compete with either sciences, humanities, or art, even though it may bring to all of them some unique insights. The common belief that it is the business of philosophers to tell people how they ought to live has been found fallacious as well. If a single phrase captures the modern perception of the role of philosophy, the best candidate may be "the study of evidence," elucidating the content of our beliefs and the reasons for holding them.[7]

All the projects associated with the descriptor "modernity" were originally formulated in the eighteenth century by the philosophers of the Enlightenment and reflected their hope in development of unquestionably objective science, universally accepted standards of morality and law, and autonomous art. They hoped that sciences and art would promote not only the control of natural forces, but also understanding of the world and of the self, moral progress, the justice of institutions, and even happiness of human beings. What actually happened is in marked contrast to those hopes and ideals. All the domains assumed to bring this progress have been institutionalized, intellectualized, and separated from the actual world and life. Unfortunately, because modernism's principle of unlimited self-realization—associated with hedonism, lack of obedience, and narcissism—became a part of the general culture, it has infected the values of everyday life and resulted in what some label as "consumer society" or "society of the spectacle." Such arguments claim that the Enlightenment project failed, including Marxism, its last variant, which is now outmoded and assumed inapplicable to new social developments.[8]

Postmodernism, a term originated among artists in the 1960s, came to its full expression in the 1970s by attacking myths legitimizing the modern age: the progressive liberation of humanity through science and the idea that philosophy can restore unity of learning and develop universally valid knowledge for humanity. Postmodern theory became identified with the critique of universal knowledge and foundationalism. It displays a deep suspicion of any form of universal philosophy, such as views associated with names like Hegel or Marx, because no one can grasp what is going on in society as a whole. In recent years, this critique resulted in "textualization" of everything. History, philosophy, sociology, and other disciplines are perceived as optional styles of writing or discourse, actually just language games. Knowledge is ceasing to be an end in itself; it is and will be more and more produced in order to be sold.

Post-structuralism is also antagonistic to the concept of totality and in its stead emphasizes fragmentation, the local, the heterogeneous, the diverse, the subjective, the spontaneous, and the contingent; i.e., it tends toward relativism. It challenges the idea that knowledge grows or progresses in any more than quantitative sense. It abandoned belief in social historical progress and despises progress-related pressures toward any kind of conformity. Post-structuralism carries a mark of strong influence by the philosophy of Nietzsche with its denunciation of the "illusion of truth" and hostility toward egalitarianism.

Deconstruction, at its outset, was an attempt to give an account to certain constitutive contradictions in philosophical systems and arguments by pointing to their infrastructure. Its procedures examine the minute particulars of the text, such as undecidable moments, nearly imperceptible displacements, and subtle ambiguities. The justification of such an approach is found in erroneous human metaphysical desires to make the end coincide with the means, to make definitions coincide with the defined, to balance every equation, to close the circle, and so on. It became one of the main features of post-structuralist theory of the self. In place of a unified and stable being or consciousness it introduced a multifaceted and disintegrating play of selves. According to deconstructionists there is nothing other than interpretation. Under the influence of Jacques Derrida this attempt seems to have deteriorated into a license for arbitrary free word play in flagrant disregard of all established rules of argumentation, traditional requirements of thought, and ethical standards binding upon the interpretative community.[9]

The most recent developments are weakening the role of philosophy even further.[10] The distinctive feature of the contemporary postmodern mind, as evidenced by frontier thinking in philosophy, is its acceptance of reality as unordered in any objective way that man's mind can discern. Contemporary postmodernism accepted the logical positivists' dictum that all philosophical problems are pseudoproblems, illusions stemming from improper use of language and logic. We have reached the post-philosophical age. One of the human intellect's major achievements, originally considered most valuable and the basis for assuring satisfying and well-directed life, has delivered so many opposing opinions that it lost its credibility.

But the admitted failure of philosophy did not invalidate the realism and importance of the initially posed questions. Common sense confirms that it is impossible to live a happy life in a world that is fragmented, relativized, without truth, without meaning, etc. So the search for the deep understanding of man's own existence must continue by investigation of other potential sources.

IDEOLOGIES

The Renaissance—the cultural movement originating in Italy in the middle of the fourteenth century and subsequently spreading throughout the whole of Europe, with its "discovery" of man and world, reoccurrence of old manuscripts combined with the invention of printing, and spectacular scientific developments—provided rich material for philosophical reflection. Critiques of the existing social arrangements, attempts to revive in Europe Rome's former greatness, together with optimism of the early humanism, provided a fertile intellectual environment for creation of new visions of man's future: the early utopias, seeds of future ideologies.[11] The importance of utopias rests with their images of potentially new social realities, records of human aspirations, and thoughts about human nature. Their often unrecognized fundamental weakness is in the conviction that the whole truth about social harmony is known, can be imparted, and should be acted upon.

The task of action started to dominate the culture of Western society in the historical periods labeled "Enlightenment" and "Age of Reason." Thinkers and actors around the time of the French Revolution started to replace philosophical speculations trying to *explain* the world by ideological prescriptions how to *change* it. In a theoretical sense, ideologies may be viewed as particular instances of applied political philosophy. The worldview represented by the majority of ideologies revolves around three principal ideas: reason, nature, and progress. A review and comparison of the best-known views of the world developed in that period is helpful at this point.

Humanism is a term of extremely varying content and significance that has been generally used to indicate a view more concerned with man than anything else, such as nature or God. It recognizes the value or dignity of man and makes him the measure of all things. It defines man's nature, with its limits and interests, as the primary theme of studies and actions. It exalts man's freedom as exercised in nature and society, and recognizes the place of pleasure in the moral life. Originally, humanism did not have antireligious nor anti-Christian character, but actually displayed a high level of tolerance toward diverse beliefs.

Liberalism is a political philosophy principally associated with the idea of freedom of the individual, of political institutions, religion, enterprise, and economic trade. It comes in many variations:

- English liberalism focuses on the individual's freedom from the constraints of the state. It is based on three principles: life, liberty, and property. It goes hand-in-hand with the classical economic doctrine of *laissez-faire,* and accepts freeing man from misery and ignorance as its aim.

- French liberalism is clearly a left-wing doctrine that mutated into two variants. The first stresses minimal state, individualism, and *laissez-faire;* the second sees freedom as ruling oneself through the medium of a state that one has made one's own.

- German liberalism perceived freedom as provision of conditions for the realization of unification of Germany. Originally, German liberals thought in terms of collective rather than individual rights, and saw true freedom in obedience to the morally perfected state. Since the end of World War II in Germany, there has been a visible shift toward the English version of liberalism.

- American liberalism is widely confused and covers a highly variable set of opinions. In the nineteenth century many associated the label "liberal" with a visionary crank. In the early part of the twentieth century, especially during the Great Depression, "liberal" was a politically tactical cover for the unpopular "socialist,"[12] but actually meant a belief in economic planning by the state, welfare, and state controls of financial institutions. In the mind of the American public, the word "liberal" is still associated with left-wing ideologies simply because not only socialists, but communists and communist sympathizers have not ceased to assume the title "liberal" rather than openly express their ideological commitments and political goals. Post-1960s liberalism seems to represent a movement committed to expansion of the welfare state, and inclines toward higher taxes, bigger government, and expanding the doctrine of individual liberation into the domain of sexual morality,[13] but is also a movement continually redefining its mission around emerging political issues of the day.[14]

Conservatism, in general terms, refers both to attachment to the customs and institutions that proved effective in the past and to the doctrines that explain and defend such an attachment. It denotes enmity to radical social changes, especially those forced upon the society by the state and justified by an appeal to abstract rights or some utopian goals. It stands on its own without connection to any religious belief. No attitude has been more common in human history because it is based on both reason and instinct and, in this modern era, is justified by the overall failure of all instituted revolutionary changes. In particular, conservatism believes that human affairs are extremely complicated and behavioral details of both individual and society unpredictable.[15] Political judgments, therefore, cannot be based on deductive application of some metaphysical or ideological principles.[16] Governments should recognize their limitations, and their role should be restrained by the nature of their instruments to simple and direct maintenance of peace and order. According to conservatism, traditions should be regarded as a beneficial heritage of skills on which new achievements must be founded, and also understood as adaptable. Therefore, conservatism is the repository of a number of verified political truths and beneficial preferences, and is self-limiting because it leads to skepticism. The instant when any particular institution, idea, or tradition is perceived as absolutely good, the related thinking and reasoning moves outside the field of the tradition of conservative thought because it does not reflect any past political or social experience.

Nationalism is a state of mind in which the supreme loyalty of the individual is due to the nation-state. It implies the identification of the state or nation with the people according to ethnographic principles, the legal concept of nationality, and self-determination. Nationalism is a relatively modern movement with its first full manifestation in the Puritan revolution of seventeenth-century England. In more recent times, many new nations, all sharing the same pride in achieved independence, have faced major difficulties being inadequately prepared for self-rule.

Totalitarianism is the word describing political systems dominated by a single party and ideology in which all political, economic, and social activities (including ordinary flow of information and education) are absorbed and subsumed, and all dissidence suppressed. This approach implies the complete control by the state of all areas of life and the unlimited power of an artificial state ideology over minds. Note, however, that competition among internal separate centers of power and bureaucratic hierarchies, parallel to the party but essential to the function of the state, preserve an element of pluralism.

Fascism is the term identifying political movements characterized by multidimensional traits of their ideology as hypernationalist, often pan-nationalist, antiparliamentary, antiliberal, anti-Communist, and populist, and, therefore, antiproletarian, partly anticapitalist and antibourgeois, and anticlerical, with the aim of national social integration through a single party. It has a distinctive style of rhetoric and combines violent actions with electoral participation to gain power and reach its totalitarian goals. Its appeal is based on emotions, myth, idealism, national solidarity, rejection of institutionalization of modern society, and offers to solve the obvious problems and injustices of the capitalist system.[17] Actions are usually aimed at youth, students, the unemployed, and all those feeling disadvantaged by social changes or political and economic crises. The leadership constitutes mostly self-appointed elite, but to be effective it needs strong mass support. Fascism can be also perceived as a political practice intended by its leaders to unite, purify, and energize nations or ethnic groups that have been under strain by internal divisions, by the fear of decadence, or by confusion caused by changes.[18]

Nazism, short for the pre-World War II German version of national socialism, had many traits common with fascism, but higher emphasis on subordination of the individual to the state, inequality of men and races, the right of the strong to rule the weak, blind obedience to the appointed leaders, and military virtues. It despised pacifism, humanitarianism, and charity, glorified conquest and hatred, and aimed at the transformation of the whole nation into an armed camp perpetually ready for war. Despite its hostility toward communism, it adopted many of its practices, including imitation of its highly centralized party organization and debased methods of the judicial process with its infamous detention, concentration, and labor camps.[19]

Socialism is a generic word for dozens of views originating with the French revolutionary thinkers, namely Voltaire, Rousseau, and the Encyclopedists. Most of the views include a belief that the existing system of society and its institutions should be condemned as unjust and morally unsound, that a different form of society, with institutions based on moral values, and with goals such as improvement of mankind, absolute equality of monetary incomes, equality of rights, etc., can be created. Most frequently stated is the dictum "From each according to his ability, to each according to his needs." Deep differences arose early in views about which kind of institutions would be best suited for a world devoted to justice, especially to "social justice."

Communism is a set of ideas with communal ownership of all property as a point of reference. It is a timeless, abstractly moral, and utopian wish to regulate individual consumption so that it is everywhere equal, and to separate morally dangerous economic activities from the ethical state. Modern communism is the Marxist version of socialism, which focuses on common ownership of means of production and distribution of goods, with the goal of forming a classless society that should emerge after the transitional period of the dictatorship of the proletariat. Actual communist movements and governments are using distinctive methods to achieve their goals—methods such as armed revolution, collectivization of agriculture and services, nationalization of industrial enterprises and banks, cultural revolution, forced labor, show trials, secret police, etc.

Pacifism is the belief and subsequent behavior of those who judge war and the employment of organized armed forces unjustifiable. Pacifists advocate settlement of disputes by arbitration and reduction of armaments, and try to influence national policies in favor of even unilateral renunciation of war.

Feminism denotes advocacy of the rights and equality of women in social, political, and economic spheres, combined with a commitment to some fundamental changes in woman's role in family and society. Feminism, like postmodernism, has sought to develop a new framework of social criticism outside the traditional philosophical basis. By the search for the one key factor that would explain sexism cross-culturally, feminists missed the importance of cultural diversity and falsely generalized thoughts of their own generation, culture, society, class, and, obviously, gender. In recent times, feminism slipped into presentation of women as possessing some unique qualities and abilities forming the basis for related special privileges. Interesting also are new charges of anti-analytic feminists that traditional epistemology, reasoning, and appeals to objectivity are inherently male-biased,[20] and apparent schisms in feminist ideology.[21]

Anti-Semitism is a unique ideology characterized by the curious fact that many of its adherents are doing everything possible to appear disassociated with it. The simple fact of feeling no sympathy for Jews, or being overly sensitive to their faults and blind to their virtues, is not necessarily anti-Semitism. Anti-Semitism is the unqualified fear, scorn, and hatred of Jewish people and a desire to subject them to discriminative measures. It has many forms and degrees, such as contemptuous nationalistic bias, aristocratic prejudice, plain desire to get rid of successful competitors, harmful propaganda, demented desire for a complete extermination of Jews, etc. But no one form is completely innocent. They all carry a seed—sometimes hidden, more or less inert or active—that in the twentieth century burst into homicidal phobia.

Why this persistent continuity of anti-Semitism from ancient and agricultural Egypt to the grandeur of militaristic Rome, on to contemporary liberal democracies? Hundreds of books, tracts, doctoral theses, colloquia, workshops, conferences, seminar, sermons, etc., have attributed anti-Semitism to capitalism, socialism, communism, political opportunism, xenophobia, father-hatred, lack of education, poverty, Jews being too aggressive, Jews being too passive, you name it. Law-enforcement officials, sociologists, psychologists, and educators study data on culprits of anti-Semitic vandalism with no clear answer either.[22] This confusion is escalated by documented anti-Semitism in Nazi Germany, czarist and communist Russia, Argentina, parts of the U.S. black community, the medieval Christian church,[23] Arabic nations, the contemporary Asian press, as well as by the variety of Jewish responses to it, such as, religious conversions, adaptations to local cultures, assimilation, fighting back, self-hatred and self-ghettoization, alliance with their persecutors, atheists, radicals, popes, presidents, civil liberty organizations, and so on. In-depth studies, e.g., by Jean-Paul Sartre,[24] point out realistically that anti-Semitism is not a Jewish problem but "our" problem, and to the fact that Jews have many powerful enemies but only one weak friend, the democrat, a friend who automatically makes concessions to the anti-Semite in the name of freedom of opinion and expression, equal rights, social integration, etc., and tries to change[25] the Jew into a generic abstract man-citizen. Sartre's own proposed solution—socialist revolution—might have been taken seriously by a few in the late 1940s or 1950s, but today it seems to have only entertaining value. This inability to explain and deal with such an obvious, long-standing, and well-documented social phenomenon points again to the fundamental weakness of all humanistic philosophies.

Neoliberalism is for liberals who still want to find some harmony in the remains of the collapse of the Enlightenment project and in the chaos of modern ideologies, and who started to assess the consequences of their own practices and institutions, as per the original goal of general welfare. Many proposals for redefinition of liberalism have emerged out of attempts for such assessment. Some emphasize the utility of wealth creation in opposition to the past emphasis on its redistribution; some try to stop the plague of lawyers and accountants in the government (i.e., bureaucrats) whose well-being is strictly linked to the redistribution of wealth created by others; some advocate a variety of industrial policies to save the favored collectivism (such as flexible manufacturing or teamwork); some are embracing globalism and dream about a borderless world, carefully avoiding the term "internationalism" strongly associated with the failed communism; and some are returning back to the age of unionism through demands for higher minimum wage, maternity leave, child-care centers, and so on. Many see this development as a reflection of short-term election goals–driven tactics, others of a turn toward utilitarianism or recasting of the liberal ideology closer to social engineering. It is also possible that neoliberalism may be just an instinct to preserve institutions favorable to their ideology, namely public schools, government regulatory agencies, welfare administration (Social Security, Medicare), and legislation such as affirmative action. But the most pernicious byproduct of such redefinitions is that it breeds in neoliberals' own ranks dissent, skepticism, and fear that rampant pace of redefinition is a sign of a dying movement.

Neoconservatism, especially as formulated by post-structuralists, takes away the dynamics upon which liberal social thought has traditionally relied. By making no distinction among large-scale social theories, neoconservatism perceives all of them as dogmatic. They offer no theoretical or conceptual argument to move into one social direction rather than the another. They see rationality as a limiting framework and mobilize the fight against what they call the imperialism of reason. Their critics say that they are afraid of being caught in any of the "metanarratives," i.e., ideologies that cannot be identified as belonging to the culture of their own generation.

It is clear that this inventory of ideologies being proposed by politicians and associated intellectual elites is not complete. The list would explode in size if attempts would be made to include their variants and mixtures. But even this short review of examples cannot hide the many contradictory conclusions reached from the principal trio of ideas: reason, nature, and progress. Besides these conceptual contradictions, a new level of confusion has been added by opportunistic changes of the political programs' contents while keeping the historical image of the ideology's name. A good simplified example may be seen in the U.S. politics of the 1990s. Conservatives, in contradiction to the meaning of the label, proposed and worked for radical changes in education, legal system, taxation, government regulations, welfare system, labor-union and minority-based preferences. On the other hand, liberals, in spite of presenting themselves as an activist group driving societal changes, have been seen fighting to maintain the status quo and opposing all proposed changes.

Looking back on the examples, we can see that the most dangerous and obviously wrong are those ideologies that envisage an end point to history because they seem to be able to convince people that these future ends justify present means and, by that, rationalize inhumanity and suffering. Such ideologies are signs of a deeply rooted subconscious lust for power. The twentieth century witnessed ideologies turned into quasireligions,[26] and many brutal and dogmatic impositions of them on major parts of the world. Their subsequent failures were accompanied by loss of many lives, enormous human suffering, and wide destruction of accumulated wealth. All this documents again the errors of arbitrary presuppositions and limits of human understanding and speculative reasoning. The tragedy is also in the high levels of deceit humanity is exposed to, tragedy caused by people unwilling to think for themselves, and the gullibility of masses still captive to utopian dreams and attractive, but impossible to implement, ideas.[27] In modern ideology-based politics, Machiavelli had metamorphosed from the *bête noire,* a person of despite, in moral philosophy to a covert teacher and hero of many contemporary politicians.

From the perspective of our inquiry, it is necessary to admit that, in contrast to philosophy, a few ideologies, especially the extreme ones with quasireligious character, were able to provide meaning and direction in the lives of many, and, for some, the ultimate meaning as reflected in their willingness to die for their convictions. But because we have seen martyrs on all, often opposite, sides of the ideological and political struggle, and also ideologies failing to achieve their goals, we know that the questions of truth vs. deception, hate vs. tolerance, or violence vs. peaceful coexistence, have not actually been resolved.

THE MEANING OF HISTORY

In politics, ideologies were and still are used to justify and legitimize the powers that be, both persons and institutions, and their goals with related actions. Looking back in time, especially in the last few centuries, ideologies served also as tools suitable to interpret sequences of historical events to demonstrate either the present's continuity with them, or departure from the observed and documented trends, as politically expedient. In this way ideologies provide a variety of answers to the psychological need to recognize some patterns in our generally mysterious social universe, a need as old as the human race. In prehistoric times, because people did not have a real history besides simple tribal memories, myths created by poets and sages were the only available interpretations. After cities and nations formed, conditions developed for actual historical narratives.

The earliest explanations were based on analogies with the seasons of nature or with the movement of celestial objects and, therefore, assumed a cyclical character of human history as well. The world has been perceived as an eternal order in which the appearance of some events as novel had no essential importance. Even in the political sphere, cyclicity of the dominant phases has been assumed: Monarchy, the original order, degenerated into dictatorship, which resulted in a revolt of the powerful and institution of aristocracy; aristocracy, by slipping into corrupt oligarchy, causes people to revolt and to establish democracy which, later, under the influence of demagogues turns into anarchy and creates an opportunity for a dictator to emerge and to start a new cycle.[28] This cycle assumed no belief in any preferred form of government.

Later accumulation of factual historical information and expansion of speculative thinking gave philosophers an opportunity to attempt more systematic interpretations applicable to dealing with contemporary problems; to conceptualize historical trends allowing philosophers to anticipate major future events; and to uncover the meaning of historical events pointing to the nature of man, society, cultures, civilization, and history itself. The ideological underpinning of those interpretations is clearly visible from the earliest times, for example, in the death penalty imposed on Socrates whose analyses were unwelcome by the state authorities.

For the purposes of illustration of widely accepted, but substantially different, philosophies of history, three examples—idealistic, materialistic, and historicistic, all stemming from the German cultural environment of the nineteenth century—are presented in association with the names of their best-known proponents. These examples are followed by more contemporary perspectives that, in some way, are parallel to the already described developments in philosophy.

Georg Wilhelm Friedrich Hegel (1770–1831) based all his views of the world on the philosophy of history.[29] His extraordinary vision was that history documents the march of freedom throughout the world:[30]

• In the Orient, only one was free.
• The Greeks and Romans provided freedom for some.
• In the Germanic world,[31] all were, or soon would be, free.

This march of freedom is interpreted as what the "world spirit" wants. This world spirit is a real, concrete, objective force, yet particularized as spirits of specific nations, and personified by particular individuals as it seeks to realize itself. For Hegel, freedom consists of a conscious recognition and acceptance of the good, which systems of values, especially the Christian system, contain. His view goes far beyond the plain freedom of will "that one can do what one wants," an opinion that frequently reflects lack of moral education. As to the individual, Hegel believed that everyone is a child of his time and, therefore, philosophies are time-compressed and comprehended thoughts. This outlook, his belief in freedom, and his appreciation of the contingent in history are the main reasons that he refused to talk about the future.

Karl Marx (1818–1883) and *Friedrich Engels* (1820–1895), fathers of dialectical materialism, believed that the understanding of history starts with understanding the principle of production.[32] Production and exchange of products are the basis for all social orders. In every society that has appeared in history, the ways of distribution and exchange of its products determined that society's division into states and classes. According to this conception, the ultimate causes of all social and political changes are to be sought not in the minds of men or their insights into eternal truth and justice, but in the changes of the mode of production and exchange. They are to be sought not in philosophy but in the economics of the epoch under study. Karl Marx transformed these philosophical statements into *The Communist Manifesto*[33] to indicate that these concepts mean that a communist revolution was not only desirable but demonstrably inevitable. The manifesto, a document written by an angry genius,[34] was therefore presented as a political program for the future.

Karl Kautsky (1854–1938) emerged in the 1920s as the most authoritative theoretician, interpreter, and popularizer of Marxism. His major contribution to the philosophy of history came with his book, *The Materialist Conception of History*,[35] written in Vienna, but published originally in Berlin in 1929. Even though this scholarly book addresses in considerable detail all the key issues, such as nature and society, the state and the development of mankind, it immediately triggers a fundamental question: "Is it of any interest today?" The key materialistic proposition, reducing ideas to mere passive accompaniments of economic activity, is, obviously, no longer acceptable.

Oswald Spengler (1880–1936) achieved both public and professional recognition through his book, *The Decline of the West*.[36] He claimed the ability to discern the outline of civilization's life cycle through which, as he believed, all civilizations must pass. The idea of civilization blossoming and decaying like a natural organism made true rejuvenation impossible. Cultures go through the prescribed stages (which Spengler called spring, summer, autumn, and winter) and fade away. World history is a sum of such cultures. In the case of Western European civilization, his status assessment resulted in extreme pessimism. His genuine historic insight, or the merit of his work, cannot be denied, even though some of his prophecies have not been fulfilled. For example, Western Europe lost its world hegemony, as he predicted, but optimism about Russia's future, or the expected flow of innovative political and economic ideas from England, did not materialize. Spengler was obsessed by politics, but political developments in the Europe of his time, unfortunately, led to frustration of all his hopes.

Arnold J. Toynbee (1889–1975),[37] probably the best-known representative of the contemporary approach to universal history, wrote his studies from the viewpoint of a participant, not as an impartial spectator. For Toynbee, history consists of innumerable angles of vision and reality. He rejected proposed biological analogies, e.g., of Oswald Spengler, but he accepted the existence of patterns and trends in history, such as "challenge and response" and "growth and disintegration." Toynbee placed emphasis on inwardly generated responses. Success or failure of civilized societies (he identified thirty-four of them)[38] depends on the severity of challenge, assessed relative to the capabilities and power of those responding. Therefore, he assigned importance to the geographical location of any given civilization, and even race,[39] for both adaptation to nature and of nature for cultural ends. Toynbee found that civilizations have not had complete meaning in themselves. He considered the study of universal states that come into existence in order to put a stop to wars and substitute cooperation for bloodshed. Regarding them as a goal of human endeavor, citizens of some civilizations idolize them and esteem them as most desirable and important. Toynbee's final interpretation of history is fundamentally religious, even though nowhere in his work is there any indication that he perceived some particular religion as having a definite revelation of spiritual truth.

Eric Voegelin (1901–1985) does not seek to identify determining forces that would explain the past or allow prediction of direction of future events. Rather he conceives history as a function of the life of man, which means that there is always present an irreducible element of freedom of the individual human being as the historical agent. History is an enterprise in which one may succeed or fail. The philosophy of history should provide criteria by which success or failure may be measured.[40] His views confirm that the philosophy of history is founded on the concept of man. Voegelin invokes a few basic principles, such as that man is a limited knower, certainty in understanding is unachievable, reality is comprehended only through experience, and faith is the only source of confidence.

Karl Popper (1902–1994), a leading philosopher of science, also considered the question, "Is there a meaning in history?" and answered it by saying, "History has no meaning."[41] All meanings seen in history were given to it authoritatively by men. He pointed to the fact that historians use in their explanations of historical phenomena general laws that are trivial, and frequently lead to interpretations based on circular reasoning. He attacked historicism,[42] the concept of historical determinism and inevitability, because of its connection with political totalitarianism.[43] He argued (1) that history is characterized by its interest in actual, singular, or specific events, rather than in laws and generalizations, which are the domain of science; (2) that proposed laws are trivial, part of already existing knowledge, and of little interest, and (3) that to avoid being flooded by unrelated material, preconceived points of view are dogmatically introduced and, therefore, all history is written from the historian's perspectives.

Michel Foucault (1926–1984) may be considered as an example of postmodern philosophers of history. He rejected the Hegelian teleological model in favor of breaking off the past from the present to demonstrate the foreignness of the past as an argument against using it to legitimize the present. Even though the gap between the past and the present is at the heart of Foucault's historiography, he allows this discontinuity to remain unexplained for fear that any explanation may lead to evolutionary conclusions. He turns away from the traditional perspective of "total history," represented by grand explanatory systems and linear processes, and from practices he calls "genealogical analysis." This allowed him to preserve the singularity of events, the neglected, the discredited, and a whole range of phenomena that have been denied their own history. Genealogy rejects the pursuit of the origin in favor of a conception of historical beginnings as lowly, complex, and contingent. There can be no constants, no essence, no immobile forms of uninterrupted continuities structuring the past (see note 8).

Computerized models of history are expected to replace the disintegrated philosophical basis for formulations of history's meaning. They represent a continuation of at least one of Enlightenment's ideas, the idea of objectivization, and are visible in the efforts to introduce computers into the historians' tool set. Data about the past—difficult to quantify because it reflects human behavior—are manipulated into categories, so they can be analyzed with "a pattern" as expected outcome.[44] The hope for quantification is that by processing vast amounts of material, beyond the capacity of the individual historian to encompass, it can bring to light patterns that otherwise would remain hidden or unnoticed. This methodology is as flawed as the other approaches. Historical data manipulation has a built-in invalidator because everything depends on the definition of conceptual categories and assignment of data to them. This, of course, depends on the historian's individual judgment and confirms that computerized models are only another way to making historical data and, by extension, history fit a pattern already established in the historian's mind.

Revisionist history responds to the need of groups and nations to justify themselves. As the means of defining identity, history becomes a means of shaping history. The writing of history turns from mediation to a weapon.[45] Revisionist history is practiced in two variants:

- *Exculpatory history* is a top-down explanation designed to justify the ruling powers, to show how noble, virtuous, and inevitable the existing power arrangements are.

• *Compensatory history*, on the other hand, is explanation invoked to justify the victims of current power, to vindicate those who reject the status quo. This underdog's history is designed to demonstrate what Bernard Russell called the "superior virtue of the oppressed."

Both exculpatory and compensatory history use the past to justify the present and to shape the future. "Who controls the past controls the future; who controls the present controls the past," runs the party slogan in George Orwell's *1984*.

Even though the interest in development of theoretical and systematic philosophies of history has lately subsided, probably due to the dismissal and loss of credibility by many ideologies, the pragmatic value of understanding history remains high, especially as propaganda material for the powers that be and professional historians. Among academicians the discussions continue.

What are the key conclusions from this short review of human attempts to understand history in natural terms and to develop a framework for best future actions of society? The first conclusion is quite obvious: no explanation, no philosophical system, no socioeconomic system, no political regime is able to satisfy all men in all places. This conclusion includes liberal democracy, because the advantages of relative liberty and equality have not been extended to everybody. Thus, those who remain dissatisfied, for whatever reason, will always have the potential to restart Plato's cycle of government.[46] The second conclusion is based on the descriptive-only character of all these explanations. Even the most logical, consistent, and systematic ones, e.g., representing the materialistic concept, do not ascribe to history any actual meaning. History is presented there as a result of some blind forces of production, distribution of goods, etc. The third conclusion, important for all of us personally, is that the intellectual constructs emerging from these studies and/or speculations are not relevant to the life of the individual member of the contemplated cultures, civilizations, nations, societies, etc., nor do they provide a credible assessment of consequences for the future, when observable agents of change operate. These studies miss completely the fact that history's impact on ordinary people does not come by new concepts and intellectual models, but through shocks and surprises of wars, uprisings, economic calamities, natural disasters, and their consequences.[47] These recurring sudden blows create a high level of apprehension and force the individual into a position of defensive insecurity. For the individual, who is the primary actor in his or her own day-to-day personal history, the grand dynamics of mankind's history is not very important, and the philosophers' and academicians' attempts to understand the meaning of history appear as a new version of the story about a group of blind men trying to describe an elephant, as told in one of the oldest Buddhist, maybe even pre-Buddhist, sutras.

It is quite interesting to observe the confluence of the populist wisdom expressed by Henry Ford, "History is bunk," with the scholarly conclusion that "History has no meaning" pronounced by Karl Popper. This fusion of ideas stands in conflict with the ideologists' and propagandists' desire to keep explanation of carefully selected historical events and facts to justify political plans and ambitions of their sponsors. Considering the multiplicity of cultures and ideologies populating the minds of American elites, it is not surprising to see the confusion in public school curricula and the inability to reach an agreement about even minimum teaching standards or guidelines, and about which historical facts should be required as a part of knowledge provided to students before graduation. The gravest social risks hidden behind this chaos are not associated with the lack of some "authorized version" of U.S. and world history to be memorized, but with the possibility that George Santayana's hint, to the effect that those who did not learn from history would be condemned to repeat it, may actually reflect historical experience.

CONCLUSIONS

Tumultuous, ill-defined, and immensely variegated proposals, aspirations, and methods of past and present philosophers represent the primary characteristics observable in the history of philosophical systems. The quantity of writings, of new problems raised, and of new ambitions indicate the irrationality of expectations that works by recent philosophers will result in anything that may approximate completeness of observations and objectivity of results.[48] In spite of the amount of time and effort dedicated to it by the best and brightest minds throughout the history of mankind, philosophy is collapsing under its own weight; speculative goals it has set for itself miss the facts of the world's complexity, inherent uncertainty, and unpredictability, and the limitations of man's mental capacities. Philosophers deserve full credit for the willingness to admit this deficient status of their field of learning.

Failing to meet the original objectives of discovery of ultimate and primary laws and causes of things and events, of the elaboration of a worldview, and of telling people how they ought to live, many philosophers turned toward another highly suspect intellectual domain of ideologies trying to change the structures and processes of human society according to their ideas packaged as ideological systems, sometimes with ultimate, sometimes with opportunistic goals. Not surprisingly, recent philosophers have found themselves members of advisory committees on contemporary policy issues and fashionable topics, such as feminism, abortion, nuclear warfare, environmental protection, multicul-turalism, etc. (a troubling array of partisan, small-interest, and groups-based policies and goals), and in competition with TV commentators, pundits, and public opinion polls. Many—with embarrassment, incredulity, and apprehension; others with gratuity—admitted that their participation in ideologies and social controversies is a fundamental step to the outside of philosophy, a confirmation of an over-one-century-old Marxist observation about the poverty of philosophy and admission that there cannot be progress in philosophy. Perhaps this also vindicates the wisdom of Socrates, who claimed that there is no merit in paying philosophers for their work. They would tend to produce only ideas and arguments favoring their paymaster's interests and lose ability to express the full range of views with which they are familiar.[49]

The malaise of our cultural life confirms "the defeat of the mind"[50] as well as the fact that the life of the mind has quickly moved out of normal man's way, making room for the terrible and pathetic encounter of the fanatic and the zombie, violent and pornographic, so well portrayed by the entertainment industry.

In the foreseeable future, philosophy proper will not disappear; it may turn its focus toward thoughts of past philosophers and ideas coming from the East. It will continue its trend away from everyday activities and may become a form of general literature.[51] But the political arena will still resonate with echoes of past utopias,[52] this time, quite possibly, with religious overtones.

The conclusions of this chapter, impacting our own search for life-critical knowledge, seem to be easy to formulate:

- All the schools of thought reviewed did not diminish the value and importance of the posed questions.

- Philosophy proposed a very diverse set of opinions about those questions, but failed to provide the desired answers. Its failure brought into focus doubts about human mind's ability to ever deliver them.

- Philosophies of history did not confirm any trends and hidden forces that may be helpful in selection of the proper direction of an individual's life.

- A few ideologies showed themselves powerful enough to give many individuals reason to live and rules how to live, even why and how to die. But the twentieth-century political and social catastrophes related to implementation of such powerful ideologies pose a serious question whether those "true believers" have not been mistaken or misled.

- Currently fashionable emphasis on diversity of beliefs, frequently perceived as a positive development, increases risks of personal and group conflicts without providing the desired answers.

- Therefore, our inquiry must continue.

Let us now take a look at another enormous domain of human knowledge, the sciences.

EXACT SCIENCES

2

The obvious conclusion of the previous chapter justifies only one attitude: skepticism about any man-created idea. Philosophical skeptics question the reliability of all knowledge claims and doubt that indubitable information about the real nature of things and events can actually be gained. They had their voice even in the euphoric intellectual atmosphere of the eighteenth century. It was David Hume (1711–1776) who showed that there are no equivalent observers (animals perceive things differently than people, different people perceive things differently, man's senses perceive the same object in various ways, etc.); how can we find who, if anyone, perceives the world correctly?[1] Man is caught between total skepticism based on contradictions involved in trying to perceive the real nature of things and natural compulsion to believe in the reality of an external world. In our times, fundamental skepticism may lead to conclusions acceptable to postmodern philosophers, but opposing common sense, namely that (1) the external world has no meaning and is not based on any general rules nor principles; it is just an arbitrary and random collection of things and sequences of events; (2) the meaning of the world and its general principles are beyond man's understanding and related knowledge unattainable; and (3) because the optimism of the Enlightenment and the nineteenth century were illusions, well-structured views of the world have collapsed, and with their collapse as frames of reference, nothing seems obvious or certain anymore.[2]

Such skepticism did not prevent initiation of a new search for true bases of certainty, knowledge, and values, an endeavor parallel to philosophy, started by work of Nicolaus Copernicus (1473–1543), Galileo Galilei (1564–1646), René Descartes (1596–1650), Sir Isaac Newton (1642–1727), and others, and later strengthened by the accomplishments of the Industrial Revolution. Emerged natural sciences provided the basis for a new optimism and new hope that certainty in human knowledge, at least about the external world, is achievable. Development of an accurate, complete, scientific view of the world seemed to be only a question of time.

At this point, it is worthwhile to remember that the word "certainty" carries two meanings. One reflects the credibility of statements and propositions, the so-called "logical certainty" or "propositional certainty," standing in opposition to "probability." Progress in natural sciences brought big volumes of such certain knowledge. The second meaning, the "psychological certainty," as opposed to "doubts" and "skepticism," refers to a state of mind (including, for example, a person's attitudes toward sets of words), strongly depends on accompanying justification, and is well outside the reach of the sciences.

In our everyday sense of the word, science is viewed as a distinctive human activity with these four primary characteristics:

1. It is practiced by special people assumed to be objective, unsentimental, and unemotional. They always try to report their findings so others can check and utilize them. Ideally, they are also honest and humble, never claiming more than they can prove.

2. Science deals exclusively with things, not ideas or feelings, with the external world and its working. This external world is anything that scientists can measure and describe, preferably in mathematical terms, and excludes everything they cannot. Scientists assume the basic conditions and laws of nature on Earth are the same everywhere in the universe.

3. Science does not deal with real-world phenomena in all their complexity; it works with their abstractions or models described by a reduced number of parameters and is concerned only with their behavior under idealized conditions.

4. Science deals with its objects and topics in a specific way, employing special methods, and its own unique language for reporting results. Its best-known method is to frame a testable hypothesis from data obtained by experimentation in a carefully controlled environment, followed by its empirical confirmation or refutation.

FUNDAMENTALS

The term "exact sciences" became more and more restricted to the domains of physical and biological disciplines (natural sciences) which, at the same time, began to claim for themselves special levels of rigorousness and credibility of conclusions to distinguish themselves from all other scientific disciplines, recently called "ironic sciences" or, somewhat pejoratively, "pseudo-sciences." But even this narrow perception of the sciences did not prevent questioning of all the underlying fundamental concepts, such as scientific laws, scientific method, scientific reasoning, scientific theories, and paradigm.

Scientific Law

Scientific law, the most desired product of science, is a general statement of fact usually, though not necessarily, expressed in mathematical form. Laws are methodically established by induction on the basis of evidence intentionally acquired by observations and experiments. In so far as it is empirical, scientific law is not a necessary demonstrable truth, but, being based on evidence, it differs from everyday, commonsense generalizations. It is further assumed that proposed laws are either true or false, confirmable or disprovable by statements obtained by observations. Once such a general statement is accepted, it usually does not matter whether it is called a "law" or a "principle." Ideally, scientific laws are strictly universal and deterministic, even though they may also be probabilistic, i.e., based on methodically obtained statistical descriptions and estimates about the proportion of the things under question. An important logical distinction is generally assumed between experimental laws and scientific theories, as discussed below.

The practical problem associated with scientific laws is how to distinguish them from lawlike statements (e.g., "All species surviving in snowy regions are white") and accidental statements (e.g., "All ravens are black"). Two tests have been proposed: the "necessity test" demanding laws to be logically stronger than the mentioned accidental statements and expressed in a modal, noncategorical language, and the "regularity test" to demonstrate that laws do not include unrealized possibilities within their scope of application, and can be used for prediction, or serve as the basis for inference from observed to unobserved matters of fact. As expected, theorists and philosophers of science raise objections to both these tests.

Scientific Method

Scientific method is the procedure by which scientific laws are established. If applied to scientific investigation in general, or something inherent in the practice of all branches of science, "scientific method" refers to the lowest common denominator of a wide range of methods devised to cope with the diversity of problems addressed. If such a common denominator exists, it can amount no more than to fidelity to empirical evidence and to simplicity of logical formulations and arguments.

Traditional views consider the scientific method as a method of research in which a problem is identified; relevant data is gathered; from those data a hypothesis is formulated; and the hypothesis is then empirically tested as per its validity. The initial formulation of hypotheses seems to be a business of inspired guessing that cannot be computerized, while the issue of their confirmation appears to be a comparatively simple, rule-governed undertaking. In practical terms, a solution to any scientific problem requires immersion in observed facts, accurate definition of universal categories describing what is observed, inductive generalization to express regularities in observations, suggestion of explanatory hypotheses, comparison of mentally imagined or experiment-based consequences of the hypotheses, and axiomatic organization of the hypotheses surviving the test.

The advancement of science was, however, secured by very exceptional persons following their own, often undisclosed, methods.[3] The most important work was usually done by addressing limited problems, not by seeking grand designs in understanding. It involved modest and limited chains of inference and abstraction related to already known truths about the problem. There are, of course, difficulties and contradictions associated with concepts underlying scientific methodology. For example, the already considered issue of equivalent observers is complicated by the need of communication among those observers. This issue brings into the field of investigation problems associated with consensible perceptions and consensual communication, with observation as an objective fact, etc. This issue is extremely important because it is not just a basic principle of Einstein's Special Theory of Relativity, but also belongs to the foundations of all sciences.[4]

The very possibility of perceptual consensibility depends upon a very ordinary ability to recognize patterns. Intersubjective pattern recognition and pattern matching are, therefore, fundamental elements in the creation of all scientific knowledge, which means that the patterns under consideration must be precise, significant, and validated. The exploitation of equivalent observers also requires assurance of observing equivalent or identical events. Therein lies an old paradox: "One cannot step twice into the same river." The very idea of reproducible experiments implies a firm belief in a certain uniformity of nature, which brings us back to the troublesome metaphysics. No other place demands higher levels of professional excellence than experimental research. But even excellent experiments are subject to some degree of uncertainty. At the macro level, they are associated with noise in observed signals, with hidden variables and interaction among variables. At the micro level, they rest with the observer's impact on the observed event, known well from quantum mechanics.

Scientific Reasoning

Arguments lead from premises to conclusion. They are designed to compel a rational person who accepts, or has certain degree of belief in, the premises also to accept, or have a corresponding degree of belief in, the conclusion. Traditionally, rational arguments are divided into deductive and inductive. Valid deductive arguments are those in which the conclusion follows necessarily from the premises, and in which the denial of the conclusion is self-contradictory. All other valid rational arguments are, by definition, inductive.

The orthodox view perceives scientific reasoning as an inductive procedure. In the general sense, "induction" covers all cases of nondemonstrative argument in which the truth of the premises, while not containing the truth of the conclusion, purports to be a good reason for belief in it. The fact that the premises cited explicitly do not entail the conclusion is the root of the problem of induction, illustrated by questions such as, "Why is it reasonable to accept conclusions of certain inductive arguments as true?" or "Why is one inductive conclusion preferable to another?" In other words, there is nothing inconsistent in acceptance of premises linked with the denial of the proposed conclusion.

The problem of induction, for some, leads to the rejection of induction as a proper mode of scientific reasoning. According to such a view, the essence of genuinely scientific reasoning about matters of fact is the framing of hypotheses as only suggested, not established, by given empirical data. Inference enters only in the control of hypotheses by the verification of their observable consequences: negative instances strictly falsify any hypothesis, while positive instances permit its use as a plausible, if unproved, conjecture pending further experimental tests. Statistical methods of hypotheses testing allow quantification of the level of belief in the conclusion and of the probability of erroneous conclusions. But such methods bring with them another set of problems associated with the concept of probability, sampling techniques, randomization, etc., and risk of misinterpreting correlations as cause-effect relations. In the past, the central issue of the philosophy of science was the desire to delimit the borders between science and nonscience in order to provide criteria whereby genuine science could be recognized, and pseudoscience exposed as illegitimate metaphysical speculation. The importance of this goal is rapidly diminishing because many contemporary scientists are involved in metaphysical speculations. The dominant thrust of contemporary work in the philosophy of science is the development of new views of science that proceed from, and tend to depend heavily on, close examination of actual scientific practice and products, e.g., theories and explanations, a parallel to the overall perception of philosophy as the study of evidence.

Scientific Theories

The number of conceptual difficulties, and their seriousness, increases significantly when scientists leave the quite secure domain of phenomena descriptions and venture into the business of their explanations. The key feature of a valid explanation is that it turns the unfamiliar into familiar, and that it removes the element of surprise. The credibility of explanations remains high when they are based on deducted models. Such are often called "causal explanations." The underlying concept of "cause" contains ideas of necessary connection between cause and its effect, of the priority of causes to their effects, of the direction of necessitation and invariability of the sequence of events, of necessary and sufficient conditions, of plurality of causes, and analytical distinction between cause and effect. But even here, philosophical problems associated with these ideas do not yield to any easy solution. Deductive explanations, and causal explanations as their special case, are perceived as the only truly adequate scientific explanations because they provide a strict symmetry between explanation (i.e., retrodiction) and prediction.

Among other types of explanations belong, for example:

- Probabilistic explanations employing observed correlation or assumed inference between an event and its probable cause.

- Functional explanations providing answers to the question, "Why such-and-such exists."

- Purposive explanations, often regarded as unscientific because they refer to mental states or events.

- Genetic explanations, which consist of sometimes lengthy accounts of a sequence of events leading up to the occurrence or existence of the fact to be explained. They may be actually a sequence of causal and purposive explanations where the underlying laws are not stated explicitly because they are taken for granted.

- Ad hoc explanations and circular explanations, which are untestable in principle because nothing could count as observable evidence for their falsehood.

Scientific theories, besides the scientific laws discussed above, are frequently used forms of explanation. The most fundamental distinction between laws and theories is that laws refer to observables, or are operationally definable, while theories contain statements that cannot be directly tested by observation or experiment. For example, laws of gravity describe observable behavior of objects in a gravitational field, while the theory of gravity attempts to explain what gravity is, e.g., by postulating existence of hypothetical particles such as gravitons. Experimental laws derive their support wholly from their observable instances, while theories are judged also in terms of their scope, internal coherence, plausibility, and simplicity. Any theory is subject to revisions or replacement, but any subsequent theory, to be acceptable, must be consistent with the experimental laws previously known to be true. Laws are usually expressed as single statements; theories are systems of statements that entail laws. Theories are more general than laws and have the task of describing, predicting, and (possibly) explaining a class of phenomena.

Theories arise from the need to explain laws. Every theory has its historical base consisting of the set of laws the theory was constructed to explain. The worth of a theory lies largely in its ability to yield new laws outside of its historical base. In addition to various premises, the truth of which is nonproblematic in virtue of their being confirmed by direct observation, theories aiming at explanation must also employ constructs that are not directly observable. This is usually called observational-theoretical distinction.

As an integral part of their structure, theories usually contain an analogy or a model. They are required to be general and predictive and, therefore, capable of assimilating an indefinite number of new observations without themselves radically changing in meaning.

Formulation of a theory is a collection of propositions that are true of the theory. Typically, a formulation of a theory consists of a few specified propositions together with all of their consequences deducted under some logic; hence, theories may be viewed as linguistic entities. Thus a change in the formulation of a theory is, actually, a change of the theory.

Some scientists assume that, in relationship to observable statements, theories have the status of instruments, tools, or calculating devices, so the question of their truth never arises.

Paradigms

To complete the overview of the foundations of the sciences, it is necessary to mention an additional concept introduced in the middle of the twentieth century, the concept of paradigm. Originally, it had been used to denote the currently universally recognized status of scientific achievement that, for some period of time, provides model problems and solutions to the community of scientists.[5] In other words, a paradigm is the constellation of beliefs shared by a given community of scientists; conversely, a scientific community consists of individuals who share a paradigm. When scientific experiments yield results that don't fit an existing set of theories, or point to their internal inconsistencies, scientific revolution may occur, bringing a new way of looking at nature; i.e., the paradigm has shifted.

The concept of paradigm brought onto the sociology of science a discomfort based on the recognition that successive paradigms may well be incommensurable (that is, lacking common problems, common meanings, and common perceptions) in similarity to successive metaphysical systems. Successive paradigms do not deny that there can be some progress in science but deny progress toward anything particular. Even the exact sciences in their historical development were often heading toward a dead end.[6] This view presents a version of radical skepticism, a view that paradigm shifts and new scientific discoveries and theories do not bring us closer to some absolute truth about nature, despite their potential or practical utility.

This brief review of the conceptual fundamentals of natural sciences and of related problems, as seen from the perspective of the theory of knowledge, suggests that the enterprise of scientific knowledge is, in obvious similarity with philosophy, unable to deliver and assure the desired completeness, finality, and certainty of our knowledge about external matters. The most valuable achievements have been delivered in descriptions of repetitive natural events and processes. This is best visible in the close partnership of natural sciences with a variety of technologies forming the industrial basis for creation of economic values and valuables bringing benefits to both producers and users.

THEORIES IN EXACT SCIENCES

Probably the best way to illustrate the problems and conflicts related to scientific theories and paradigms is to discuss three of them that dominate current scientific and public opinions, namely cosmogonies, theory of evolution, and theories of everything.

Cosmogonies

Cosmogony is a term describing any scientific theory, religious doctrine, or myth about the origins of the universe. It should be distinguished from "cosmology," which studies the physical universe as a whole with the aim of explaining the variety of observed phenomena. Human interest in cosmologies has been always relatively high due to our natural fascination with and awe of the mystery of starry skies (*mysterium tremendum et fascinosum*) and to the frequent conviction about the stars' impact on an individual's life (astrology). Cosmogonies, on the other hand, were and still are of interest to a limited number of persons, from poets to priests and thinkers. While cosmologies developed into considerable systems, e.g., Ptolemaic or Copernican, cosmogonies remained quite simple.

Early cosmogonies were mostly products of poets and priests. Even the early philosophers' improved versions were plagued by inconsistencies and missing time segments. For example:

- The Babylonian epic Enuma Elish attributes the existence of the universe to sexual congress between primordial divinity Aspu (the Begetter) and Mumu-Tiamet (She who bore them all).

- Early Greeks believed that in the beginning there was chaos, a confused and shapeless mass of earth, sea, and air mixed up together. The story opens with Gaia (Earth) and Uranus (Heaven) who, through a series of sexual unions, produced the world, divine offspring, e.g., Cronos (Time) and Zeus, the father of gods and men.

- The original Japanese cosmogony centered in three creative deities who are said to have come from the primeval chaos: Ame-No-Minakanushi (central deity) with two subordinates, Takami-Musubi (creator of heaven) and Kami-Musubi (creator of lesser deities). The creation of the universe began with two deities, Izanagi (male) and Izanami (female), who descended from the high plain of heaven and through spontaneous sexual generation created the terrestrial world, including the islands of Japan with their mountains, rivers, grasses and trees. Their offspring, the Sun Goddess Amaterasu Omikami, eventually sent her grandson Ninigi-No-Mikoto to rule over Japan, whose great-grandson Jimmu Tenno became the first ruler whose Yamato clan spread its authority over the whole country.

- In Maori myth, the world parents who brought the cosmos into being arose themselves from "po," a kind of antecedent pulp, pushing the drama of creation into infinity.

According to the majority of early cosmogonies, the universe started at some finite time due to universal feeling that it must have some "first cause" to come to existence. Thinkers not comfortable with the idea of some divine intervention at the beginning concentrated on advancement of the belief that the universe had always existed and will continue to exist forever, a belief, even though reformulated, that is still shared by many scientists. Observable and documented setbacks through a variety of natural disasters and catastrophes were the main explanation for the cycle of history resetting the human race back to the beginning of civilization.

The ultimate questions of how, when, and why the universe came into being have been put aside for centuries. The search for answers lost its appeal when all involved—scientists, philosophers, and theologians—grew weary of them. But currently, scientists aided by new astronomical observations and powerful computerized mathematical tools renewed their speculations with all seriousness. The present age is actually fascinated with cosmogonies, and we see most accomplished physicists proposing, developing, and popularizing a variety of scenarios how the world began, how it looked initially, the time of its beginning, how the physical time began, and why the world is the way it is. The impetus to this new interest came from Einstein's Theory of Relativity claiming universal constancy of the speed of light, observation of the red shift of spectral lines from distant galaxies, and from the discovery of the cosmic background radiation. The critical idea of many current theories lies in the explanation of the red shift by the hypothesis of an expanding universe.

Steady-state hypothesis is a theory proposed in 1948 by Hoyle, Bondi, and Gold, which explained the hypothesized expansion of the universe by compensatory continuous creation of matter throughout space. Its attractiveness for minds of physicists naturally inclining toward materialism rested in the conclusion requiring neither an initial moment of creation nor a limit to the extension of the universe.

The *Big Bang hypothesis* is a theory of the origin of the universe accepted by most scientists today. Einstein's General Theory of Relativity assumed that space-time began at the Big Bang singularity and could come to an end by collapsing into another singularity, either a Big Crunch, or black hole. At the big bang itself, the universe is thought to have had zero size and infinite temperature. As it expanded, both temperature and radiation levels decreased, allowing elementary particles and antiparticles to form, and their later conversion into helium, hydrogen, and other elements. Local irregularities caused gravity forces to slow down some regions of expansion, increased their density, and initiated their rotation. This way galaxies were born. Continuing regional collapse of matter resulted in formation of stars and other astronomical objects.

The original singularity associated with the Big Bang openly invites creationist explanation. The birth of the universe means not only that matter and energy, but also space and time have a finite and instantaneous beginning that calls for explanation by the idea of creation out of nothing.

Even though the Big Bang hypothesis is an admirable, mind-pleasing theory, it leaves many questions unanswered. The theory's technical contents-related questions are, e.g., Why was the early universe so hot? Why is it so uniform on a large scale? Why is it still expanding at nearly critical rate? What is the origin of local irregularities and density fluctuations? Is ours the only universe initiated by the Big Bang? Conceptually, the theory is based on some lately weakened assumptions, such as:

- The appealing but questionable assumption of the validity of known laws of physics over the whole universe and over the duration of its existence.

- The hypothesis of the expanding universe, conjectured from the observed red shift in spectral lines of faraway galaxies as a linear function of their distance, held in spite of the disturbing evidence that this relation fails in quasars and particular sections in the sky and wave bands and suggests a need for a new explanation of the red shift.

- Statistical inferences from data about only a few samples of galaxies, making contravening evidence more significant.

- The assumption of the homogeneity of the universe and its isotropy, which is nothing more than mathematical convenience, a simplification contradicting astronomical observations and pointing to often forgotten or neglected substantive differences between mathematical models and reality.

- Acceptance of mathematical models' singularities without acceptance of the related failure of physical laws.

- Accepting violation of the Second Law of Thermodynamics but failing to provide any explanation where the original energy and information needed to start and run the universe had come from.

Recent discoveries of the existence of mass in neutrinos, of fainter-than-expected supernovae, a possibility of an accelerating expansion of the universe, and the question of the "information paradox" (whether information disappears forever if it goes into a black hole) indicate that the cosmological evidence keeps shifting, and revisions of current cosmological theories and related cosmogony may be inevitable.[7]

Anthropic cosmological principle. One of the most critical sets of questions relates to the initial configuration of the universe, and the origin of laws of physics and the values of the cosmological constants figuring in those fundamental laws, i.e., questions related to the so-called "boundary conditions," both necessary and sufficient, at the beginning of time. One well-known, but still controversial, answer has been proposed under the concept of the anthropic cosmological principle[8] that relates the existence of the universe to the existence of humanity. It indicates that if the initial conditions of the universe and the laws of physics were different, mankind would not be here! In other words, not only man is adapted to the universe, but the universe is adapted to man as well. There are three versions of the principle:

- Weak anthropic principle: The observed values of all physical and cosmological quantities are not equally probable, but they take on values restricted by the requirement that there exist sites where carbon-based life can evolve, and by the requirement that the universe be old enough for it to have already done so.[9]

- Strong anthropic principle: The universe must have those properties that allow life to develop within it at some stage in its history.[10]

- Final anthropic principle: Intelligent information processing must come into existence in the universe, and once it comes into existence, it will never die out.[11]

The anthropic principle reformulates a boundary on human mental ability represented by a longtime recognized impossibility to conceive a universe forever empty of life. Post-Copernican attempts to do so (universe as a machine, universe as a clockwork, man as a biochemical system, etc.) failed because even the most pure materialistic views of the universe have been developed by man as an observer. Hopes that the anthropic cosmological principle will be proven false are alive and based on quantum theory's picture of multiple, even infinitely many, universes, and on the belief in future successful formulation of a complete and consistent unified theory.

In summary, the current theories about the origin of the universes can be classified into three different types,[12] with numerous variations in all of them:

1. The universe is not eternal but has no beginning, because when going back in time, Heisenberg's principle of uncertainty erases the distinction between space and time, i.e., time becomes spatialized. This four-dimensional space forms a closed surface curled back upon itself, so it has no edges nor boundaries.

2. The universe began as a microscopic quantum fluctuation out of empty space, as virtual particles do. The basic idea is that if the total mass-energy content of the universe is zero, then Heisenberg's uncertainty principle allows it to exist for an indefinite period of time.

3. The universe began as a quantum fluctuation in a previously existing universe, i.e., it is imaginable that universes might reproduce themselves. A newly created universe would not necessarily remain within its parent universe. Individual universes may not be eternal, but the cosmos of multiple universes would be.

From this review it is clear that proposals of cosmogonies are impossible without confronting questions philosophers clearly identified as metaphysical. Such proposals are untested and possibly will remain untestable, opening an ever-growing rift between theory and experiment. They also frequently contain variables that no one can interpret. Such developments cause alarm among scientists who recognize in them a transformation of hard and exact sciences into something that, in the past, has been appropriately called myth. It would be better to admit that there seem to be certain basic questions that may not have answers in the domain of sciences, even though some scientists will insist on asking them. The most disturbing development seems to be the fact that contemporary cosmologists feel free to postulate astronomical objects beyond observation (black holes, white holes, wormholes, false vacuum, vacuum energy, zero-point energy, virtual particles, etc.) and theories of many stripes that cannot be confirmed by experience. This shows either calculated or careless erasure of the difference between disciplined physical inquiry and speculative metaphysics.[13] The products of current theoretical physicists are much closer to works of Homer or Dante than those of Faraday, Einstein, or Teller. Proposing new myths may be an interesting, intellectually challenging, and profitable business, but as a contribution to man's factual knowledge it has no value.

Theories of Everything

Socrates expressed his ultimate dream in his desire for superlative knowledge and explanation of everything, why it comes to be, why it is, why it perishes. For the ancients, it was breadth of knowledge alone that was the indicator of intellectual success. In our world, it is both breadth and depth that count. People always try to formulate some initial cause for the existence of the world beyond which explanations will not be sought. Today, the real goal of the search for a Theory of Everything is not just a desire to understand the structure of all observable forms, but to understand why there is any matter at all; to attempt to show that both the existence and the particular structure of the physical universe can be understood; to discover whether, in Einstein's words, "God could have made the universe in a different way."[14]

Can we hope to develop an ultimate explanation of the universe, a single all-embracing picture of all the laws of nature from which the inevitability of all things seen must follow with unimpeachable logic? What if our human frame and our cognitive processes are placing real limits upon the concepts we can accommodate? Despite the suspicion that human mental powers are not adequate to handle an understanding of nature at its ultimate level, optimists view our recent successes as indicative of an emerging golden age of discovery, of the fact that fundamental science will soon be more or less complete, with missing links expected to be discovered during a few coming decades.[15]

Even though many contemporary theoretical physicists believe that they are close to the keys that will unlock the mathematical secrets at the kernel of the universe, it is necessary to keep in mind that "everything" is a tall order, a big subject. There is always the risk of forgetting the original question asked when drifting through the space of encountered problems.

The most famous attempts to develop a Unified Theory of physics, a subset of a Theory of Everything, were those of Eddington and Einstein. For many reasons they both failed, even though we may excuse their failure by pointing to the seriously incomplete knowledge of the world of elementary particles by both scientists. But the presently increased knowledge also identified new challenges, such as increasing complexity, limits on algorithmic compressibility of sets of physical laws, insufficiency of experimental techniques, and missing logical reasons that the universe should not contain arbitrary elements which do not relate to the rest. Even if we do discover some unified theory, it would not mean that we would be able to predict events in general[16] because the uncertainty principle of quantum mechanics[17] sets limits on our predictive powers, and because of the many limits of mathematics itself not allowing exact solution of the theory's equations, except in very simple situations.[18]

The current status of attitudes toward this grand intellectual aspiration can be described by these two clear but contradictory positions:

- A theory which would provide the complete set of underlying rules that control, in finest detail, every action of inanimate or animate matter is within the actual grasp of today's physicists.[19]
- Theory of everything will never be found.[20]

Faraday expressed well that it is difficult to abandon the hope that an identifiable single force rules nature. Yet even on the practical level, the necessary breakthroughs in technologies, such as particle accelerators and supercolliders, and in mathematics and information processing are not even under consideration; furthermore, dealing with frequent conceptual absurdities, such as superstrings and Higgs particles,[21] is quite awkward, making it difficult to see how any real and substantive progress could be achieved. The so-far failed search should lead to the long overdue admission that science does not represent the only means to the discovery of ultimate truth, if such truth exists.

Theories of Evolution

The concept of evolution sees that the existing variety of plants and animals does not exist more or less unmodified from the beginning of biological time, but has come to being through a progressive diversification that has accompanied their biogenetic descent from their ancestors. Even though this idea has been adumbrated many times in history, Darwin gave it a form of acceptable theory. It is naïve to suppose that the acceptance of evolutionary theory is based on evidence and proofs. Actually, its acceptance rests more with its attractive simplicity, rationality, apparent self-explanatory power, strong ideological appeal, and support from the scientific community.

Darwinism. One theory with many characteristics of a Grand Unified Theory (GUT) of everything, or at least of "many things," has been proposed by Charles Darwin in his theory of evolution. Using Darwin's own words (slightly paraphrased),[22] the theory is based on these primary propositions:

- The more complex organs and instincts have been perfected not by means superior to the human reason, but by the accumulation of innumerable slight variations, each good for the individual possessor.

- Variability is governed by many complex laws: by correlated growth, compensation, the increased use and disuse of parts, and the definite action of the surrounding conditions.

- The complex and little-known laws governing the production of varieties are the same, as far as we can judge, as the laws that have governed the production of distinct species.

- There is a struggle for existence leading to preservation of profitable deviations of structure and instinct.

- In the survival of favored individuals and races, during the continuing struggle for existence, we see a powerful and ever-acting form of selection.

- Natural selection has been the main, but not exclusive, means of modification.

- As according to the theory of natural selection, an interminable number of intermediate forms must have existed, linking together all the species in each group by gradation as fine as are our existing varieties.

- There is a grandeur in this view of life, with its several powers, having been originally breathed by the Creator into a few forms or into one. From so simple a beginning, endless forms most beautiful and most wonderful have been and are being evolved.

Darwin resolved the two major limitations of older versions of evolutionism by producing a well-organized body of evidence that evolution had occurred, and by formulating what seemed to be a verifiable or refutable explanation of how it occurred. Darwin's biological theory of evolution by natural selection did not occur to him in an intellectual vacuum, but in a supportive environment of cosmological beliefs that nature operates everywhere and always by the same sorts of law (uniformitarianism), and of accepting change as a fundamental feature of nature, i.e., belief that observed structures and patterns of behavior have to be regarded as historically conditioned. Darwin was aware that some aspects of his theory are hard to believe and that many objections may be advanced.

In fairness, Darwin's theory influenced almost all aspects of human thought. Darwinian ideas spread rapidly into the whole intellectual domain of Western culture. They renewed interest in cosmogonic speculations in philosophy and caused the social sciences to become strongly evolutionary. Darwinism is credited for the destruction of the quasitheological frame of mind in the sciences. Because of their ability to inspire and lend appearance of scientific support, Darwin's ideas became all things to all people, a clear sign of difficulties ahead. The fate of Darwinism in the twentieth century and beyond has been and is, therefore, mixed. Darwinism itself mutated into many variants that are subject to natural selection with the possibility of extinction as well.

Neo-Darwinism is Darwinism reformulated into the language of Mendelian genetics, and, by that, revised in its doctrinal kernel. It assumed inheritable variations providing the recombinations and reassortments of genetic factors that Mendelian heredity allows for. This makes the process of natural selection an umbrella concept for inequalities of survival, or of reproductive rates—in other words, for inequalities in the contributions made by the different organisms to the ancestry of future generations. Those hereditary endowments represent the organisms' fitness. Evolution by natural selection could thus be described in terms of the survival of the fittest.

Emergent evolutionism, in contrast to classical Darwinism's assumption that all changes in living things take place gradually, maintains that modifications are events characterizing discontinuity with what happened before. Whatever comes to be for the first time must do so suddenly and abruptly. Such discontinuity has a character of emergence which implies that the variety, diversity, and complexity engendered by evolution are irreducible, cumulative features of the creative advance of nature.

When the concept of emergence is used in cosmogony, it is closely connected with the concept of levels, e.g., living things form a level that emerged from the nonliving, physicochemical level. Emergent evolutionists did not resolve the question of how many levels there are. The fact that occurrences and characteristics of all genuine emerging novelties are unpredictable and unintelligible, being causally disconnected from antecedent conditions, is something to be simply accepted. The more comprehensive versions of emergent evolutionism that purport to apply to the whole spaciotemporal universe, or to the totality of existence, remain speculative possibilities at best.

Pragmatic evolutionism, a distinctly American generalization of Darwinism, uses chance variations and natural selection to explain the role of human thought and its numerous and varied products. Pragmatic evolutionism provides a bridge between biological and cultural evolution.

Social Darwinism is the common term covering the seizure of selected aspects of Darwinism by academicians, political ideologues, and public speakers to justify their own proposals for solution of ethical, economic, and political problems. Social Darwinism interestingly seems to fit both the left and right political wings. Karl Marx wanted to dedicate the first volume of his *Das Kapital* to Darwin (he refused the honor), while Darwinism also provided a rationale for Adam Smith's doctrine of the "invisible hand." Particular emphasis on the struggle for existence and the survival of the fittest provided pseudobiological justification for power politics, imperialism, and wars, and served well even in Hitler's justification of Nazism. It has been used to justify *laissez-faire* policies, but it also has been attacked as unethical by arguments that man represents an island of cultural evolution in a sea of Darwinian change. Currently, Social Darwinism is rightly regarded as philosophically naïve and of no interest to contemporary ideologies.

Popular Darwinism is a version falsely portrayed as established fact of science instead of just a hypothesis that currently dominates public educational institutions, and which is promoted by the majority of communication media. This makes Popular Darwinism suspect as a possible cause of observed social and moral problems. In this way, with their implication, Darwinistic evolutionary speculations disturb the whole human society and, therefore, stimulate all kinds of responses that can be clustered into four general groups:

- Documentation of the theory's development over time[23]
- Unquestionable support of the theory[24]
- Questioning some of the theory's selected aspects[25]
- Opposition proposing alternative theories[26]

Such a diversity of opinions of both proponents and opponents itself suggests that Darwinism is more a philosophical position than a scientific theory. This suspicion is intensified by some of its defenders' favorite tactics: to attack its critics' intelligence and character (a method used by Darwin himself), writing off alternative theories as indicative of a religious bias, and use of legal means instead of scientific argument to enforce its acceptance.

Anti-Darwinism

In spite of the high visibility and legal success of imposition of the Darwinistic evolutionary theories upon public schools, the ideas revolving around the concept of creation did not disappear either from the scientific community or from the religious part of the population. But the real dialogue, sometimes more a legal contest, is taking place only between atheists among scientists and other thinkers. It is interesting to note that non-Christian creation stories—e.g., those of native Americans—are never criticized and are taught in some public schools, and also that non-Christian religions are not part of the debate. In most cases, the anti-Darwinian thinking concentrates on these two principal themes: Design in nature and creation.

Creation science, a clearly antievolutionist view, is based on the description of God's activity as presented in the first chapters of the Old Testament book of Genesis. The originally literal reading of the biblical account of creation in six days has been met with ridicule because it is in conflict with generally accepted validity of carbon dating in geology, paleontology, and archeology. More recent opinions see in that story a symbolic representation of mankind's beginning. The fundamental conflict of creation science with early Darwinism is between the belief in instantaneous creation and the belief in evolution by the accumulation of slight variations over long periods of time.

Christian Science is a term for convictions that Christian beliefs may, and actually are, influencing the content of scientific theories, so that the scientific laws and theories might have a different meaning for Christians than for non-Christians. This position rejects the assumption that sciences and their methodological naturalism are religiously neutral. Therefore, it cannot accept that Darwinian evolution is somewhat compatible with theism. The sciences' antireligious stance is visible in reductionist statements such as "everything, including our minds, can be reduced to its material base," or "mankind's existence is a stroke of good luck rather than a planned outcome."

Theistic evolution is the view probably closest to Darwin's own opinion. It implies that God called matter and living organisms into existence, and then abandoned the universe to itself to be controlled by chance and necessity without setting any final goals and without any intervention or guidance. This view actually consigns the creator to nonexistence and, by that, it becomes virtually atheistic. Theistic evolution seems to be a very naïve combination of two opposing positions and, probably, rests on misunderstanding what contemporary scientists mean by the word "evolution."

Intelligent design theory, a highly sophisticated version of creationism, starts with the conviction that information cannot and does not spring spontaneously from matter, which is understood, from this point of view, as inert. The second principal idea reflects the notion of "irreducible complexity,"[27] the idea expressing that certain parts of living organisms, being so complex and composed of many separate parts, cannot function on their own. In other words, a system is irreducibly complex if it consists of several interrelated parts so that removing even one of them would completely destroy the system's function. Because of the complexity, living organisms cannot be considered a product of random blind selection (in reductionist perspective); they are a result of a preconceived design.[28] Natural selection is not able to propose a detailed model by which complex biochemical systems might have been produced in a gradual step-by-step fashion. In a similar way, it is believed the concept of natural selection does not have the power to explain how the original building blocks of living organisms were formed.

We may conclude this short review by confirming that the value of presented challenges to evolutionism is in uncovering its inadequacies, in affirming that some real causes of natural events might not be purely mechanistic, and in requiring people to think more critically about evolution and admit the existence of tough questions associated with it. This review also makes clear that the issue here is not a matter of science against religion; one may be religious and hold either of the views. In their essence, creation and evolution are differing worldviews, two different belief systems in conflict. They are antithetical; if one is true, the other is false. Evolutionism assumes that nature is autonomous; creationism views nature as permanently dependent on its creator.

Gaia hypothesis is another perspective standing outside the domain of evolutionary theories but also outside traditional creationism. Using the vocabulary of biology, it restates an old Greek belief that Earth is a living creature, a living organism. The principal idea is that the earth's lower atmosphere is an internal, regulated, and necessary part of life itself,[29] and existing in a state of planetary equilibrium for eons. It perceives humanity and its activity as inconsequential because of its almost unnoticeable impact on the ecosystem. In the case that man will disrupt the environment, Gaia's response will result in humanity's extinction. Such strong statements about Gaia's purposeful regulation of Earth's ecosystem have been toned down lately.

Metaman, in opposition to Gaia which is not human-centered, is a theory that acknowledges humanity's key role in the formation of a global superorganism, the metaman, consisting of humans merged with machines. Its collective memory is stored in minds, libraries, and electronic data banks; its nervous system is built by flow of traveling humans, physical and electronic mail; its consciousness is identified with mass media; it acts through individual markets, competition, and innovation; it makes decisions through political and industrial institutions, and so on. Metaman is absorbing human cultural diversity, and its growing capabilities diminish its dependence on Gaia.[30]

CONCLUSIONS

Any attempt to assess the value of sciences for the modern society and for our own individual lives must start from the position of high respect. A simple look around confirms their enormous application value in many ways; from the big number of conveniences and improvements brought into our life through a variety of technologies, through better understanding of nature allowing us to more effectively harvest its powers and processes, to making it possible to protect ourselves from environmental extremes.

A similar respect is due to the discipline science brought into many of our mental processes, namely reasoning, decision making, and evidence gathering and evaluation. Our mental models about the objects, processes, and events in the material part of nature we directly interface have improved significantly since Newton's times and have stabilized enough to become a part of public knowledge and culture. This applies also to many leading scientists whose names are now familiar to every well-educated person. This highly positive image gets cloudier when considering some of the scientific results that lead to the availability and proliferation of weapons of mass destruction.

Since Descartes's times, there has been a tendency to insist that not only philosophy, but the whole culture, is to be led by science. Programs have been proposed to coordinate developments in social sciences, humanities, and fine arts with natural sciences, e.g., through alliances in conflict with religion, mysticism, and even philosophy. This attitude of putting science on a pedestal, on assigning to it higher value than to other bodies of knowledge, is technically called "scientism." In the past, scientism reflected the enthusiasm created by the successes of natural sciences and the Industrial Revolution. Recently, it may be seen as an ideologically flavored defense against those whose explanations, supposedly, display ignorance of the actual status of modern sciences, or defer too much to intuition and common sense. Generally, scientism is a hazard for all engaged in developing theories in all domains of human knowledge and, therefore, should be recognized and combated.[31]

Much less positive images, as well as directly negative views of the sciences, have emerged from the communities of philosophers of science, and from people studying economic and social consequences of science and behavioral patterns of scientists, especially those venturing beyond scientific boundaries.

The most serious blows against the foundations of scientific inquiry, even though not very well understood by the public, came from the top scientists themselves.

- Einstein's Theories of Relativity (1905 and 1916) denied existence of any absolute frame of reference, led to relativity of motion and mass of all objects in space, to relativity of time, to curvature of space, etc., making all descriptions of the inanimate part of nature equal and, by that, pushing descriptive explanations of nature beyond comprehension and into latent conflict with common experience.

- Heisenberg's Principle of Uncertainty (1927) stated the impossibility of measuring the position and momentum of a subatomic particle simultaneously with more than strictly limited precision. This makes our knowledge of the present state of the world fundamentally uncertain and incomplete and, therefore, all predictions doubtful.

- Gödel's Theorem in mathematics (1931) showed the impossibility of proving the consistency of any formal system with its own tools. This also implies the impossibility of translating scientific laws and theories into a unitary and provable deductive system.

These developments were clear indicators that the Enlightenment's dream of complete, objective, and accurate understanding of nature will not be realized in the domain of the sciences, a defeat more humiliating than the collapse of metaphysics.

The other serious danger is in the fact that practicing scientists must make certain assumptions that are not susceptible to proof simply because they are essentially philosophical. For example, physicists must assume that there are such things as physical laws, not just observations of repetitive sequences of events, and that they do not change with time. So, even scientists who have the reputation of disdaining philosophy are actually trapped in it. The same situation is at the research frontiers, in explanations of theories going beyond the accumulated evidence, or beyond their testability. Answers that past scientists considered metaphysical are quite often being proposed by current scientists for public consumption.[32] We may consider comparing, for example, Newton's wisdom in leaving the mysterious nature of gravity untouched and dealing in his Theory of Gravity only with descriptions of its consequences with contemporary freewheeling fathers of untestable concepts of black holes, white holes, wormholes, false vacuum, etc., or with Darwin, who knew that his theory is not testable. The slippery slope toward metaphysics is always there.

This long-suppressed presence of metaphysics in the exact sciences has been brought to the open and explained by the post-structuralists. Jean-François Lyotard pointed to the fact that scientific knowledge cannot know, and make known, whether it is true without appealing to some narrative knowledge (popular stories, myths, legends, tales, etc.) which, from the postmodernists' as well as the scientists' perspective is no knowledge at all. Because modern myths are embedded in various ideologies and, sometimes, dressed in formulations using scientific language, the conditions for confusion, even deceit, are always present.

Two myths[33] most frequently used by scientists, and acceptable to governments seeking to improve their own credibility and progressive image by supporting scientific research, are:

1. Science is indispensable in the liberation of humanity. This myth, which has the form of emancipative narrative, has its origin with the intellectual environment of the French Revolution.
2. Science provides the only solid basis for achieving unity of all knowledge. This speculative narrative represents the Hegelian tradition.

Because of these two myths, the traditional notions of scientific truth and progress in knowledge were subjected to many attacks. Karl R. Popper proposed that theories can never be proven but only falsified. Imre Lakatos contended that scientists ignore falsifying evidence. Thomas S. Kuhn argued that science is actually a political process. Paul K. Feyerabend, by deconstructing scientific milestones, concluded that there is no logic to science and that modern scientific theories are proposed under an "anything goes" strategy.[34]

In addition to the crumbling foundations of scientific disciplines traditionally perceived as exact, we can see also the deterioration of the credibility of scientists and their work. A small but growing segment of the scientific community has encouraged a trend toward toleration of political influence, compromise, and even fraud in scientific research.[35] Although the majority of scientists have not participated directly, many are silent onlookers, or are looking the other way. This loss of objectivity and impartiality may be seen in the breakdown of the peer review system; in fake research reports based on bogus data; in the profit motive behind suppression of knowledge about adverse consequences of research-based conclusions; preoccupation with publication and, most importantly, the creation of "super science" projects patronized by powerful politicians.[36]

The closeness, and sometimes open servility, of many scientists to the state and its ideology, even though understandable when considering the amount of money governments spend on the sciences or their unscrupulous enforcement power, make even the social position of the sciences suspicious, and confirm Bertrand Russell's warning that science always gravitates from knowledge to power, and from contemplation to manipulation. The frightening conclusion, already observed in the ideological slavery of science in Nazi Germany[37] and Communist U.S.S.R.,[38] is that the scientific community is as "pure" and unbiased as the political machine dispensing its patronage and its funding. This view is shared by Brian Appleyard,[39] whose argument develops in three steps:

- Science has no value and is based on essential amorality.

- Because science is irresistible, it becomes spiritually corrosive, burning on its own stakes past authorities and traditions, and unwilling or unable to coexist with anything.

- Therefore, it is reasonable to hold science responsible for the general moral and spiritual decline of the West and resort to resisting it.

The tragic conclusion from the history of science and, especially, from its development in the past hundred years, is that human desire to find absolute truths, however noble, too often culminates in tyranny of the mind or, worse, in tyranny of the elite claiming ownership of the way to those truths. In short, contemporary science not only lost the certainty associated with its laws and theories but, due to its ideological engagement, also its credibility.[40]

There is no need to add too much to these conclusions by philosophers of science and scientists themselves. From the perspective of our particular inquiry it seems obvious that science does not have the answers, nor do its developments diminish the validity and importance of our questions.

SOCIAL SCIENCES

3

Every study of organized knowledge considers the sciences in terms of the material they study, their objectives, and their relationship with other disciplines and bodies of knowledge. The issue of methodology is considered secondary, as per its overall importance, because of its strong dependence on both subject matter and goals. The history of the sciences as a whole shows that methods leading to successful attainment of certain objectives are more easily developed for some materials than others. The study of social phenomena can benefit from a variety of methodological approaches, but the following four are emerging as the most frequently used:

The *historical approach,* which is always reconstructive, creates probably the most difficulties because the studied phenomena frequently include an extreme variety of distinct intellectual activities and social behaviors. The essential characteristic of this approach appears to be the endeavor to conceptually integrate those phenomena while preserving their individual qualities. Its weaknesses are in the need to preserve the phenomena with high levels of concreteness, which may lead to unrealistic static views of historical periods, and in the dominance of ideology-contingent narratives.

The *logistic approach*, even though distinctly logical, is not purely formal. It is being applied mostly to common observations and experiences, and aims at the development of useful, logical constructs suitable for analysis and argument.

The *scientific approach* aims at conversion of social qualities into measurable quantities. It seeks understanding as an end in itself; it starts with given phenomena but destroys them by transmuting them into abstract concepts, such as laws, models, mathematical expressions, and the like.

The *practical approach,* on the other hand, does not aim at understanding per se, but for tangible effects that are perceived as profitable and desirable, for both the present and the future.

Of course, these four approaches must be integrated to achieve the most adequate representation of the material under study.

History is the mother of the whole field of social sciences. Because history is taking place in ethnic, national, cultural, and civilizational realms, the realistic studies of social phenomena must account for the fundamental role of these realms as well. It is, therefore, quite surprising that the domains of, for example, sociology, economics, and governmental studies remained for a long time unconscious of that strong underlying influence assuming that human society is driven by some yet to be identified, from man and society independent, objective forces similar to laws of physics. They still quite often operate in a framework of denial or ignorance of these realms, or hope that they can succeed, as the exact sciences did, without understanding of their nature and impact.

In other words, people working in fields other than the exact sciences, fascinated by their successes, began to imitate their techniques and vocabulary, instead of their spirit, in attempts to reach and vindicate equal status. This approach has dominated social studies for more than one century and a half. This methodology-based perspective is finally being questioned because it has scarcely contributed anything to our understanding of social phenomena. The methods forced upon the social sciences were not always necessarily those followed by the exact sciences. In contrast with natural sciences, dealing with object-to-object relations, social studies address the relations between men (subjects) and things (objects), and the relationships between man and man (subject-to-subject or I-thou). Man's conscious or reflected actions are making collected data substantively subjective, and the "facts" of social sciences include beliefs and opinions about actions that are the object of studies.[1] Results of such critiques condensed into a new label for disciplines studying man as an intelligent social being, namely "ironic sciences." The purists, recognizing only the exact sciences as real science, often use the label "pseudosciences" to indicate their disrespect and disapproval.

The huge domain of inquiries about man and society prevents even a review of the field. For the purposes of our own study it will be sufficient to touch upon issues related to sociology, economics, and studies of civilization and cultures.

SOCIOLOGY

In short, sociology is the study of societies with the primary goals of developing observation-based, objective descriptions of social phenomena, and a coherent conceptual framework for their explanation.[2] Auguste Comte (1798–1851) was the first one to designate the word "sociology" to the dream of developing a science of society. Sociology's genesis can be traced to folk, political, and legal thinking as known from the earliest records of human thought in ancient civilizations. The study of human society is a reflection of natural curiosity of how a society is held together, whether or not societal changes indicate a progressive, or any other, direction of history, and how the actual facts of social life can be translated into some intelligible, general scheme. Most of the concepts used in sociology can be traced to the philosophical works of four men: Karl Marx (1818–1883), Herbert Spencer (1820–1903), Émile Durkheim (1858–1917), and Max Weber (1864–1920). They all had perceived the observed changes in their societies as signs of a major modal transition from traditional to modern, from a society dominated by personal relationships to one with relations impersonal and bureaucratic, from feudal to capitalist and socialist societal arrangements, and from a society dominated by retrospection to one clearly oriented toward the future. This interpretation of changes observed in their times has already been identified as a pseudohistorical claim. Though analytically distinct, the sociological aspects of social systems are so closely interdependent with economics and politics that defining a clear line of demarcation is difficult. Strong influences of psychology (e.g., of Sigmund Freud) and of Darwinism also cause some overlap with other bodies of knowledge.

At the current time, sociology's results are far away from the originally stated aims because no clearly articulated and credible theory has emerged. The thousands of detailed empirical studies, often leading to contradictory conclusions, cast doubts over the goals themselves. On the other hand, lately we have seen an increase in practical application of methods of sociology in the fields reflecting more current and real problems of society, for example, education, social work, criminology, marketing, propaganda, public opinion polling, industrial relations, and so on. The proximity of sociological theories to ideologies is causing even such applications to be perceived as controversial.[3]

In spite of its twentieth-century shift from speculative thinking to empirical research, it has become evident that sociology cannot be viewed as a science, but as an intellectual position or a mode of consciousness closely related to humanities (literature, philosophy, history, cultural studies, anthropology, art, language, theology, etc.).

Faddish for a short period, Social Darwinism is now almost universally perceived as a bad thing because it provides a rational explanation and excuse for wars, imperialism, racism, militarism, eugenics, poverty, and exploitation. Social Darwinism also proved a convenient weapon in the humanist assault on realism and naturalism. These are, of course, ideological assessments that may be used as an indictment against both liberals and conservatives trying to benefit from it during the interwar years. From the more serious analytical evaluation, its failure can be traced to the illogic and incompatibility demonstrated by the attempts to fuse ideas of Darwin with those of Spencer. The ultimate defeat is in the recognition of Social Darwinism as a social myth, even though effective, associated closely with liberal ideology and metaphysics.[4]

Critical Social Theory

The ideological underpinning of all branches of social sciences is again being confirmed by the continuous, often vociferous, debates about human sameness and otherness. On the one side stand post-structuralists, postmodernists, some feminists, and others who would base an identity-politics on the absolute otherness, the radical incompatibility of different intellectual traditions, and even sometimes the impossibility of full communication across lines of cultural or other basic differences. On the other side stand defenders of the Enlightenment with its universalism, modernism, and rationality as a basis for communication. In short, the tension between universality and difference is still in full force as the central issue of contemporary debates in social and cultural theories.[5]

Critical Social Theory has been proposed to facilitate a constructive engagement with the social world, starting with the presumption that existing arrangements—including currently affirmed identities and differences—do not exhaust the range of possibilities and allow for discovery of new arrangements that could be introduced. In spite of such a noble aim, even the most recent attempts have come under widespread criticism, and Critical Social Theory has been charged with failure to recognize the full impact of the cultural diversity of human existence. The tacit universalism has often allied it to aspects of the liberal political tradition. Part of the problem is that liberal sociologists have assumed that human beings normally live in only one social world at a time and on this assumption developed a notion of bounded and internally integrated societies. Yet this assumption is in conflict with reality, making clear that people inhabit multiple worlds simultaneously and want and are able to maintain connections with all of them. The idea of strict exclusivity forming the kernel of the liberal ideological position, in actuality, reflects a confused focus on, and generalization of, a deviation.

Sociological Theory of Knowledge

From the perspective of our objectives, these sociological controversies and ideological fights are mostly irrelevant; they only cast more doubts about the whole business and meaning of sociology as such and, especially, about its claim to the status as a branch of science. The only subject of importance to us seems to be the Sociological Theory of Knowledge because we are seeking knowledge needed to answer our questions.

The philosophical tradition of the theory of science rests on a hypothesis about the relationship between the form and content of thought, i.e., between the categories and the ingredients of knowledge or, in other words, between scientific method and the object and goal of science. The truth of this hypothesis has been widely accepted as unquestionable and self-evident. Its conclusion leads to the belief that a science is identified by its use of a particular method, not by the specific character of the subject matter. Truth of this hypothesis is now being questioned because, on one hand, some viewpoints take scientific knowledge for granted and, on the other hand, some schools of thought deal with all knowledge as exclusively socially determined, i.e., believing that nonideological scientific knowledge of natural and social worlds does not exist. The prevailing sociology of knowledge neglects the question of what conditions, if any, allow prescientific myths and ideologies to develop into supposedly scientific theories. Therefore, the sociologists who put themselves in the role of destroyers of myths are finding themselves as maintaining some of the old ones by translating them into the language of science, or creating new ones.

Crisis of Sociology

In 1970, when Alvin Gouldner warned about the coming crisis in sociology,[6] neither he nor his readers could have anticipated how severe that crisis would be. Today, the crisis is still far from over, and it is not even clear whether it will end. The crisis follows the trend and patterns of the present world that only a few serious sociologists can praise, especially when still caught under the spell of the Enlightenment's vision of a new man and a new world. This becomes quite apparent when comparing the world we live in with the visions announced in 1960s—for example, the dream about a world in which: " . . . through nonviolence, courage displaces fear. Love transcends hate. Faith reconciles doubt. Peace dominates war. Mutual regard cancels enmity. Justice for all overthrows injustice. The redemptive community supersedes [the] immoral social system."[7]

It is hard to look back at such sociological imagination with conviction that sociology can provide a realistic and credible assessment of the society's future. Today, dreams of a moral society are, at best, local hopes of those who actually suffer, and, at worst, platitudes hiding the meanness of arrogant seekers of power, but not anymore the irrational or emotional outbursts of intellectuals in the luxury of their academic environment.

The strangeness of the crisis in sociology relates to the fact that the problems of the current world (late 1990s) do not appear as crises, at least not to those in position of relative comfort. Today, sociology has lost its way in the public's eyes because of the collapse of the welfare state, which bankrolled the profession's Golden Age, and because the ideological underpinning made it unfit as the desired position of decisive measurer and assessor of social facts. Sociology missed the fact that a credible social maturity rests with accepting the world for what it is, learning to speak carefully of it and its details, and with avoidance of creating utopian visions no matter how painful the current situation may be.[8]

STUDY OF CIVILIZATIONS

In the simple explanatory wording of dictionaries, the word "civilization" provides the broadest identification for large groups of people or nations that achieved an advanced state of their society, as reflected in high levels of culture, science, industry, and in organizational structures of their governments. Civilized societies differ from primitive ones because they are settled, urban, and literate. Based on specific times in history, location, and group uniqueness, civilizations acquired different characteristics. Human history is, therefore, history of civilizations. Encyclopedias, with their bewildering range of subjects and contributors, provide, probably, the best and fullest condensed description of a particular civilization.

Newer views of civilization are concerned, besides descriptions, with its general nature, origin, progress, changes, and recent chief developments. The continuous discoveries about man's past, about behavioral and cognitive differences, as well as investigations of still-existing primitive societies, are forcing scholars to frequently recast the concept of civilization, interpretations of its past, and assessment of future possibilities.

During the Cold War, the essentially ideological bipolarity masked many underlying differences and similarities between nations. Now, the most important distinctions are expressed in the language of cultural and civilizational characteristics, not in the traditional terms of ideology, politics, or economy. Peoples and nations are now attempting to answer for themselves the most basic question humans can face: "Who are we?" instead of the old one, "In which ideological camp do we belong?" The search for an answer follows the obvious path leading to the things of highest perceived value, such as ancestry, religion, language, history, customs, morals, or institutions, as defining their group identity.

The most important groups that emerged in the post–Cold War world seem to represent seven, or eight, or even nine, civilizations:[9] African, Buddhist, Hindu, Islamic, Japanese, Latin American, Orthodox, Sinic, and Western.

Every civilization sees itself as the heart of the world and writes its history as the central drama of the history of the whole human race. This has been perhaps more true of the West than of other civilizations. This monocivilizational viewpoint has decreasing significance in our multicivilizational world. But this truism does not fit the concept of "The only remaining superpower" and is, therefore, resented by many politicians and some scholars. There is no more use for the assumption of the unity of history for the parochial concept that the European civilization of the West is, or will soon become, the universal civilization of the world. The fact that our world is a multipolar, multicivilizational world is being evaluated from basically four major perspectives.

One World: Euphoria and Harmony is based on the view that the war of ideologies is at its end and will result in harmony, international partnership, peacekeeping, and overall liberal democracy.[10] A similar illusion, which was prevalent right after World War I as well ("War to end all wars"), collapsed with the emergence of fascism and communism. Recent developments in the Middle East, Africa, the Balkans, etc., are bringing the post–Cold War euphoria to its end quite fast.

Two Worlds: Us and Them. This picture of the world carries some resemblance of reality because of the known differences between rich and poor, developed and developing, East and West, North and South, etc. This perspective is being eagerly embraced by extremists of many different ideological flavors.

The *many and more states* perspective reflects the belief that states are, and will remain, the dominant entities in world affairs. This statist paradigm is quite realistic, but it probably underestimates the power of rising international institutions, such as The World Trade Organization, International Monetary Fund, The World Bank, United Europe, trade blocks (e.g., NAFTA), and so on, pointing to a varied, complex, and multilayered international order, in many ways similar to that of medieval times.

The *sheer chaos* paradigm stresses the breakdown of states and governmental authority, proliferation of international crime organizations and terrorism, and intensification of local conflicts into massacres and ethnic cleansing.[11] This view is also close to the reality of our times and furnishes a graphic and accurate picture of the events and changes taking place. But the image of universal and undifferentiated anarchy does not provide any guidance for the future and could be missing the fact that the world may well be chaotic but not totally without order.

Considering the world we live in from any realistic perspective, the urge for destruction of opponents, characterizing the twentieth century, is easily recognizable. Mankind did its best to destroy itself in two major wars, in release of a flood of evil that many intelligent people tried to justify with praise of violence and cruelty as means of liberation and as a painful, but necessary, aspect of the dawn of a perfect society. From the humanitarian viewpoint, the biggest tragedy stemming from the growth and subsequent collapse of this heroic and aggressive materialism, associated with the name of Karl Marx and his theater of evil, rests with the fact that the only alternative humanistic vision that has emerged—the ideology of "human rights"—is actually a new justification of wars and military interventions. One may be optimistic and not feel that we are entering a new period of barbarism, but one can't exactly be joyful at the prospects before humanity either.[12]

CULTURAL STUDIES

In the search for personal answers to the basic questions of life, the framework of civilizations, even though important to consider, may be too broad and too general. The narrower concept of "culture" may provide better guidance.

Culture, as a concept, is not susceptible to simple definition. Cultural anthropologists insist that virtually no aspects of culture are common to all human societies and, therefore, observable cultural factors—such as religion, small-group or public behavior, language, humor, holidays, and ceremonies—cannot be systematized and translated into universal laws. They will remain a randomly construed grab bag of those aspects of human behavior that cannot be explained by some other, e.g., psychological or economic, theories. In spite of these difficulties, anthropologists, psychologists, sociologists, and others proposed hundreds of definitions of culture.[13] Many of those focus on issues associated with the meaning of symbols in which societies develop, perpetuate, and communicate their knowledge about, and attitudes toward, life. This quite broad perspective encompasses ideas, values, and other phenomena usually systematized by religions and ideologies. Among the variety of formalized approaches, it is quite popular to propose and emphasize a small number of factors, frequently called "dimensions," suitable for comparisons among different societies. But even those reflect multiplicity of perspectives by focusing either on patterns of communication (context, space, time, information flow), or values (acceptance of existing power structure, risk avoidance, individualism, etc.). Another approach is using descriptive metaphors[14] discussed in the following chapter. Dimensional approaches are instructive but somewhat lifeless and narrow, and metaphors may help to understand and deal effectively with actualities of a given culture, but have too many controversial elements to be accepted as a norm.

For the purposes of our study, culture may be understood simply as the total set of inherent ethical and social habits that covers ideas and values, as well as relationships and behavior. This view stresses that choices influenced by culture arise out of habits, and that they are not rational in the strict sense. The most important habits that make up a culture are reflected in moral codes and laws by which societies regulate behavior, especially when they seek to restrain the raw selfishness of their members.

To identify culture with ethical and social habits does not mean to classify it as irrational. Actual cultures are based on historical experience and display a high degree of rationality in well-structured patterns of successful behavior and valuation. Habitual choices are an effective way of life because no one has the time or inclination to rationalize formally and in detail the vast majority of required normal daily decisions. Such habits assure, for example, that the majority of people display a certain degree of honesty or prefer to avoid social risks. Because culture is a matter of habits, it changes very slowly, much slower than ideas or fashions.

Culture Wars

The importance of culture in the life and future directions of society became once more highly visible in the U.S. in the period from the 1970s to the 1990s under the label "Culture Wars." Even though twentieth-century philosophical developments, and experience with World War II and the Cold War, indicated the failure of ideologies of both right and left orientation, their appeal to politicians and their loyal academic supporters as tools for influencing the electorate remained irresistible. This is especially true when ideological biases are masked by ambiguous cultural vocabulary of family values, human rights, equality, pro-choice, pro-life, alternative lifestyles, etc. These empty shells can be filled with vague content as situational opportunities demand.[15]

On the conceptual level, this movement made crystal-clear the subjectivity and ideological dependency, not only of all the interpretations and explanations of cultural and sociological phenomena, but of their definitions as well. The dominant relativism permeating the whole society is a sign of the last phase of humanism, which made man the ultimate measure of all things. Originally "man" was the short form for "mankind"; now "man" means an individual. Originally the conflict was between man's empirical knowledge and knowledge revealed; then one body of human knowledge was put in conflict with other bodies of knowledge; and now the conflict is sliding toward the domain of one man's knowledge or belief against beliefs of others. From the medieval contempt of the world to the belief that man can save the world and himself, the world has now moved to the postmodern chaos of ideas and society weary of both perspectives. This vacuum of credible humanistic ideas brought into the picture, almost overnight, a variety of religious groups, some leaning toward political left and others toward right ideologies, making this chaos in the individual's mind even more complex and dense.

This highly visible culture war between dying ideologies is masking another silent war between society's traditional values and the lowest-common-denominator values now emphasized by the powerful entertainment industry. There is no question who is winning this war and who is defining the set of values for the future generation. Here the dangers and risks are the highest because those who define the value set in the pop culture are not just defining some patterns of thinking, but patterns of behavior of the majority as well. A humanistic ideological framework, which slipped into sheer relativism, does not provide an individual member of society with any means of defense against this serious threat.

ECONOMICS

Economics, beside linguistics, seems to be the best-developed branch of social sciences. It covers a wide variety of topics associated with understanding how individuals, households, businesses, and governments behave. It studies activities of production and exchange of goods; trends in prices, output, and unemployment; commerce among nations; and also money, banking, capital, and wealth. A frequently used technical definition of economics is simple:[16] Economics is the study of how societies use scarce resources to produce valuable commodities and distribute them among different groups.

Economists stress their desire for scientific approach through observation, statistics, analysis, and experiments, but have a difficulty convincing others about the adequacy of the level of control in their experiments, in subjectivity of observations and collected data, and in uncertainties related to the inherent unpredictability of human behavior. Another risk is seen in the well-known pitfalls in economic reasoning, such as focus on a single variable, seeing cause-effect relation in simple sequential order or statistical correlation, false generalizations, and neglect of cultural influences.

Economic theories, sometimes accompanied by mathematical models, are being developed to provide an explanatory framework for policies, norms of behavior, and regulatory actions of the government. For our inquiry, these frameworks are most important subjects of study. They all have essentially subjective character because of the always-present underlying concept of value. The following theories serve as examples.

Planned Economies

Planned economies are perceived as tools for deliberate creation of societies with certain structures to fulfill certain purposes: in Bertrand Russell's term, "artificially created societies." The rationality of this approach, which in its essence treats the whole society as encompassing a centralized methodology of production and resources planning as if a single manufacturing company with the assumed expertise of the planners, is expected to assure the most effective achievement of the stated purposes. In planned economies, the planners and economists consider human civilization entirely as the product of conscious reason, even as the product of human design, and their own role in combating spontaneous and irrational deviations caused by natural calamities or imperfect implementation of their plans and aims.

The ideologues of planned economies see them as an ideal tool of a collective humanity self-determining its own progress through "scientifically" determined and planned processes and institutions. This explains their affinity with socialist societies where the means of production, distribution, and exchange of goods are wholly, or substantially, in the hands of the state or strictly controlled collectives. Probably the highest level of ideological arrogance has been displayed by the followers of Saint-Simon when characterizing his ideals by the term "scientific socialism." In other well-structured and submissive societies, planning may be implemented only partially through, for example, preferred technology policies, subsidies of selected industrial sectors, and price controls.

The critical error in the concept of any economic or social planning is the unrealistic assumption that a complete concentration of all relevant knowledge is possible. Its tragic consequences were demonstrated in the arrested economic growth and the collapse of the socialist bloc, and in the prolonged economic crisis in Japan in the 1990s.

Market Economy

Market economy is a term describing an economic system in which the greater part of the activities of production, distribution, and exchange of goods and services are conducted by private individuals or companies, rather than centralized institutions of the government. Market economy is a fundamental characteristic of capitalistic systems where "market" is understood as an economic minisystem in which particular goods and services are exchanged at price, with the traders free to sell or not to sell what they have for what they want. The exchanges are voluntary because both parties see some advantage in them taking place; in other words, market exchange is not what some theoreticians call "zero-sum game."[17] The exchange price is determined by the interaction of supply (the varying amounts of goods producers are willing to offer at different prices) and demand (the quantity of any good that would be bought at different prices). In general, prices are the function of the consumers' real income, but price mechanisms are also the prime determinant of the income distribution across the population of consumers, although government interventions (e.g., income redistribution via fiscal policy) can strongly influence it as well. Competition among suppliers is considered fundamental for the market health because it provides freedom of choice for the consumer.

Market economies are criticized for unequal and arbitrary distribution of income, and sometimes for excessive rewards to entrepreneurs and owners of the means of production, distribution, and exchange. Another criticism comes from the perception that in advanced economies markets are dominated by producers and biased against consumers' interests.

Keynesianism, recognizing the fact that capitalist economy is subject to booms and depressions, redefined the problem of economic theory as the determination of aggregate demand and, therefore, of employment in the short run. This approach provided a theoretical framework that legitimized the use of fiscal policy and government spending as instruments helping to attain full employment and stabilize the economy.

Monetarism assumes that past rates of growth in the stock of money are the major determinants of the growth of the GNP. Consequently, monetary policy should be exclusively guided by this variable and disregard other factors, such as interest rates, credit flows, and free reserves. It also believes that fiscal policies do not significantly affect nominal GNP, though they may alter its composition and affect interest rates. Monetarism acknowledges a variety of tactical economic tools, which include managing the quantity of money, controlling interest rates, government borrowing from the public via government bonds, or cost-of-living indexing, but recognizes that their application may bring adverse side effects in the form of slower growth, temporary high unemployment and, in some situations, social pressures to introduce price and wage controls.

Supply-side economists are proposing to cut the tax burden on the economy—e.g., by moving to flat or generally lower tax rates, and by reduction of the tax on capital gains to stimulate investment—boost economic growth by shrinking the size of the government, and keep the currency strong.

New Keynesianism is an attempt to redefine the government's role in the economy. So far, the main results are great critiques of simplistic free-market policies, but coming up with new ideas that really work turned out to be much more difficult than originally assumed.

Theory of rational expectations, a recent attempt to demolish Keynesianism, assumes that ordinary people can understand and forecast economic trends, on average, as well as professional economists do. This stance leads to preference for government inaction even in times of rapid economic change. It also implies that most unemployment is voluntary, which for most people is an unappealing conclusion. Despite its intellectual attraction, it has not lived up to its original promise; its forecasting models still have Keynesian core, and they do not reflect the real world as well as the old Keynesian ones that they were supposed to replace.

Globalization, in the 1990s, seems to be the only economic principle accepted by academic economists, by Wall Street and corporate executives, by most European political parties, and, in the U.S., by both Republicans and Democrats. The enthusiastic embrace rests with the fact of enormous success of the U.S. economy in general, and U.S.-based international companies in particular, as well as with the explosion of international trade. Globalization essentially means negotiating away trade, investment, and licensing barriers of all kinds. U.S. internal deregulations and corporate downsizing are perceived as contributing to the goal of globalized trade and are justified as a removal of obstacles to increased efficiency. These actions are seen as supporting the master-remedy for all economic woes: faster economic growth. Financial crises in the Pacific region and Russian economies of the 1990s, with their potential to destabilize the rest of the world as well, are damping the original enthusiasm in parallel with the growing suspicion that the underlying philosophy takes for granted that the society exists to serve the economy, not the other way around.

Protectionism, the opposite of globalization, is reemerging as a response to its adverse consequences, namely, to the economic difficulties and anxieties faced by working Americans.[18] The presumed villains are the "transnational power elites" and local politicians who do their bidding. The problem-solving cornerstone is seen in renewal of tariffs on goods produced in areas of low-paid foreign labor. Call for government intervention in the form of new trade barriers reflects an underlying discomfort with *laissez-faire* capitalism. While an unfettered free market is the most efficient mechanism to distribute goods, there are higher values than efficiency; the economy is not the country, and the country comes first. Protectionism carries its own potential for causing economic damage by inviting reciprocal actions by foreign governments and, internally, by creating potential for dulling the market-based incentives to boost productivity.

Behavioral economics, a controversial combination of psychological insights and economic methods, seems to be the latest hope (or fad?) after the failure of speculations and mathematical models. In reaction to the well-documented, erroneous assumption of the traditional economic schools of thought that well-informed people make better decisions, behaviorists are factoring in egotism, greed, stubbornness, and downright foolishness of excessive optimism, expecting to uncover reasons for people's behavior leading to changes in their investment strategies, stock market panics, saving levels, acceptance of high debt, etc. The biggest risk lies in the repetition of, in the past, observed tendencies leading to degeneration of psychological insights into psychobabble.

Laissez-faire is a term describing market economy in which activities of the government are kept at an absolute minimum. In the *laissez-faire* philosophy of economics, private property is considered as the natural and untouchable expression of personal freedom. Therefore, this practice is highly compatible with the doctrines of individualism, especially of the rugged American variety: the love of freedom and pride in it, encouragement of competition, unregulated industry, and open opportunities.[19] The principal problem of *laissez-faire* capitalism rests with the high probability that in an entirely free market nothing is sacred and everything is for sale,[20] including babies, human organs, maternal surrogacy, as well as politicians[21] and presidential pardons.

In the latter part of the nineteenth century, attempts were made to use Darwinism in support of *laissez-faire* capitalism, and to justify those who benefited from it as winners in the process of natural selection, as those who are simply better adapted to the actual conditions of social and economic life. This Darwinian flavor supports the idea that poverty is the result not of social or economic dislocations, but of personal failure or character deficiencies.

The confidence in leave-it-alone economics went through a crisis during the Great Depression of the 1930s, from which other schools of economic thought emerged.

Welfare Economics

This term describes studies and resulting proposals for creation of conditions under which the so-called "social welfare" function (aggregate utility) can be maximized, subject to the constraints of scarce economic resources and limits set by political and administrative conditions. Such maximization requires satisfaction of the requirements of production at marginal cost as a necessary, but not sufficient, condition. This wide term embraces all policy-oriented economies. When actually realized, the state (i.e., the welfare state) assumes responsibility for the promotion and protection of the welfare of its citizens in many forms, such as unemployment benefits, universal medical insurance and care, public housing and education, old-age pension, support of the handicapped, etc., quite often on the "cradle-to-grave" basis.

Critics of such systems point to the fact that beneficiaries become less industrious and self-reliant, that free personal choices are restricted by state controls essentially similar to serfdom, and, in the long run, that the rate of wealth creation will unavoidably drop below the levels demanded by policy goals and society wants.

Capitalism

This exceedingly broad and vague term covers variously organized societies, different market structures, and many different levels of the mixture of private and public enterprises, legal rules, and government intervention. Capitalism is frequently described in ideological language as a system preferring private property ownership over communal ownership. Marxists see in it class-structured society (bourgeoisie vs. proletariat) favorable to exploitation. Non-Marxists define it in terms of resources, their use and control, and profit generation. Ideologically, capitalism encompasses a doctrine of social justice, implicit assertion of income and wealth inequalities, and expectation that citizens will employ their energies and resources in the wealth-creation process.

The collapse of the Soviet socialist bloc historically documented the advantages of free-market capitalist economies. But their introduction into highly variable cultural and economic conditions created new problems, exposed their limitations, and opened the door to corruption and frequently irrational experimentation during the transition phase. These events documented once more that capitalism has both virtues and vices.[22]

The *British-American* form of capitalism stresses individualistic values of brilliant entrepreneurs, individual responsibility for skills and profit maximization, and accepts conditions allowing for easy hiring and firing of employees and hostile takeovers. Individuals are supposed to have a personal strategy for success, and companies possess strategies for achieving goals set by their owners and investors. In general, British-American capitalism is close to the *laissez-faire* economy.

The *German-Japanese* variant, actually a communitarian capitalism, highly values teamwork, firm loyalty, industry and technology policies, and social responsibility for available skills; requires profits to be sacrificed to maintain employment and wages; and assumes that government plays a significant role in economic growth. In other words, this variant is quite close to a welfare economy. Some historians see communitarian capitalism as a relic of the past local military-industrial complex where military and economic strategies were so close that they could not have been separated.

Petty capitalism, frequently seen in developing countries, is a system of private production of agricultural or other commodities more for market than for the producer's own use, through firms organized in the idiom of kinship. Therefore, ownership, although private, is usually not individual.[23] It has proven itself highly imaginative and creative, as well as economically productive. Household enterprises are managed by men who, ideally, are members of the household and rely on labor of a finely graded spectrum of blood kinship. Outsiders are hired primarily to make up for any family-labor deficit.

The economic activities of petty capitalists are frequently embedded in, and subordinated to, tributary economics managed by state officials who put their own and rulers' requirements of reliable revenues and continuing dominance above any need for economic expansion. Petty capitalism is often a desperate attempt to deal with overburdening and aggressive tributary extraction.

Along with commodities, petty capitalists produce deep-rooted and subtly effective resistance and a sophisticated repertoire of self-protective measures aimed against the predatory ruling class. Therefore, despite their importance for the rulers, they are perceived as an expanding irritation and target for rulers' focused response. This subtype of capitalism, in general terms, never achieved any significant level of hegemony, but because of its creativity, persistence, and frequent reinvention of itself, it remains quite common.

Crony capitalism is a journalistic term for a capitalist system characterized by the dominance of government-dispensed rewards, privileges, and protection from competition, oriented toward loyal elites: a system the economists call "rent-seeking." It is often instituted in authoritarian political environments where military, financial, economic, and political powers are all fused. The larger the state presence, the more the economy is characterized by rent-seeking. Because of the role government budgets play in such arrangements, the industries are actually government owned, or government financed. This usually results in fraudulent accounting practices allowing money (usually foreign investment) to be squandered on the elite's personal wealth, ill-conceived real estate development and industrial projects inflating property values, and also to hide the actual foreign currency debt of big conglomerates and banks. In its early phase, with the help of foreign investors, such a system may show spectacular economic growth. Later, the reality of unpaid debts will cause a financial crisis and, quite probably, a prolonged stagnation as well.

The unquestionable historical success of capitalism, from its simplest petty form to its most elaborate German-Japanese variant, presented ideological challenge to institutionalized Christianity. The traditional focus on the poor members of the community caused many churches to have strong affinity with left-wing politics, despite the open atheism or antireligious position of the leading socialist ideologues. The ideological fight cast a spell over many Christian scholars and authors and produced highly imbalanced results: high levels of tolerance for the excesses and flaws of planned economies, and strong critiques of the weaknesses associated with capitalism. Even though new perspectives have been emerging recently,[24] in Christian circles the voice from the left remains louder,[25] confirming the quasireligious character of its source: humanism.

Trust-based Economy

From the recognition of the historical inertia, it is not unreasonable to consider that values, habits, and cultural styles may as well be the key ingredients of economic success because they influence the ways economic behavior rules are set, processes are constructed, communities managed, achievements rewarded, opportunities created, and conflicts and tensions resolved.[26] One specific aspect of culture that closely relates to economic activity is the ability to create new associations. Its fundamental importance rests in the facts that

- Major economic activities, in today's world, are carried out not by individuals, but by organizations demanding a high degree of social cooperation.
- Property rights, contracts, and laws of commerce, which are indispensable for creating market-oriented economic systems, have their content strongly linked to culture.
- The extent and quality of economic relations depends on levels of culturally determined mutual trust. This trust reflects the expectation of regular, honest, and cooperative behavior based on commonly shared norms.

This ability of people to work together for common purpose in groups and organizations represents "social capital" with mutual trust as its major component.[27] Social capital differs from other forms of human capital, e.g., skills and knowledge, in many ways. It cannot be acquired by individuals acting on their own, nor through rational investment decisions. Social capital is based on the prevalence of social, rather than individual virtues, and is created and transmitted through cultural mechanisms like tradition, habits, or religion. The accumulation of social capital is a complicated and, in many ways, mysterious process. While government policies may deplete the society's bank of available social capital, governments have a great difficulty building it back again.

This culture-dependent characteristic of a society strongly influences the nature of the industrial economy that the given society will be able to create. Even though working groups can be formed on self-interest or formal contract, the most effective organizations are based on trust and shared values. They do not require extensive legal regulations of their relations due to the prior moral consensus. By contrast, low social-capital societies force cooperation regulated by formal contracts that must be negotiated, agreed upon, litigated, and enforced. The legal apparatus substituting the missing trust increases the cost of doing business. Widespread distrust in a society imposes a kind of tax on all forms of economic activity, a tax that high-trust societies do not have to pay. The lesson is that modern capitalism, shaped by technology and operating in a high-trust society, allows selection of the best forms of organization and cooperation for given market situations, both valuable economic advantages.

More recent studies[28] point also to the influence of favorable geography (e.g., a temperate climate of mild winters and wet summers that permitted hard and uninterrupted work and farming without large-scale irrigation) as another key factor in wealth creation, especially when assisted by supportive behavior (thrift, honesty, hard work, patience) and positive motivation.

It is interesting to recognize the ideology-based fear of many recent researchers and writers in the field of economy to address the biodiversity of societies visible to everyone in differences in manual dexterity, in some measurable aspects of intelligence, gender-related levels of ambition and resulting specialization, disparities in population-growth rates, and so on, and their influence on the wealth-creation ability of a given society.

The preceding review of proposed economic theories, and of the economic reasoning associated with them, leads to conclusions that may be as confusing and mutually contradictory as the theories themselves. The most positive one may relate to the demonstration that fundamental questions of economy—those related to social good—can be formulated coherently and subjected to reasonable open-ended discussion and inquiry. It has also been demonstrated that distinction between whether there can be an objective answer to a given question, and who should be thought of as possessing it, is of central importance. The recent developments confirmed that economic theories cannot lead to unquestionable normative proposals of what ought to be done simply because there are no unquestionable theories. They also provided justification of doubts about the possibility of some unified economic theory by illustrating the manifold diversity of the so-far-acquired knowledge and understanding.[29]

Focus on the abstract mathematical theories, often rewarded by Nobel prizes (e.g., William Vickrey in 1996) brings much less admiration due to their very minor significance in terms of human welfare, as admitted by some of the laureates themselves. The fundamental concept of mathematization of economic theories is itself suspicious. A century ago, Alfred Marshall persuasively argued that most economic phenomena do not lend themselves easily to mathematical expression and warned against assigning wrong dimensions and proportions to economic forces and variables. F. A. Hayek also perceived economics as doubly condemned: first, by employing questionable methods different from those of exact sciences, and then, after adopting them, claiming to have demonstrated both their power and limits. Mathematization, being past-data-driven, is a sign of lost vision.[30]

A general opinion prevails that academic economics has taken a very bad fork in the road, is becoming useless to the business community, and has no policy implication either. Economists are now involved in intellectual pursuits that have very little to do with the social issues dominating the newspaper headlines, such as inequality, continuing poverty, welfare reform, protection of the Social Security system from bankruptcy, and so on. Consequently, politicians also increasingly tend to ignore academic economists and are turning for guidance to ideologies, bureaucrats, public opinion polls, and self-styled public-policy experts, often from the media. What is gospel today is gone tomorrow.[31] Paul A. Samuelson confirmed that current developments do not justify the millions of dollars a year the taxpayer is forced to give the government to subsidize economic research. In other words, developments in the twentieth century showed clearly that economics is still a peculiar science, a "dismal science" as referred to by Thomas Carlyle. F. A. Hayek even called economics a pseudoscience, indicating for a long time that if it were possible to outwit the free markets or society's judgment regarding what is profitable, economists and social scientists would be rich—his own version of the all-American question, "If you're so smart, why ain't you rich?"

The intellectual failure of economists fades into insignificance when compared to the tragedy of lives and wealth lost through forced or legislated implementation of erroneous theories turned into bad policies. It breaks one's heart to contemplate the murders committed in the name of collectivization of agriculture in the now-defunct Soviet Union, the extent of arrested growth in society's living standard and for decades maintained poverty in some states of Asia and Latin America in the name of planned economies, and the pervasiveness of organized crime and corruption in many so-called market economies. On the other hand, there is not enough appreciation of the hard work of entrepreneurs and skill- and knowledge-workers in the industrial and business trenches who actually create the wealth of their society, wealth many others freely consume, arbitrarily redistribute, and even shamelessly waste.

CONCLUSIONS

The preceding short reviews indicate that all studies of social phenomena are characterized by deliberate suppression of individuals as individuals, as well as by elimination of individual human behavior. They investigate the interrelation of collective and patterned products of the behavior of personalities, with these personalities and their behavior no longer taken into account. This view is not only collective; it is also inevitably long-range because the dimension of time adds to the social phenomena the quality of dynamism, change, flow, or growth. In the long run, the individual, even the outstanding one, necessarily fades away.[32] Therefore, it is not only easy to slip into the belief in undefined immanent forces and strict causes (determinism) behind observations and experiences, but also to deny the individual consequential influence, or freedom to avoid the traps of the cultural and intellectual environments he or she lives in. Our individual experience of frequent creative striving and the role of personal will in value-related decisions, together with the observation of the noise of "cultural wars," indicate the high level of naïveté of many social theories, their ideological foundation and, therefore, that they are much closer to opinions, expression of attitudes, or speculations than to accurate, scientific knowledge.

Social theorists' demand for approaches modeled on natural sciences can be traced to the early decades of the twentieth century. The enthusiasm for scientific social studies, with emphasis on statistical surveys and attempts for exact generalization, is best visible in economics. The idea that social studies might resemble a natural science has provoked skepticism because social scientists are often participants, not detached observers, in the study matter, so objectivity can be only pretended at the price of credibility. In contrast to the natural sciences' search for causes, social sciences seek the meaning of events.

When considering the traditional belief in intellectual rigor, objectivity, and central position of science in learning about human society, the obvious conclusion will lead to scientism, an occupational hazard of all modern thinkers, stemming from the willingness to put too high a value on science in comparison to other branches of learning and culture.[33] This form of silent worship of science in social studies reconfirms the earlier conclusion about the quasireligious character of ideologies and the difficulty in controlling their influence.

It has become evident that in our search for answers in the domain of social sciences we have encountered a chaos very similar to the one observed in the field of philosophy: chaos of many often contradictory ideas, explanations, and interpretations of social phenomena forbidding the assessment of their objectivity, accuracy, and certainty. Society and the individuals submerged in it remain mysteries, demanding that we continue our search by reviewing additional sources of information.

STUDIES OF MAN

4

When we accept Karl Popper's incisive critique of inductivism, W. V. O. Quine's repudiation of the analytic-synthetic distinction, and the critique of scientific theories and explanations by Paul K. Feyerabend and Thomas S. Kuhn, it begins to be prudent to question the usage of the term "science" for identification of almost any body of knowledge. This feeling of linguistic insecurity intensifies when top experts from the field of exact sciences, e.g., Roger Penrose, cast their eye across the whole panorama of modern sciences and find it wanting. This is even more pertinent in the field of social sciences addressing man and his social environment, considering F. A. Hayek's convincing argument about influences of metaphysics and ideologies in these domains. Therefore the title of this chapter is "Studies," not "Sciences," of Man.

It surely is ironic that the only two fields of exact science that can approach man with the same rigor as other objects of nature are anatomy and genetics,[1] both a sort of bodily geography, which can use cadavers, inanimate objects, as the main source of data. Any other study of man as a living being encounters difficulties when prudently taking into account the influences of the human mind on all bodily processes, including mechanical, chemical, biological, and physiological.

The most modern discipline studying man's existence, experiences, and anxieties is philosophical anthropology, which was established in the 1920s. It studies both man as a creature and as a creator of cultural values. It tries to interpret philosophically the facts concerning the nature of man and the human condition that other studies have discovered. It seeks to elucidate the basic qualities that make man what he is and that distinguish him from other beings. Its program aspires to a new, scientifically grounded metaphysics by combining the critical tradition of the Enlightenment with the emphasis on dogmatic certitude.

Philosophical anthropology tries to correlate and integrate anthropology's own various subdisciplines, such as historical, political, juristic, biological, psychological, phenomenological, theological, and cultural anthropologies. It embraces most of the social sciences. In general, philosophical anthropology is an attempt to construct a scientific discipline out of man's traditional efforts to understand and liberate himself. At the same time, it has been unable to escape controversies surrounding all sciences, as pointed out by existentialist and phenomenologist critiques.

The rise of scientific rationalism cannot be regarded as a process of liberation from the shackles of superstition, conventions, and fallacies, as originally expected. It turned into a process that has deprived Western man of his life's "center of gravity"—seen, for eons, in the transcendent dimension—and has alienated him from his authentic spiritual nature. At this point, it is proper to mention that neither anthropologists nor archeologists ever discovered a tribe of atheists.

The central theoretical insight credited to philosophical anthropology consists in an affirmation of the individuality and sociability of man as ultimate values. But this is, in essence, the utilitarian image of man that has prevailed in the Western cultural environment since the early nineteenth century. The controversy between individual freedom and collective justice, inherited from the distant past, remains unsolved.

Then who is this "man," this subject-object of a variety of investigations we plan to review? Not even anthropologists agree, or consistently employ, the terms "man" and "human." It seems to be beneficial to distinguish between human nature, as the sum of man's potentialities, and human personality, the total sum of his actualities. From this distinction it is quite clear that the concept of human nature is much wider than that of human personality.

One of the earliest scientific definitions of man was included in the first edition of the *Encyclopædia Britannica* (volume 2, p. 789), published serially in sections from 1768 to 1771. It defines man (*Homo*) as ranked under the order of primates, and characterized by having four parallel foreteeth both in the upper and lower jaw, and two mammæ on the breast—not a very complimentary assessment of man's difference from an ape, but characteristic of all scientific perspectives. According to Linnæus, who contributed to this definition, there are two species: The *Homo Sapiens,* subdivided into five varieties (the American, the European, the Asiatic, the African, and what he called the monstrous), and the *Homo Troglodytes,* orang outan, a native of Athiopia, Java, and Ambodia, not endowed with the faculty of speech.

It is obviously impossible to satisfy all schools of philosophy by one precise definition, but as a matter of convenience, most frequent humanistic understanding sees similarly as humans those representatives of the family of Hominidæ who posses a level of intelligence enabling them to design and fabricate tools for a wide variety of purposes. Such a view invites additional discussion about the concept of human nature.

HUMAN NATURE

Different meanings have been associated with the concept of human nature, but everybody agrees that it strongly relates to the obvious differences between man and other living things. The nature of man is both familiar and almost indescribable; none of the scientific and scholarly disciplines captures it in the fullness that common sense recognizes in it.

Part of the human nature is inborn; the rest seems to be acquired and deepened through learning and experience. Therefore, we can say that human nature is the result of man's hereditary endowment and unique experiences, both local and universal to the whole of mankind, and could be characterized in terms of the states of mind and feelings. Among those characteristics, moral judgment and preferred methods of action are often perceived as of dominant importance.

The commonsense view sees human nature not as innate and inferable from certain behavior, but as present in man's conduct. It implies a probable range of conduct that is "just what is to be expected" from people. Literature is a rich repository of commonsense descriptions of human nature exploiting narrative of behavior, deliberation, and musing, quite often at, or close behind, the edge of normal expectancy.

Modern intellectual developments are fragmenting the concept of human nature, and sometimes actually discarding characteristics previously considered permanent, even eternal, namely man's soul. What is left, some sort of "mutable man," is again cut into pieces to fit the material focus of individual branches of sciences—man as a toolmaker, as a biological system, as an information processing machine; what is left immutable fits only the interest of anatomy. There is real concern that such perspective will render not only the concept of human nature, but man himself, meaningless. So, it will be profitable to look over some of the past and contemporary perspectives and see whether there are some possible answers to our inquiry.

Examples of Beliefs About Human Nature

Rival beliefs about human nature are usually part of political and socioeconomic systems and are reflected in preferable patterns of life. Different views about human nature lead naturally to different conclusions about what the meaning of life is, what we ought to do, and how we can do it. But a few main elements are common in all views,[2] namely the background assumptions about the nature of the universe, assumptions about man's position in nature, diagnosis of what is wrong with man, and prescriptions for the remedy and desired improvement.

Plato (427–347 B.C.) held a dualistic view of man as a mortal physical body and indestructible nonmaterial entity, called soul or mind, that can exist apart from the body. Because knowledge is attained by the mind, not the body, intellect should be emphasized. Considering also man's social nature and the individual's dependence on others, morality in the form of virtues is equally important. Requirements of knowledge and virtue lead to an ideal society governed by a perfect philosopher-king. How he should be found or educated and how to prevent him from sliding toward absolute power are still unanswered questions.[3]

Karl Marx (1818–1883) thought that, apart from a few obvious biological facts, there is no such a thing as permanent human nature.[4] What characterizes men in one society or period is not necessarily true of them in another place or time. Whatever a person does is an essentially social act, i.e., an act reflecting acknowledgment of the existence of other people in certain relationships to that particular person. Therefore, the real nature of man is the totality of his social relations. Because these relations are different for different persons, there is no rationality in the assumption about some universal generalized human nature.

As universal man vanishes, two fictitious personalities, the worker and the capitalist, stand in a hostile confrontation. Neither is fully human. The worker is a nonman, an abstract proletarian devoid of every human attribute save the essential one: class hatred. On the other side, the productive entrepreneurial urge within most men is transformed into a fleshly, semihuman form, the capitalist, whose behavior is a function not of his individual decisions, but rather that of an objective historical power which transcends human control.[5] In this view Marx deviated from Darwin, whom he admired, and insisted that more than natural evolution was involved in the emergence of the human species. Endowed with the capacity for consciousness, humanity began to influence its own evolution in a way radically different from what takes place in the merely animal realm.

The primary problem man faces is what Marx called "alienation," a concept that encompasses certain characteristics of the capitalist society, namely private ownership, and related wrong value judgments. In this respect, capitalist society is not in accordance with basic human nature. Out of this assessment follows the obvious conclusion: if man is formed by circumstances, these circumstances must be humanly formed. If alienation is caused by the features of the capitalist economic system, then the system cannot be reformed or incrementally improved. It must be abolished and replaced by a better one. This opinion has serious consequences for the individual because it perceives the cure of all observable ills in some revolutionary transformation of the society.

The view of *Sigmund Freud* (1856–1939) is based on acceptance of strict determinism, assuming that all events, including events in the realm of the human mind, have preceding sufficient cause. Dreams, slips of tongue, faulty actions, etc., previously considered insignificant are now looked at as determined by hidden causes in a person's mind. Nothing that a person does or says is, therefore, accidental or haphazard, which, in extreme interpretation, may suggest denial of human free will. Another implication is the need to recognize uncontrollable causes determining some choices of behavior, and to postulate existence of unconscious mental states, which brings Freud's theory into the area of quasireligious faith.[6]

The unconscious is perceived as a natural driving force that actively exerts pressure and influences a person's thoughts and behavior. Freud points to unconscious desires that a person cannot explain rationally to others, or even to himself. But the question of the ultimate nature of such mental states has been left unanswered.

Originally, Freud talked about a tripartite structure of mind: conscious, preconscious, and unconscious. Later, he distinguished three major systems within the human mind: the id, which contains all the instincts demanding immediate satisfaction; the ego, involved in dealing with the outside world; and the superego, a special part of the ego that contains the conscience, the social norms acquired in childhood and early youth. The superego has, of course, connection with both id and ego.

The least systematic is Freud's view of human instincts and drives. Sometimes he claimed the ability to distinguish an indeterminate number of instincts; in other situations he thought that they all could be derived from a few basic ones. Because of his focus on sexual instincts, his ideas have been misinterpreted to the point that all human behavior is sexually motivated.

He also assumed that individual human character is a product of hereditary endowment and of forgotten particular traumatic experiences in infancy and early childhood.

About 1930, Freud remarked that man has gained control over the forces of nature to such an extent that with their help man will have no difficulty in exterminating one another to the last man. Mankind knows this, and hence comes a large part of the current unrest, man's unhappiness and widespread mood of anxiety.[7]

The ultimate goal of Freud's studies seem to be the achievement of harmonious balance between id, ego, and superego, and between the individual and his world. The primary strategy leading toward this goal can be summarized under the umbrella of self-knowledge, with the potential help of psychoanalytical treatment as the key tactics suitable for remedial cases.

The position of *Jean-Paul Sartre* (1905–1980) directly contradicts Freud's postulates of complete psychic determinism and of unconscious mental states because he held the conviction that every aspect of man's mental life is intentional and responsibly chosen and, therefore, transparent to the individual. Anguish, for example, is not fear of an external object, but the awareness of the ultimate unpredictability of one's own behavior.

From Sartre's perspective, the crucial problem of modern man is self-deception, the unwillingness to admit that his attitudes and actions are determined completely by himself, his character, his situation, his assumed role in life, etc. In other words, man tries to escape his responsibility by pretending that he is not free. But man is condemned to be free. Every human individual is completely free to decide what he or she wants to be and wants to do. Individuals are not determined by the society or anything else, and they cannot escape the necessity of choice. So, the only realistic attitude is to accept this situation and make choices with full awareness of their possible results. This opinion of Sartre's existentialism is clearly reflected in modern liberal democracy, which acknowledges the right of each individual to freely pursue his or her own concept and understanding of happiness, and assumes the existence of no objective values for human living, only of subjective individual choices.[8] The dark aspects of existentialism found their expression in the random killings observed in the last decades of the twentieth century.

B. F. Skinner's (1904–1990) interest in the scientific method provided the reasoning behind his conviction that empirical studies of human behavior are the only way to discover the true human nature. This approach led to a rejection of all postulates about unobservable inner mental causes of behavior and to a general perception that a person is an organism whose behavior has identifiable and manipulable causes, a frightening conclusion considering the twentieth-century experience with totalitarian ideologies and political regimes.[9]

Skinner holds that circumstances and environment control human behavior via the mechanism of conditioning. Therefore, they should be humanly formed. In parallel to Marx, he suggested that social environment should be changed deliberately so the new man, the product of such change, will display better patterns of behavior. This prescription looks naïvely optimistic, but the underlying demand to voluntarily hand over individual freedoms to social engineers is quite sinister.

Konrad Lorenz (1903–1989) is one of the founding fathers of the scientific study of animal behavior. He sees man as an animal who has evolved from other animals; therefore, man's patterns of behavior are fundamentally similar to those of animals. To think of man as different in kind, whether in virtue of free will or anything else, is an illusion. Man's difference is only in degree because man is so far the highest product of evolution.[10]

The crucial point of Lorenz's view is the belief that, like many other animals, man has an innate drive to aggressive behavior toward his own species. In this belief he sees the only possible explanation of the conflicts and wars throughout all human history, the principally unreasonable behavior of supposedly reasonable beings. This militant enthusiasm, the aggressive excitement associated with loss of rationality and moral inhibitions, is a product of evolution of the instinct of the communal defense response of our prehuman ancestors.

Lorenz knows that appeals to rationality and moral responsibility have been notoriously ineffective in controlling human conflicts, confirming his belief that aggression really is innate in man, but also introducing pessimism into his view of man's future. The only hope is that reason will influence the evolutionary selection process in the right direction.

Jacob Bronowski (1908–1974) assumes man to be a singular creature with a set of gifts, in body and mind, which make him unique among the animals.[11] Man is not a figure in the landscape, but a shaper of the landscape, the explorer of nature.

Every human action goes back in some part to man's animal origins, but man's behavior is not driven by his immediate environment, as animal actions are. The radical difference is in the sense of foresight, in imagination of the future, in the ability to fix an objective ahead and rigorously hold attention on it. This foresight drives cultural evolution, a sequence of progressive changes that have made man master of the Earth.

The most powerful drive in the ascent of man is his pleasure in his own skills. Man's hand is the cutting edge of his mind; therefore, the tool that extends the human hand is also an instrument of vision, of imagination of new structures and of new combinations of things. Such imaginations bring the objective, descriptive, and anonymous knowledge into the domain of personal discovery, personal knowledge. This knowledge creates desire to understand nature on both macro and micro levels and paves the way toward conviction that every man can and should be master of his own life. But real mastery demands certain, indubitable, and complete knowledge attainable only through science.

The key human dilemma rests with the possibility that even the most accurate and certain knowledge can be, and already has been, misused. Science may lead to dehumanization of man; it stimulates the human itch for power related to the ages-old conflict between intellectual leadership and civil authority. No animal is faced with this dilemma. So the imagination, which is the root cause of the cultural evolution toward a new future, is also the source of man's fear of that future, fear that mankind could even cease to exist.

Martin Heidegger (1889–1976) completely rejected the Darwinian, naturalistic view of humanity. He perceived the paradox of rationalistic humanism in its attempt to integrate the view that humans are like other animals struggling for survival, with the view that humans are different, being endowed by a rationality that gives them the right to define, evaluate, and use things in any way they choose. This perception is nothing more than self-elevation of the human animal to the level of god. Heidegger maintained that modernity and industrial technology are the result of mortal humanity's hubristic attempt to make itself godlike, to act as if there were no transcendent dimensions beyond human reason. In short, the question, "Who is man?" is a proper one, but the answer, "Man is an intelligent animal" is wrong.

Heidegger also maintained that humans are not animals at all, that the human body is something essentially other than an animal organism, that the human hand especially cannot be conceived as equivalent to an animal's appendage. Animal life is driven strictly by impulses and instincts, while utilitarian considerations drive human actions.

Heidegger's analysis of the human being, like the human being itself, includes a complex totality of mutually related discrete items of experience reflecting everyday existence with its three aspects: contingency, forfeiture, and transcendence, all of which are relevant to his concept of the world. In Heidegger's technical terminology, the only meaningful view of man is as "Being-in-the-world." Only this view allows explanation of why a finite creature can reflect upon infinity. Outside of this perspective man remains blurred and formless.[12] The problem with this view, which had been developed before the explosion of visual mass media, is the fact that man in front of a TV set is not "in-the-world." He has become only a spectator, an eavesdropper, a Peeping Tom, a listless and passive consumer of the strongly biased phantom images presented to him as the world. If Heidegger is right in his analysis, the nature of today's man is significantly poorer than that of the members of previous generations and cultures.

Hannah Arendt (1906–1975) argued that three basic kinds of human activity require recognition:[13]

- Labor, which produces goods for immediate consumption and is aimed at sustenance of life.

- Work, which produces enduring structures where human behavior can take place.

- Action, which opens up and preserves the historicopolitical world through language.

She noted that economists (e.g., both Adam Smith and Karl Marx) define humanity in terms of its capacity for productive labor, which leads people to become preoccupied with appetites and desires and other urges of the body. Dominated by the never-ending cycle of production and consumption, humanity is in the danger of declining to Nietzsche's "herd," concerned only with a full belly and warm shelter. The consumerist society is able to bring the "laboring animal" to the deadliest, most sterile passivity history has ever known. In consonance with Heidegger's view, she warned that the destruction of earth can easily go hand-in-hand with a guaranteed supreme living standard for man, and just as easily with organized establishment of a predefined and unified state of happiness for all men.

Robert Nozick (1938–) sees the ability to achieve a meaningful life as the key characteristic of human nature. Meaningful life is perceived as a life organized according to a plan and a hierarchy of goals that integrate and direct it. Such a life has certain features of structure, pattern, and detail that the person intends his life to have and show forth. This means to live transparently so others can see the plan man's life is based upon, and thereby learn a lesson from his life—a lesson that includes a positive evaluation of these weighty and intended features in the life lived transparently. It is generally agreed that people do not want their lives to provide others with any negative lesson.[14]

Michel Foucalt (1926–1984) concerned himself not with the past evolution of the concept of human nature, but with the influences and consequences associated with the rise of the technological era, especially with the resulting transformation of man.[15] He studied the disciplines imposed on man by modern institutions, such as factories, military barracks, hospitals, etc., and by the impact of the growing importance of sexuality. Modern institutions subject people to constant surveillance and impose rules designed to achieve, from their point of view, a state of "normalcy," designed to turn human beings into the "bio-power" suitable for the totalizing aims of political, economic, and technological systems.

He sees dangers in the changed character of power. Traditional forms of power are visible, brought into the open by police and military, and kept on display, while ordinary citizens are kept in the shade. Now, power itself seeks invisibility behind political, marketing, financial, medical, etc., databases continuously fed with new information obtained in frequent and flagrant violation of privacy, and behind an ever-increasing number of laws, lawyers, and bureaucrats. Now the individual is in the open and with constant visibility to the hidden powers that be. The most curious aspect of this transformation is that, somehow, the disciplinary practices themselves seem to embody this power. This trend leads to a situation in which the original, historically emerged social ends and intentions of this transformation fade away, resulting in some sort of social and cultural pathology: nihilism, narcissism, depression, apathy, despair, low self-esteem, etc. This psychopathology is as much a result of political economy and ideological hegemony as it is a question for biology, medicine, and psychiatry.

The Fourth Man. Since the early 1960s, an opinion has been formulated suggesting that from among the three types of man produced by Western culture—the Christian, the Renaissance individualist, and the bourgeois moralist—a new "Fourth Man" has emerged. This new man is, obviously, post-Christian (even postreligious), postindividualist, and postmoralist. For this "Fourth Man" all the old beliefs have no meaning.[16] The defiant behavior of young people of the post-World War II generation, illustrating their deep indignation at the world they inherited, may be considered as a sign of the

"Fourth Man" coming. The results of such rejectionist attitude are best described by the term "dislocation," indicating that the "Fourth Man" has no homeland. He has wandered away from his cultural roots, from his heritage, from his past, from his community identification, and from his family, and found himself facing the complex and fast-changing contemporary world with an extremely high level of anguish, uncertainty, and without any credible guidance.

This self-inflicted disorientation, characteristic of impersonal cosmopolitan society, is accompanied by loneliness, high mobility reflecting both flight from problems and search for some security, risk of being enslaved by a crass subculture, mediocrity and shallowness in personal relations, and predisposition toward narcissistic gluttony, hedonism, desensitized emotions, and dulled empathy.

The "Fourth Man" looks like a spiritual amputee looking for mood implants, and finding them in, for example, the peace movement, New Age mysticism, promiscuous sex, and drug use. But regaining spiritual health looks almost impossible due to his complete and fatalistic rejection of all metaphysical and doctrinal systems.

The possessed man. The French postmodernists observed the changes in the post–World War II society and changes in the direction of its cultural development as well. They were familiar with the original "possessive man," the calculative owner of values that can be appropriated on the free market or acquired by manipulative ideological power. This possessive man has been the hero of all early political economies and terminal subject of ideas about property ownership and property ownership–related rights. He has been the energizing agent driven by economic inequality and was eager to sacrifice himself to the rules of the production system. The social system of possessive individualism has been characterized by state capitalism, state socialism, and state fascism. The final crash of these statist systems has defined the division between the demise of the possessive individual of the age of classic liberalism and the emergence of the possessed individual as the inheritor of the nihilist legacy.

Now, after the crash of those statist systems, this possessive individual has become himself an object of consumption and has been overcome by the "possessed man," who became the sign of the disappearance of ideology as a social force and of its transformation into plain rhetoric. Possessed individualism is the condition of today's freedom because it involves perfect forgetfulness of the history of humanity, and even of the history of man's own life. For the postmodern philosopher, the possessed individual—limited by forgetfulness, charmed by seduction, and disciplined only by the codes of cynical power—embodies the form of nihilism associated with the last days or rationalism.[17] He represents the new order of domination, which is the result of mutation from hierarchically defined powers to self-appointed, often violent leaders, bringing with them many quite alarming events.

There are, of course, many other views of man and his nature, perhaps less prominent in the West, but significant in other parts of the world, such as:

Hinduism, which may be characterized as a system of means for man to attain liberation from the common destiny of continuous rebirths, which, due to human malice and eternal retributive accountability, may lead to being reborn in a lower condition.[18]

Buddhism, offering belief and practices leading toward attainment of man's freedom and enlightenment in perfect existence through a life of efforts in following the views and life of Buddha.[19]

Islam, inviting man to believe in an unknowable god (Allah), who works in mysterious ways, sustains men, teaches and guides them, is merciful, or leads unbelievers astray according to his will.[20]

HUMAN PERSONALITY

The majority of attempted conclusions in the study of human nature, directly or indirectly, addressed the sociability dimension of human nature, and some assigned to it very high, if not the highest, value. It is, therefore, quite natural to consider that human nature will be reflected in the character of the society he lives in and contributes to, and, vice versa, the surrounding social environment will influence the feature set describing human nature. It is understood that, because of differences among cultures, no single generic definition of human nature can emerge from human studies. But the stereotypes, sociotypes, or metaphorical descriptions of dominant personality traits might bring, if not valuable insights, then at least better appreciation of real men and their individual uniqueness.

That this is a real concern is demonstrated by managerial experience from multinational companies pointing to the fact that local culture influences employees' attitudes and behavior more than professional role, social class, gender, race, or age. It is also well known from experience that small cultural mistakes can have enormous consequences. Very strong cultural influence is also easy to recognize in works of art and literature, which may help in mutual understanding among people approaching their self-realization differently.

Let us keep in mind also that it is quite natural that, while a given group or society may have a distinct mind-set, it can be united with other groups by a cultural worldview that they all share. For example, although culture tends to differentiate societies, social class or ideological identification tends to unite them.

Cultural portraits, in the form of metaphors, provide valuable learning mechanisms about dominant cultural characteristics influencing human behavior.

Cultural Metaphors

Constructing cultural metaphors represents a relatively new method leading to understanding the cultural mind-set of some social or ethnic group and of its members, and to compare findings to those gained in studies of other groups. In essence, the method involves identifying some phenomenon or activity of a group's culture that all of its members consider, consciously or unconsciously, to be very important, if not critical, and with which they identify closely.[21] Cultural metaphors emerge as the dominant profile from structured interviews with natives when attempting to identify and prioritize well-established behavioral patterns, such as public behavior, leisure pursuits, socialization, greeting behavior, humor, eating behavior, sport, work ethics, characteristics of successful social status, and so on. Thus the metaphor is a guide to understanding personalities and, therefore, provides basic insight into human nature as adapted and molded by the given cultural milieu. Although the metaphor itself cannot encompass all of the reality, it represents a good starting point. Because it is difficult to verify cultural metaphors empirically, they must be simple, to the point, and reflect consensus between the analyst and subjects of his study.

In the following examples, the presented lists of observed characteristics are, of course, incomplete. The first example illustrates the logic of the methodology; the following examples summarize the primary observations about the individual's personality as it reflects the local culture. The study results are then expressed in descriptors of two complementary terms: individualism and collectivism, and in the form of the primary metaphor.

Americans. Considering its popularity, professional football seems to be the best metaphor describing and explaining various critical aspects of American culture. Americans will instinctively recognize the link between life in the United States and what is happening on the football field. Here is the list of observations:

Football is a team sport, but only the individual player is glorified and celebrated as an icon possessing superhuman traits; the professional football team is actually a multimillion-dollar corporation subdivided into departments with specialized functions; it is an embodiment of profit, fame, and glory; importance of sponsorship is high; winners are glorified and praised while losers are forgotten and ridiculed; victory demands ceremonial celebration; there is a defined set of collective rituals; deep religious and patriotic sentiments are displayed; values are shared by one dynamic group; homogeneous crowd of spectators; intense competition; rules of the game are slowly changing, but not its purpose; emotional intensity; mystical appeal of the outstanding athlete; high degree of specialization; consistent aggressiveness; constant movement; outlandish speed; huddling; cheerleaders are highly valued; special gear and gadgets.

Out of these observations, a few obvious characteristics readily emerge:
- Goal orientation (Beat the Joneses, get rich, retire early)
- Short-term job orientation (Changes creating opportunities)
- Regulated team competition (Antitrust laws, minimum salary)
- Emphasis on individualism (VIPs, celebrities, CEO compensation)
- Competitive specialization (Dislike of fixed job descriptions)
- Innovation encouraged, but not in the domain of values and ideals
- Aggressiveness (Intense motivation, profit focus)
- Extrovertedness (Extended personal relations)

The concluding characterization of an American personality may be then stated in terms of competitive individualism, in conjunction with flexible, purpose/goal–based collectivism.

British. The traditional British house may serve as the appropriate cultural metaphor. Being built to stand the test of time and assure a familiar and unchanging way of life, it provides a simple model of the preferred social institutions and conservative behavior.

The primary observations about the personality of a typical Briton are: Preference for long-lasting, traditional style of their buildings; monarchy as a vital part of the political scenario; socialistic bias reflected in services provided by the state—health, education, and housing; insistence on private, personal space; enjoyment of camaraderie in the local "pub"; behavior characterized by orderliness, patience, and unexcitability; social roles and status are generally well-defined; speech patterns are related to social and regional differences; quintessential leisure activity is afternoon tea; preference for bland food with no surprises; love of biting and satirical humor; vagueness in communication is favored because exacting details are considered trivial, unnecessary, and somewhat distasteful; social conversation is characterized by politeness and modesty.

Resulting characteristics: tradition-bound and iconoclastic individualism combined with social class–based collectivism.

Frenchmen. French wine and wine making is the obvious cultural metaphor because of wine's important role in the local history and economy, because the wide variety mirrors the variety of personalities, and because French wine's reputation supports the French predilection to think in terms of greatness.

The primary observations about the embedded personality of a typical Frenchman are: a romantic view of his country as special and unique; tendency to give the impression that France is the center of the universe; society is clearly stratified and divided into classes; each person knows his place in society, is comfortable with it, and does not feel inferior to anyone; rules, regulations, and procedures are perceived as guarantors of certainty and order; preoccupation with form over substance is evident in the sense of style and a flair for elegance; when honor is an issue, keeping one's word is more important that profit; centralized social structures demand and receive acceptance of autocratic behavior; emphasis is on low-context behavior in the form of excessive bureaucratic rules; conversational restlessness is necessitating long and lively exploration of the topic's details; Frenchmen are quick to criticize; although romantic in love, marriage tends to be approached in a practical manner; government instability seems to be welcomed; one of life's greatest pleasures is seen in having friends; there is resentment, prejudice, and discrimination against newcomers, especially against those arriving from former colonies.

Resulting characteristics: Rationalistic individualism in combination with ethnicity-based collectivism.

Italians. Italian opera serves as the closest cultural metaphor very well, considering its emotional language, dramatic actions, spectacle, pageantry, and sense of fate.

The primary observations about the personality of a typical Italian are: acceptance of insecurity as a fact of life; ability to enjoy life; love of spectacle and pageantry and clothing sophistication; importance of voice based on belief that Italian language is the most beautiful in the world; exteriority reflecting conviction that emotions are so powerful that an individual cannot keep them within and must express them to others; minimalist private life—everything of importance occurs in public; family is at the center of life, including business relations; relatively low level of mutual trust among individuals outside the family circle resulting in difficulties to integrate immigrants; in the North respect is achieved through prosperity, in the South respect means to be obeyed, admired, and envied; importance of the family meal ritual.

Resulting general characteristics of Italian personality: subordinated individualism in combination with religion and family-based collectivism.

Japanese. The Japanese Garden seems to be the best cultural metaphor when considering the ever-present water as a symbol of social fluidity combined with retention of essential characteristics and its centrality in agriculture, and the Japanese keen awareness of natural beauty as well.

Observations: Post–World War II society, as a whole, is fluid and changing while retaining its essential character manifested in these four elements: harmony, the proper way of doing things emphasizing form and process, combining the energies of individuals into group activities, and spiritual training and aesthetics; acceptance of self-discipline, self-mastery, and devotion to duty; importance of martial arts, flower arranging, and tea ceremony; excessive amount of love and attention given to children, especially to boys;

abundance of social interest groups; in negotiation, preferred partners are open-minded, generous, and capable of appreciating the other person's position, even when neither logical nor rational; situational ethics is prevalent; drinking and drunkenness are good-naturedly tolerated, even encouraged; sex is not strongly associated with love; personal status is of great importance, because it provides basis for self-identification; appearance does not always reflect reality; contemporary society is experiencing a high rate of cultural change carried mostly by young people, namely tendency toward diversity and individuality, desire for instant gratification, and need for stability and maintenance of status quo.

Resulting characterization: disciplined individualism in combination with undifferentiated, family-based collectivism.

Spaniards. Dominating metaphor: The bullfight (*corrida de toros*). Here bulls represent foreign invaders to be conquered by a team (*cuadrilla*) of fighters, of heroes facing a genuine danger to assure conditions for the following communal enjoyment of food, drink, and the opportunity to display hospitality.

Observations: Fear of loneliness resulting in living close together to achieve a sense of security; preference to deal with long-term friends and acquaintances rather than outsiders; feeling comfortable in crowds and delight in communal festivities; loyalty toward family, friends, town, does not extend to the larger collectives; upbringing of children is characterized by highly protective spirit; husbands see their wives as if they are saints, accord to them due respect and know that they are their family's stronghold, but the macho "Don Juanism" is perfectly acceptable as well; harshness of Spain's climate is accepted but is reflected in sadness and tragedy of folk songs and dances; key values are honor, dignity, and pride, associated with a contempt for manual labor; belief that men are not born to realize any social goal but to realize themselves, resulting in lack of collective effort, poor government, and inefficient bureaucracy; work is seen only as a means to an end—survival; there is a visible disdain for commercial activity; violence and death are faced with dignity; emotional expressions (*"Olé!"*) are interactive forms of communication and participation; acting on emotions, Spaniards are incredibly generous and hospitable; religion is incorporated into life's both mundane and most dramatic moments.

Resulting characterization: Proud and self-sufficient individualism together with limited, selective, loyalty-based collectivism.

Cultural metaphors seem to support an intuitive view that the dynamics of culture is a function of only a small number of mechanisms. Into the most basic set belong geographical closeness, common language, and a common system of values. The influence of religion on the contents of the value system, strong in the past, is now declining. Among additional mechanisms, the most visible are common ethnic origin, extended family, education system, form of government, group history, social class structure, and rate of change, especially of technological change.

The examples reviewed provide a very reasonable initial insight into people's behavior in different cultural environments, into their personalities, and by that, a new perspective on the problem of human nature. But we may continue our inquiry by opening a new, although obvious, question: "What is meant by 'behavior'?" Answering this question is not as simple as it seems.

Suppose that "behavior" is understood, according to common sense, as any movement of an organism. The immediate difficulty is uncovered by a follow-up question, "Does this include physiological processes?" B. F. Skinner proposed a more restrictive definition of behavior as "the action of the organism upon the outside world." Here the difficulty stems from consideration of speech as "verbal behavior," and of dreaming, reflecting, observing, inferring, and so on. Perhaps behavior should be considered only "whatever an organism does, provided that it acts upon the outside world," but this definition will open questions related to observability and about unintentional movements.

These problems, accompanied by the conviction that what is termed "behavior" is in some way the matter of central importance in the study of man, are at the beginning of behaviorism, a philosophical theory expected to resolve the key issues. It is interesting to note that all three dominant branches of philosophical, theoretical, and psychological behaviorism accepted the perspective of reductive materialism, assuming that all psychological phenomena can be ultimately explained in terms of molecular motions and publicly observable circumstances as their cause. Critics hold these maxims too restrictive and, therefore, do not expect full understanding of human behavior to be achieved when a behaviorist perspective is adopted.

MENTAL PHENOMENA

The previous reviews confirm the helpfulness of distinguishing between human nature, the widest sum of man's potentialities, and human personality, the sum of his actualities. With the benefits of the method of cultural metaphor, we have procured some insights into the external, cultural influences on man's personality. But it does not take more than common sense and personal experience to recognize that man's personality and observable behavior strongly depend also on his will, mental capacities, intelligence, accepted personal moral standards—in other words, on his conscious mind-set defining his personal identity and uniqueness in the cultural environment. The truth of this simple conclusion is so self-evident that it does not require any assumption about the ultimate nature of man's mental processes, being either nothing more than a product of material processes of the human brain, or reflecting man's endowment by a unique, nonmaterial entity called the soul or mind.[22]

Human Mind

Plato made a sharp distinction between the body and the mind, holding that the mind can exist both before and after its residence in the body, and could rule the body during its residence. But it was Descartes who systematically investigated the nature and interrelationship between them. For him both body and mind were substances, although of completely different basic natures. In opposition to Plato, Descartes considered the body more fundamental.

Because Descartes's concept of mind, the mental-substance or pure-ego, remained obscure, other philosophers, like David Hume, suggested the "bundle" concept as an alternative. In this view, the mind is a bundle or collection of different perceptions, which succeed each other with a high rapidity and are in perpetual flux and movement.[23]

Criticism of Hume's view led to William James's proposition that the human mind is a stream of consciousness, which failed to account for occurrences of states of unconsciousness. Later, the focus shifted from search for unity of the mind to its relation to the body. The fact of the matter is that, in spite of many theories, there does not as yet exist a satisfactory account for the concept of human mind.

Dualistic theories, in general, hold the view of differences between the mental and the physical, some of substantive difference, others of difference in properties, relations, or states.

- Interactionism assumes that mental events can sometimes cause bodily events and vice versa.

- Occasionalism rejects the possibility that there could be causal interaction between these two.

- Parallelism assumed correlation between mental and physical events, using an analogy with synchronous mechanisms to point to preestablished harmony between the two.

- Epiphenomenalism presents the perspective that causal relationships work only in one direction, from body to mind; that mental events are effects only, never causes.

Monistic theories, on the other hand, deny that there are two things to be related. It is not difficult to recognize that the majority of such theories are based on a materialistic view of the world.

- Extreme materialism holds that whatever exists is physical. From this radical perspective comes the conclusion that statements about mental events are either synonymous with reports on physical events, or meaningless. In psychology, this position is identical with behaviorism.

- Identity theory uses a philosophical distinction between significance and reference to claim that mentalistic and physicalistic expressions differ in significance but both refer to the same underlying physical phenomena.

- Neutral monism sees the difference between mind and body not in the nature of its ultimate constituents (atoms and molecules) but in the ways they are arranged.

- Double-aspect theories view the mental and the physical as different aspects of something that itself is neither mental nor physical.

Bishop Berkeley attempted to develop a monistic theory of human mind under the umbrella of idealism. For him, the physical objects exist only in the mind as classes of perceptions. His underlying assumption was a claim that statements about physical objects are meaningful if, and only if, they are taken as statements about the perceptions of perceivers.

The mind-body problem remains a source of acute discomfort to philosophers. There have been attempts to show it as a "pseudo-problem," but none have stood up under test. Currently, not one of the proposed solutions can be classified as markedly superior to the others.

Consciousness

In the discussion of the mind-body problem, there are two separate issues: "How is it that the brain, a material object, can actually evoke consciousness?" and, vice versa, "How is it that a consciousness, by the action of its will, actually influences the motion of material objects, which seem to be physically determined?" These questions, together with the obvious advantage consciousness gives to those possessing it, indicate that consciousness is the essence of mind, that all mental phenomena are actually, or potentially, conscious.

Since the early seventeenth century, consciousness became an issue in philosophical debates. It has been assumed that man is always conscious to himself of thinking; therefore, consciousness has been defined as the perception of what passes in a man's own mind. Attempts to explain it considered it as (1) a peculiar substance, quite different from the material substance of which physical objects are composed; (2) as an attribute, a property of the brain or of the mind; or (3) as a group of cognitive relations that are unique and can be directly apprehended.

In behaviorist psychology, consciousness is a concept referring in a general way to the behavior of an organism, characterized by alert awareness and responsiveness as contrasted with the lack of awareness and relative unresponsiveness of deep sleep or anesthetic coma. Between these extremes, there are varying degrees or levels of consciousness. Although detailed understanding of the neural mechanisms of consciousness has not been achieved, correlations between states of consciousness and brain function are possible, and some were actually identified via electroencephalography.

Recently, a widely held view looks at the brain as a giant computer, and at the relation between the brain and mind similar to that of computer hardware and software. But computer models of the brain remain doubtful and imperfect, and may be totally wrong.[24] Reasons for rejection of the computer model are principally two: One, none of the familiar materialistic analyses of mind can deal with conscious experience; they either leave it out or identify it with something else that has nothing to do with consciousness. Two, computers, which do not have a mind, can be described as information processing systems only because they are constructed by people, who, having minds, can interpret their physical operations in that way. In John Searle's view, subjective consciousness is not reducible to anything else. It is the essence of the mental, even if most mental states are not conscious at any given time. One cannot study any aspect of mental experience without including it, or its possibility, in the definition of what one is trying to understand. In particular, intentionality is inseparable from it.[25] Such a view confirms the irrationality of the belief that consciousness is actually a scientifically describable "thing." Indeed, there is no universally recognized criterion for its manifestation. Explanations that unconscious actions of the brain are algorithmic in their nature may be acceptable, but the actions of consciousness are quite different, characterized by judgment-forming, aiming to ascertain the truth of a statement, creating insights and comprehensions, providing inspiration and aesthetic criteria, and allowing for nonverbality of thought and perception of time, all processes of nonalgorithmic nature.[26]

Considering that in the mid-1980s concepts of "mind" and "consciousness" were both actually excluded from scientific discourse, to see now cognitive scientists, philosophers, and neuroscientists revisiting these issues is very interesting, even though there is still no agreement on how consciousness should be studied or even defined. But many of the participants of this new discourse remain quite skeptical: consciousness and free will are mysteries too profound for humans to decipher, scientifically or otherwise; they see the current wave of enthusiasm as misplaced and reflecting participants' misunderstanding of quantum mechanics, assuming that quantum computation "somehow" gives rise to consciousness.[27] In spite of the sporadic optimism, mainly on the part of mental materialists, Ludwig Wittgenstein's advice, "Whereof one cannot speak, thereof one must be silent," is still pertinent.

CONCLUSIONS

Although there are thousands of scientific studies concerning almost every aspect and detail of human life, the principal question, "What (or who) is man?" has been overlooked by most of the branches of science involved, and the basic fundamental answer remains unknown. Our review indicates that, from the earliest times up to today, men have held widely divergent and even contradictory views about man's nature. Man has been thought of as essentially a spirit accidentally and temporarily imprisoned in the flesh, as an animal essentially no different from other animals, likened to a machine deterministically producing its acts, as a system of mutually dependent and supportive chemical and neurophysiological processes, as a complex information processing system, and, recently, even as a spiritual machine.[28] All these and other searches for the nature of man and meaning of life, sometimes supplemented by visits to sages and wise men, by reading poetry or using drugs, indicate the fundamental importance of the expected answer, man's vulnerability to becoming a victim of intellectual uncertainties or fraud, and the naïveté of beliefs in arbitrary connections between a person's life and some speculative formula of behavior.

In general, theories and explanations of human nature available at the present time are too mixed a bag to provide any assurance about the value of their individually assumed perspective. Some of them may deserve attention, but it must be attention closely guarded by extreme care in distinguishing between those of analytical or empirical character and those that may well be meaningless. If we do not know for sure who or what man essentially is, we are in a state of tragic fundamental ignorance of everything else about him as well. Man must know who he is if he is to know anything else about himself specifically as a human being.

ETHICS AND LAW

5

Presented reviews of different bodies of knowledge—speculative, scientific, and in narrative form—illustrate well that philosophers' and scientists' aspirations to accurately and credibly interpret and explain the reality of nature and man for everybody have not been fulfilled. Now, even more, there seems to be a real possibility that these aspirations are unrealistic, some say even immodest. In addition, questions of virtues and values, or of truth and goodness, do not have a place in the contemporary scientific picture of the world, because answers to them cannot be tested by any scientific procedure. While all the information presented so far is highly illuminating, the problems encountered did not allow us to reach our objective. So, let us now reduce the scope of our questions to only those that deal with the direction and guidance of man's behavior, especially his behavior in social settings. On the strictly human level of reasoning about those, philosophy still remains the most suitable principal framework for investigation.

It will be necessary to ask not only if we can ever know the rules of proper behavior, but whether such rules can be justified as a consequence of the available knowledge of the external world, questions endemic in most branches of philosophy. In ethics the problems are even more difficult to resolve because, while skepticism in the domain of metaphysics may be questioned, it is almost impossible to accept any human claim of knowledge of objective truths about what we ought to do. Furthermore, the disagreements concerning major moral issues seem to involve deeper principles that often have no common ground for mutual resolution. Lessons learned from Hume's skepticism should help to accept the eventuality that general and final answers may not be possible, that the questions posed have no universal meaning, that they may be unimportant in the overall scheme of things, and so on. Let us also keep in mind that issues of behavior have at least two aspects, the motivation of and the impact on the individual carrying out the particular behavior, and the influence of and impact on surrounding environments.

Despite difficulties, the fundamental character of the question about life's direction and sources of guidance seems obvious, and its importance unquestionable. Who has not asked—if only when depressed—"How should I live, and how can I find out?" Let us, therefore, take a look at two domains of knowledge with intuitively the highest probability to provide the necessary insights: ethics and law.

ETHICS

Plato reported[1] that Socrates knew well that to talk about how one should live is a serious, nontrivial, philosophical concern. They both were convinced that philosophy can answer behavior-related questions, that it can help man to direct, or if necessary, redirect his life through general and rationally reflective understanding.

Socrates' wisdom comes through when taking a closer look at his question, "How should one live?" This question avoids suggestivity of other similar questions, such as, "What is our duty?" or "How may we be good?" or "How can we be happy?" or "What should I do from a self-interested point of view?" His question is silent about the person whose life is in question, noncommittal about the considerations to be applied to it, and, in itself, does not bring in any apparent moral claims. In addition, it is not immediate; it is not about what one should do now, or next. It is about a manner of life. If ethical reasons, for example, emerge as an important component of the answer, that will not be because they have been presented by the question.

The question naturally invites the idea that there must be some preferable way to live human life that is better in some impersonal or interpersonal sense. Under Socratic reflection, even the practical question "What shall I do?" seems to be driven toward generalization of the "I" involved, and to accept some commitments, at least to examine one's own life. The unexamined life, as he put it, is not worth living.

For the Socratic-era Greek philosophers, the satisfactory state of life is characterized by well-being (*eudaimonia*) of the soul, a state which can be described in terms of knowledge and discursive reasoning leading to development of a universal set of virtues reflecting certain excellence of character. Such virtues are an internalized, intelligent (i.e., not based on habit) disposition of action, desire and feeling that also involve favorable and unfavorable reactions to other people, their character, and actions.

It is the part mentioning "reactions" where conceptual risks are quite often encountered. It may invite suggestion of involvement of judgment, assessment, approval or disapproval, all containing a flavor of, at least, temporary superiority. They also suggest some binary judgment of guilt or innocence, and in the modern mind, they collectively invite skepticism about this particular view of virtues. Modern times' understanding gives no reason to expect that any set of virtues can be fully harmonized with other personal and cultural aspirations that have a similar claim to represent human development. There is a gap between the individual's perspective and the outside view, which may consist of many beliefs equally compatible with human nature.

Principal Concepts

Ethics may be viewed as the systematic study of the nature of "value concepts," such as good, bad, ought, right, wrong, etc., and of the general principles that justify and guide their application. There is an obvious distinction between a philosophical theory of ethics and the everyday tasks of making moral decisions, but both benefit from clarification of the mentioned concepts.

Value. In the contemporary culture, the terms "value" and "valuation" and their cognates are used in a confused and confusing way.[2] In the past, the meaning of value as the worth of a thing was relatively clear and its use limited to economics. Today, meanings and uses are various and conflicting. Value enters easily into the talk of the man on the street and the man in the White House alike; it passes readily among philosophers and scientists, literary critics and political ideologists. In some indirect way, this currency points to the importance of the concept. Value may prove to be the key that could release all human and social sciences from their present position of pathetic, dignified futility.[3] The following meanings of the word "value" are encountered quite often.

- In the narrow sense, the term "value" covers such terms as good, desirable, or worthwhile.

- In a wider sense, it covers also all kinds of rightness, obligation, virtue, beauty, and truth.

- In its widest sense, it is the generic noun for all kinds of critical, or pro and con, predicates as opposed to descriptive ones, and is contrasted with existence or fact.

- Value is often thought of as a general predicate like "color."

- The term "value" is used in reference to something that is valued, thought to be good, or desired.

Some cognitivists see in value a metaphysical property that can neither be observed by or in ordinary experience, nor can be made an object of empirical science. For other cognitivists, value is a natural and empirical property that can be ascribed to objects. Extreme emotivists and existentialists assert that basic value judgments are arbitrary, irrational, and incapable of any justification. Although idealists, naturalists, and pragmatists offer different theoretical bases for the concept of value, and interpret it in different ways, they all see knowledge as the principal generalizing and unifying factor. On the other hand, this unity does not solve the classic distinction between fact and value.[4]

The Good is understood, in ethics, as what is intrinsically good, good-in-itself, not what is good only as a means to something else. This view is obviously very relevant to the question of what we ought to do, what is the supreme purpose of human life. There is a general agreement that an inanimate object, or its state or quality, cannot be good in itself. What is good-in-itself must be a kind of experience or state of mind. The difficulty is that this view is compatible with many opinions as to the exact nature of the good. The good is frequently perceived as follows:

- Happiness as the only good, a position that generally makes no distinction between happiness and long-lasting pleasure. Psychology pointed to the close connection between desire and pleasure.[5] Hedonism is not necessarily an expression of selfishness, because universalistic hedonism, aiming at the total sum of happiness, makes sense.

- The good as a unity of personality[6] assumes that no humans can be satisfied by purely physical desires, that all people embrace some sort of ideals controlled by consciousness. The unifying power of consciousness never exists apart from the content of consciousness. If we regard this unifying power as the personality of each individual, then the good resides in the development and maintenance of personality.

- Perfection as the good reflects man's desire for the fullest development of his faculties. Perfectionism may take an egoistic form, but it will still remain close to common sense. The real issue is, "What are the faculties?" They cannot be anything actual, apart from their actualization in states of mind. They remain hypothetical. This reduces the concept of perfection to a certain state of mind related to actions.

- The pluralistic view reflects the difficulty of finding a single formula that will cover all forms and cases of intrinsic goodness. It points to virtues, knowledge, love, and aesthetic experience as potential candidates for key variables in the desired formula.

With the concept of the good is closely associated the concept of obligation. When a man knows what the good is, he is obligated to produce it. This view makes obligation a moral consequence of the knowledge of good. The concept of obligation then relates to problems of motivation, sanctions, and duty.

Moral sense is the capacity to experience feelings of approval and disapproval as related to observed behavior or expression of knowledge. In a narrower view, it can be expressed by a phrase of ordinary language as a "sense of right and wrong." It documents the ability of moral discrimination.[7] The reactions caused by man's moral sense are akin to the kind of love or admiration that naturally arises toward beauty; therefore, virtues may be seen as a sort of beauty. Modern perceptions of the moral sense are found in the emotive theory of ethics,[8] which holds that moral judgments are expressions (exclamations), but not descriptions, of the speaker's emotion of approval or disapproval.

Behind all the principal concepts of ethics is hidden the even more fundamental concept of consciousness, already encountered in the previous chapter. In its simplest form, it enters ethics as a slogan: "Let your conscience be your guide." Despite its appeal, consciousness alone is insufficient and, quite often, untrustworthy. It varies from person to person, and can be altered by training, experience, and circumstances. The reliability of man's consciousness is not self-certifying, and, therefore, always subject to doubt.

Principal Perspectives

Traditionally, ethics had a practical purpose. Its goal was not that people should simply know what is good, but that they should become good. Later, expectations shifted toward generality and a systematic nature of ethical claims, and toward credibility of evidence proving those claims.

With these new demands, important disagreements have arisen. For example: Should ethics discover new truths or give systematic account of existing knowledge? How to unify the diversity of moral beliefs? How to define the ultimate rationale of the moral knowledge and practices man already has? These and other problems were approached from a variety of perspectives, presuppositions, and beliefs.

According to the *ethical naturalism* perspective, moral judgments just state a special subclass of facts about the natural world. This position has been accepted by utilitarians, evolutionists, and pragmatists. Critics point out that questions about rights are certainly different from questions of facts. Naturalism's attempts to define goodness in natural terms, thus declaring it also a natural property, have been considered its major fallacy. With this view is also closely related the problem of the assumption that it is possible to deduce an "ought" from an "is."

Ethical objectivism holds that the truth of what is asserted by some ethical sentence is independent of the person who uses this sentence, the time at which he uses it, and the place where he uses it. *Ethical logicism,* a variant of this perspective, believes that true ethical judgments are true because they cannot be denied without self-contradiction. Another variant, *intuitionism,* considers that, although ethical generalizations are not true by definition, those of them that are true can be recognized by any person with the necessary insight.

Ethical relativism is used by contemporary philosophers to designate positions they disagree with or consider absurd. The most important disagreements relate to the claim that diversities in values, and therefore in morals, are fundamental. *Metaethical relativists* reject the thesis that there is always one correct moral evaluation. *Normative relativism* asserts that something is wrong if some person or group thinks it is wrong. All relativist perspectives have difficulty supporting themselves by scientifically valid evidence, to derive meaning and purpose of ethical statements, and to explain the role cultures play in ethical controversies. The key consequence of relativism is that moral convictions of a society have, in themselves, no direct implication for what an individual member of that society is morally bound to do.

Ethical subjectivism assumes that moral judgments about men or their actions are judgments about the way people feel or think or react to these men and actions. It follows that ethical qualities are not inherent in actions and actors, but reflect judgment of the observers. This view has been the target of an enormous number of objections, most of them associated with the reference to feelings, inclusion of the words "I" or "now" or "here" in moral judgments, and the possibility that an action can simultaneously be judged "right" and "wrong."

Ethical skepticism is a position which leaves open the possibility that some actions or principles are right or wrong, and claims that we can never be able to know that this is so. This position puts limits on what is logically possible to do with ethical statements and, thus, casts doubts over the nature of moral concepts. In other words, skeptics accept commonsense moral beliefs intact, but question whether it is possible to give them an objective foundation.

The *existentialist perspective* recognizes that existence is met only in the individual who creates himself in free choice while facing the reality of an enormous load of responsibilities and his limitations, especially the ultimate limitation, death. Existence becomes even more complicated by life in the modern world, which is dominated by man-created industrial and bureaucratic institutions, and which imposes on man the recognition of the insignificance of the natural world and of all human values. This view is peculiarly appropriate to a time when the Western civilization seems to breaking up, with social bonds mostly vanished. Morality thus becomes something completely beyond reason, with no absolute values or principles, unless virtues such as authenticity, fidelity, or sincerity are counted.

Logical positivism, which began as a reaction against metaphysics, views moral judgments not as statements about facts, but as expressions of the emotional attitudes of those who utter them. There is an agreement that moral judgments are not propositions expressing belief or knowledge about matters of fact involving actions or states of affairs; they only communicate psychological conditions or attitudes of feeling or will, but not cognitive attitudes. Much of ethical thinking is, therefore, an attempt to state clearly what these noncognitive attitudes are. Logical positivists accept the basic propositions of morals (that pleasure is good, that truth ought to be told, etc.) as synthetic propositions apprehended by intellectual intuition, but do not associate them with any examination of moral assertions or arguments on their merit.

Despite the obvious controversies among different ethical perspectives and interpretations of ethics' fundamental concepts, for most of the modern era, the belief in moral progress remained strong. Only the postmodern times brought disillusionment undermining this belief in progress, recognizable in practical calls for restoration of family values, for some restrictions of violence on TV and pornography on the Internet, and in debates about abortion, assisted suicides, affirmative action, cloning, etc. When assessing the current state of affairs, the conclusion is that ethical concerns are secondary, trailing behind the dominating, "It's the economy, stupid!" interests.

Ethical Theories

The desire for discovery and formulation of some impartial position is reflected in proposed ethical theories. They address questions about proper thinking patterns of people generally committed to thinking in ethical terms. They express a wide variety of attitudes and beliefs, and serve as instruments of ethical arguments.

An ethical theory is an account of what ethical thoughts and practices are, an account that either implies a general test for the correctness of basic ethical beliefs and principles (a positive theory), or implies that there cannot be such a test (a negative theory).[9] It is necessary to distinguish between theories (1) that make substantive claims about what one should do, how one should live and what is worthwhile; (2) that are concerned whether these claims are a form of knowledge, how they could be validated, whether they are objective, and so on; (3) that are linguistic inquiries into the terms used in ethical discourse; and (4) that see substantive ethical judgments as different from philosophical analysis.

Ethical theories may have many different starting points, both inside and outside ethics. Ethical experience, belief, or intuition may serve as examples. In contemporary philosophy, they are formally divided into two major classes: teleological (utilitarian, consequential) and deontological (duty-based). In the modern social environment, the issues of individual rights and justice gained importance, thus providing two additional classes of contemporary ethical theories. It is probably worthwhile to accept the fact that all ethical theories are viewed by their authors as normative, openly or in disguise.

Utilitarian theories are formulated around the thesis that action or practice is right if it leads to the greatest possible balance of good consequences, or to the least possible balance of adverse consequences, in the world as a whole.[10] The purpose of morality is to promote human welfare by minimizing harms and maximizing benefits. The key concept is that of "intrinsic value," a value in life that we wish to possess and enjoy just for its own sake and not for something it brings. Pluralistic utilitarianism believes in many intrinsic values, while hedonistic utilitarianism focuses on acts and practices that maximize pleasure.

The contemporary view understands the concept of utility not in terms of happiness, but rather in terms of the satisfaction of individual preferences, as determined by a person's behavior. This means, to maximize a person's utility is to provide that which he or she has chosen, or would choose, from among the available alternatives. To maximize the utility of all persons affected by an action or policy is to maximize the aggregate utility of all persons in the group. A major difficulty is encountered when individuals have morally unacceptable or harmful preferences. This situation creates problems of how to formulate the range of acceptable preferences, and how to measure and compare them. These two problems are the focus of principal criticism.

Utilitarianism is also challenged on the grounds that it can lead to injustice. The goal of the greatest value for the greatest number of people may result in unjustifiable harm or disadvantage to a minority. In modern social and political environments the requirement that the rights of the individual be surrendered in the interest of the majority is plainly unacceptable. Utilitarian response to this criticism points to the short-term and superficial character of that critique; in long-range view, utility never eventuates in overall unjust incomes.

Deontological theories deny that, in ethics, only the consequences of actions and rules are important. Deontologism maintains that the meaning of duty is independent of the concept of good, that the rightness of actions may be determined by other factors, such as friendship or parent-child relation, which enrich the moral life.

Deontologists refuse to accept means/ends reasoning in the domain of ethics. They believe that we are called to observe the rights of others and to help them through difficult times. They commonly insist on the importance of motives and the character of the agent, pointing to the importance of distinction between the motive for an act and its consequences.

Deontological theories rely on the Kantian view[11] of ethics, which emphasizes performing one's duty for the sake of duty and not for any other reason, i.e., a person can act not only in accordance with duty, but also for the sake of duty. Some deontological theories expand the concept of duty toward duty of reparation, fidelity, gratitude, self-improvement, justice, etc. Such *prima-facie* duties are a form of *a priori* laws that hold unless overruled by some superior moral obligation. Kant tried to establish the ultimate basis for the validity of moral rules of duty in pure practical reason, not in intuition, conscience, or the production of utility. Ethics should provide a rational framework of principles and rules that constrain and guide everyone, independently of an individual's own personal goals and preferences. Therefore, an action has moral value only when performed by a person with an autonomous good will that reflects a valid rule as the sole motive for the action. Kant perceived a person's autonomy as the ability to govern himself in knowing acceptance of universally valid moral principles. In that case, immoral behavior involves a person trying to make an exception of himself.

Kantian tradition also affirms respect for the human being as possessing human dignity and, therefore, the only rightful determiners of one's own destiny. A stretched interpretation of this view holds that we should never treat another person as a means to our ends. But respect for persons thus constructed may easily come into conflict with, for example, constraints of economic interactions.

The most severe criticism of deontological theories claims that they covertly appeal to consequences in order to demonstrate the rightness of actions. Determination of actions to be right or wrong is impossible without consideration of consequences, so it is no surprise that the Kantian system has been found unsatisfactory.

Theories of justice. Philosophical concerns about the concept of justice revolve around the term "cooperation": what gives one person or group of people a right to expect cooperation from others in situations where the former benefit from it and the latter do not? Some ethicists have held that principles of justice have a moral priority over all other moral principles, and explicated the basic notion of justice, or equality, in terms of fairness and "what is deserved."

Systematic theories of justice attempt to be more specific than those principles. They aim at precise elaboration of the notion of equality and detailed specification of how different individuals are to be compared, and also at identification of what it means to give people their due. They attempt to systematize and simplify moral institutions by selecting and emphasizing one or more of the available principles.[12] Some emphasize equal access to primary goods, some emphasize needs, others emphasize rights to social and economic liberty. In most current systems, it is easy to recognize distinctions between just procedures, equal opportunities, and equal or just results. Ideally, it is preferable to achieve all, but this is seldom possible.

One of the many difficult problems of justice in a cooperative society is to design a system of procedures that provides as much justice as possible. Because of the inevitability of unfortunate outcomes, shifting the blame from results to procedures intensifies the inherent contradictions. The purpose of moral principles and ethical theories is to assist persons in making difficult decisions about these dilemmas, but they are not always successful in that mission (see also pp. 101, 102).

Theories of economic justice. Contemporary Western society's unprecedented ability to create wealth also creates, as an unintended consequence, easy-to-notice economic disparities among individuals and nations. This discrepancy triggers demand for development of new ways to distribute this wealth, which then stimulates desires to formulate theories of economic justice in general, or theories of distributive justice in particular.

Egalitarian theories assume that individual differences are no more significant in the economic and social domains than in the ethical domain. John Rawls[13] contends that society should distribute all economic goods and services equally, except in those cases where an unequal distribution would actually work to everyone's advantage. His views are a direct challenge to utilitarianism in the Kantian tradition. He perceives two principles of justice as acceptable to all, namely that each person should be permitted the maximum amount of equal basic liberties compatible with similar liberties for others, and that once this equal basic liberty is assured, inequalities in access to primary social goods, such as income, rights, and opportunities, are to be allowed only if they benefit everyone.

Libertarian theories challenge egalitarian theories directly by concentrating on individual rights, which reflect Adam Smith's view that people acting in an individually self-interested fashion exhibit behavioral patterns that collectively enhance the interest of everyone in the larger society. People are freely entering and withdrawing from economic arrangements in accordance with a controlling perception of their own interest. The concept of free choice is central to their account of justice, including the fundamental right to own and dispense with the products of their labor as they choose. This right is so fundamental that it must be respected even if its unrestricted exercise leads to great inequalities of wealth in society.

More recent critiques point to the fact that claimed redistribution is actually far less redistribution of free income from the richer to the poorer than a redistribution of power from the individual to the state. It inexorably results in atrophied personal responsibility and hypertrophy of the bureaucracy, instead of relief to the minorities its proponents pledged to serve.[14]

Robert Nozick's theory[15] aims at the justification of citizens' fundamental rights or entitlements. It presents social justice as embedded in states' pronounced steps to actively redistribute the wealth acquired by individuals exercising their economic rights in accordance with laws of free-market economy. This seems to be a pure procedural justice devoid of any substantive criterion or pattern.

Marxist theories, still alive in some academic and political circles, challenge the adequacy of any purely procedural account of justice, as well as lower-level concepts, e.g., of consumer sovereignty. These theories substitute all free-market conceptions of justice by some materialistic principle specifying people's need and their fulfillment as the key measures of economic justice.

Theories of rights. Much of the modern ethical discussion turns around the ideas about rights and how to secure them. Natural rights, such as the right to life, liberty, property, a speedy trial, and the pursuit of happiness, are considered universal natural rights not to be interfered with. The principal purpose of stating them in major political and legal documents is in the need to check the power of the state.[16]

Rights have various origins. Many philosophers have maintained that all people have fundamental rights, irrespective of merits, just because we are humans. Examples may be found in impartial treatment in matters of justice, freedom, equality of opportunities, etc. One of the principal problems is the recent proliferation of diverse rights, or right claims (such as rights to privacy, to confidential information, and to executive privileges; rights of children, elderly, animals, and of special-interest groups) causing unavoidable conflicts among them.

Developers of the theories of rights are forced to carefully distinguish between moral and legal rights, *prima-facie* and absolute rights, and to develop sufficient justification for the claim, or desired overriding status to avoid protracted controversies already experienced in the politics of liberal societies.

Most of the theories of rights are weak in recognizing the correlativity of rights and obligations. Every right granted to an individual, or a group, entails an obligation on the part of others either to provide something, or not to interfere with one's liberty. This indicates the need to supplement theories of rights with theories of obligation for their justification.

The world of ethical theories is, of course, much richer than the presented examples would suggest. In ethical studies one can encounter also moral-sense theories, ideal-observer theories, emotive theories, and theological theories.

We may close this simple review by concluding that ethical theories provide rival and controversial answers to the important moral problems individuals and groups are facing. Philosophers point to the conceptual problems, but individuals and groups are facing real problems and the need for acute decisions. The controversies inherent in the variety of ethical theories provide an excellent opportunity for reflection on moral problems and the limit of philosophy and of human mental capacity to resolve them. But as an aid in helping the individual man to answer Socrates' question they are of low value. They actually failed to demonstrate the bare minimum: that, in the larger scheme of things, there is any importance to ethical behavior.

The total enterprise of ethics, including its principal concepts, perspectives, and theories, is currently complicated by the tension between the past influences and modern, or postmodern, circumstances and needs. The resources of the most temporary moral philosophy are still not well adjusted to the current world and its social, ethnic, and technological dynamics. This situation paradoxically makes the old philosophies a richer source for ethical investigations and contemplations. There is a deep irony in this development, for perhaps no other segment of human history has presented more difficult and urgent problems concerning the quality of human life than the twentieth century.

MORALITY

The admitted weakness of the philosophy of ethics, and the unquestionable importance of knowing how to lead a good life, make it impossible to neglect an inquiry into the practical aspects of the problem.

It is now almost a tradition to use the term "morality," instead of "applied ethic" or "ethic in practice," when dealing with beliefs about right and wrong conduct. In contrast to ethical theories, morality is a social institution with its own history[17] and code of learnable rules. Like natural language, morality exists before people are taught its rules, and its requirements are learned as part of the process of acculturation. In other words, in the broadest sense, morality is a pattern of sanctioned behavior: acts, customs, and habits. Though there is a decisive personal element in all aspects of morality, there is not such a thing as a "private" morality. Even the most unbending individualists cannot escape sanctions authorized by their legitimate community.[18]

The processes of sanctioning or authorizing acts of individuals or groups reflect either a sense of obligation or are validated by the consequences of those acts. They themselves may be a cause of moral dilemmas because of the tension between the present situation and the previously accepted morals and manners accumulated for the purpose of protecting the group members from misconduct in known, already experienced situations. Recognition of potential dilemmas leads to the acceptance of the view that all morality is goal oriented, and to a new perspective that understands morality as sanctioned conduct aimed at rescuing men from the social risks of the human predicament.

In practical life, it seems to be important to distinguish moral rules from rules of prudence (self-interest). In some real situations this may be difficult because they are often bound together in a single statement.

The basis for formulating moral rules can be illustrated by the following few moral concepts and practical concerns of the contemporary society.

Manners

In a simple literal sense, manners are means of getting along. They constitute a class of actions, gestures, and rhetoric that are currently at hand, sanctioned by an appropriate community to be used for success in social encounters. Because they include everyday social conventions, they have a trivial connotation of politeness, etiquette, or civilized conduct, which degrades the perception of their importance. Manners relate to acts, in contrast to morals which deal with attitudes that shape those acts. Both manners and morals are institutions of the society in general, while laws, in their statutory sense, are special, precisely defined institutions of the legislator. In some societies, all may be united in some major legal document, such as the U.S. Constitution.

Conventional manners are those that reflect the satisfaction and tacit approval of society's dominant groups. Dissenting manners (bad manners), on the other hand, trigger dissatisfaction. The relation to approval brings into the picture problems of potential disadvantage to less powerful groups, and of conflict with strong individuals or celebrities, which, in best case, may result in mixed manners, or in less fortunate situations, in segmentation of the society and double standards. For example, in the U.S. individualism produces one set of manners (e.g., self-appointment syndrome, self-congratulatory attitudes, boasting), while the equalitarian impulse produces another set (e.g., conformism, tendency to compromise, win-win business attitude).

Freedom Versus Responsibility Dilemma

People are normally held morally responsible for their actions, but under some conditions, they may be held responsible for almost everything. Personal responsibility is generally regarded as a necessary condition of justice. For some, this means no need for distinction between responsibility and liability to punishment. Conceptually, the key problem is identification of conditions (necessary and sufficient) under which a person is responsible for his acts. In the current social environment of scientism and scientific determinism, a view can be advanced that external conditions specified in scientific laws are sufficient to produce in each human choice and action. This view, however, opens the old dilemma between moral responsibility and freedom, a dilemma going back to Aristotle.[19]

Utilitarian thinkers argued that the claims of justice are satisfied if the rules, according to which a person is judged to be morally responsible, are based on the principle of maximized social utility. In this case, the problem of freedom is bypassed. Libertarians claim that the fact that a decision or action is not fully determined by antecedent conditions, which does not automatically imply that it occurred by chance or as an accident, will justify exemption from moral responsibility. Hard determinists allow that blame and punishment may be useful, but they deny that they are ever morally deserved. The crux of this dilemma may be seen in attempts to presuppose that freedom can be specified in abstract, independently of a specific moral outlook, and independently of the concept of justice.

Envy

Envy is a drive that lies at the core of man's life as a social being, an urge to compare oneself antagonistically to others. Only social inhibitions prevent man from retarding the quality of his social relations. In all cultures of mankind, the emotion of envy is condemned, and envious persons exhorted to be ashamed of themselves.[20] Some societies display instances of institutionalized envy, which destroy the possibility of individual economic advancement, make innovation unlikely, lock in primitive, traditional manufacturing and agricultural practices, and instill fear of success.

The origin of envy is still unclear. Freud attempted to explain it on the basis of the herd instinct. Others talked about "royal envy" preventing subordinates from enjoying the privileges of those in power. Still others suggested that envy is a by-product of dislike of another person caused by the feeling that one's own status is being threatened, or, in general, by perception that the behavior of the other person deviates from accepted standard or norm. Some sociologists equated envy with jealousy, and studied its correlations with hostility, power, resentment, revenge, appeasement and conformity. Even though no credible explanations emerged, envy's relation to revolutionary ideologies and behavior (e.g., the slogan "Ownership is theft" or the practice of social banditry) has been clearly established.

Humility

Traditional views of humility as a meek lack of self-respect, of low self-esteem, or of undervaluing one's good qualities have been declared erroneous because they may lead to resignation, discouragement, and in general to mistaken assessment of one's own personality. Another set of critiques points to the covert demand never to take offense and almost automatic forgiveness, to the easiness of pretense of humility, of displaying false humility, and to the puzzling high value assigned to it.

A more meaningful perspective sees humility as a realistic assessment of one's own accomplishments.[21] In this view, to be humble is to understand oneself and one's moral entitlements clearly enough that one is disposed not to exaggerate about them. In this way, humility is no longer paradoxical. It provides an understanding that one is not special, not an exception to be treated differently than others. Such humility protects a person from the mistakes life offers in abundance. This view also permits being resentful and withholding forgiveness, as long as there is consistency in the underlying assessments and avoidance of self-absorption.

The benefits of such humility are visible in the lack of bitterness, control of envy and jealousy, avoidance of unnecessary competitions, freedom from elitism, protection from arrogance, aversion to coercive and manipulative measures, and the preference for simple living unencumbered by too many possessions. In general, being humble is a good way for a person to be.

Contemporary Moral Concerns

Philosophy has been trying for more than two thousand years to sort out the basic issues of fairness, empathy, self-sacrifice, and so on, without too much success. Philosophers have pondered the intangible, enjoyed the paradoxical, and focused on the peculiar. Their failure opened an opportunity for another group, the ideologists, who, on the other hand, have "solutions" to every imaginable social problem, including all the rhetorical tools and skills able to persuade the undecided, to convince the uninformed, and nauseate the rest. The real tragedy is when unjustified and controversial ideological solutions become legalized and solidified in society's laws, or are used to divide the society by politicians seeking power by exploitation of the millennia-old maxim *divide et impera,* divide and conquer, actually meaning "divide in order to rule." The long list of such controversial moral issues with only dogmatic solutions can easily be interpreted, at least in the U.S., as a drift from democracy toward judicial autocracy. A few examples may illustrate the intellectual controversies stemming from contradictory arguments.[22]

Suicide, the decision to take one's own life, is a private and socially uncontrollable matter. The uninvolved spectator is unable to appreciate the feelings, worries, and anguish of the person contemplating suicide. Liberal attitude toward suicide rests on the assumption that any self-destructive action is *prima facie* evidence of mental derailment. This reasoning fails in cases of suicide motivated by preservation of a person's own dignity, as in the Japanese tradition of *hara-kiri,* by the purpose of freeing one's own family from some burden, and in cases of request for assistance. But it may be supported by "The right to die" slogan.[23]

Euthanasia and assisted suicide, originally perceived as moral issues and condemned, probably due to World War II events, are now being considered as factual issues concerning only whether there are reliable means of ensuring that the decision to end life (one's own or someone else's) has been rational. Two arguments are usually forwarded: "The right to die," and the possibility that taking another person's life is an act of mercy.

Abortion opponents base their objections on the sanctity of human life, on protection of a defenseless human being which, even when still inside of mother's womb, is genetically different from her, or on the doctrine of natural rights. Proabortionists invoke the mother's right to choose and the potential harm done by prohibitive laws.[24]

Capital punishment is claimed to be useless because it does not deter others from crime. It is also regarded as unjust because it may lead to execution of an innocent person, and because the guilty poor and disadvantaged are more likely to suffer this type of punishment than the guilty rich. Arguments for capital punishment call for retributive justice, point to the saving of lives of potential future victims, and to its value as a deterrent. It is interesting to note that in the former U.S.S.R. capital punishment had been abandoned, but systematic killing had been justified by an analogy to weeding out fields to assure better harvest.

Affirmative action opponents perceive it as a case of reverse discrimination in conflict with the Constitution and with the concept of equal opportunity. Proponents see in it a strategy of dealing with past injustice.[25]

The importance of morality and moral issues is recognized beyond the boundaries of the society as a whole. They are being addressed in the general business environment[26] (see also note 10), and as individual company concerns[27] as well.

All these reviews and examples confirm that universal development of ethical judgment and moral behavior is still an unsolved problem at home, at schools, at the workplace, and in society at large. Modern philosophy, as an academic discipline, very seldom becomes engaged in issues of applied ethics. The early desire for objectivity in higher education, reflected in deliberate avoidance of moral indoctrination, actually caused an influx of ideological indoctrinations into the fields of ethics and morality which, by frequent dogmatic postures, brought their controversies into the public domain. The originally intellectual-only chaos has been transformed into divisions of the society.[28]

LAW

In contrast to morality, which is oriented toward expanding and strengthening sanctioned patterns of behavior, law and legal systems are concerned more with behaviors and acts violating those sanctioned patterns. They are distinguished from mere customs by the nature of their sanctions—the physical force—and by the special social position of the persons who may apply them.

Law is eminently a social phenomenon. It is a system of rules in action, a system that must be effective to be acceptable. It must be recognized that formal law plays only a partial role in areas it purports to regulate. It is a component of the "living law" that applies to all sectors of human conduct, and which can be described only through careful observation of actual behavior. On the other hand, aspects of the living law, such as locally preferred virtues, customs, and commercial practices, are sources of the norms of the formal legal system. This has become an imperative after the failure of the positivist view of separating law from morality in the brutalities of European dictatorships of the twentieth century.

A legal system is the most explicit, institutionalized, and complex mode of regulating human conduct. The difficulties in the workings of such systems are usually traceable to their complexity, or to the tensions between legal and moral rules, i.e., to situations when a legal prescription of human behavior is in conflict with man's consciousness. The first step toward a legal system has been the abolition of private settlement for murder. Because murder is not the only offense that could provoke revenge and civic violence, states continued to expand their jurisdiction toward lesser and lesser crimes.

Like any other knowledge-based system, law is founded on a few principal concepts, such as evil, justice, property, retribution, due process, etc., discussed by jurisprudence, which studies the meaning, nature, and purpose of law and its relation to other disciplines. Review of these topics is more enlightening than an in-depth review of legal systems, or technical terms, such as damages, evidence, *habeas corpus*, indictment, injunction, and so on.

Problem of Evil

The idea of evil, and the problems it has presented to thinkers throughout history, expresses incisively the great divide in man's outlooks on nature and human experience: natural-scientific view and spiritual-religious view. Scientific naturalism has been concerned with descriptions and explanations, while trying to stay neutral to any basic evaluation.[29]

Ethical theories distinguish themselves by their alternative views of what is the highest good and how achievable it is. Plato, not a docile optimist, declared that evil will never pass away, for something must be antagonistic to good.[30] The optimism of the early eighteen century held that evil is like the shadow set off by the light of the universal system of cosmic perfection. Pessimists of the nineteenth century saw human life as a continuous frustration, as a selfish, ruthless, and futile enterprise. Existential dialectic refused valuation via good and evil and held that the only measure accepted is continual self-assertion and self-attestation. The idea of evil has been expressed forcibly in appraisals of the historical process, namely in the denial of progress.

The resulting general view of the idea of evil prefers a graduated perspective, forming a hierarchy of choices with the choice between good and evil as the principal direction. Evil may be categorized in evil originated by humans, evil associated with pain and suffering, evil caused by natural disasters, and metaphysical evil reflecting imperfections of all nature. The traditional explanation of evil was that the inner man had failed in the cosmic frame of his external system. Modern view blames the inadequacy of the external system in accommodating the intrinsically good man. The interesting point is that the logic of both explanations strongly indicates that evil is personal.[31] This fact is confirmed, in spite of the world crises of the twentieth century that aggravated and confused man's moral outlook: Every time the good guys in the cowboy movies win, the audience cheers.

Justice

Justice, in similarity to the idea of evil, has also been conceived historically either as a suprahuman eternal idea or a temporal man-made ideal, with occasional intermediate perspectives, usually those that mix theory with practice.

Plato and Aristotle proposed that justice does not consist of giving equal rights to men naturally unequal, but in giving everybody his due, including to the rich their richness and to the poor their poverty. Besides this "give and take" type of justice, other types are characterized by concepts of reciprocity (*quid pro quo*), equivalency, or retribution. Justice has been considered synonymous with aspiration, a mood of exaltation, or desire for what is fine or high. It has been thought of as constant and absolute, but again, not in a strictly uniform way. In summary, justice is a principle reflecting
 • That the like should be treated alike (fairness, equality, impartiality)
 • Harmony (ethic, morality)
 • Reason (reciprocity, vengeance, contract)
 • Utility (pain, pleasure)
 • Custom (virtues in groups, tribe, polis)
 • Man (his interests, needs, order, charity)
A similar list of injustices may reveal the positive content of the idea of justice more clearly.[32]

Despite its obvious importance and eminent practicality, the question of justice seems to come and go as a topic of social concern, culminating at the beginning of the twentieth century and falling out of favor in the contemporary world. Today, the prevalent metaphor is "social contract," independently whether the contract is a historically real or just imaginary event. The key topics of interest shifted from distributive to retributive justice, with the issue of punishment providing the focus point.[33] The recent emergence of terrorism brought into the field a new concept of "wild justice"[34] as the most dangerous source of repression of our time, and with it, the revival of interest in retribution.

Property

In its widest sense, property denotes the exclusive relationship of a person, or a group of persons, to an object or a complex of objects of material value. The acknowledgment of the importance of property is shared by many conflicting ideologies. At one end of the ideological spectrum, the right to own private property is regarded as one of the most basic natural rights essential to the existence and dignity of man. At the other end, property is condemned as the source of evil and the most important single instrument of oppression of many by few.

In the legal sense, property is a bundle of powers, which may include the title to a mortgage on another man's land or share in a company. In modern times, social necessities led public policies to restrain the originally unfettered use of property rights. The intermeshing of private rights and public laws brought a much more complex concept and regulation of property, with an idealistic aim to create higher economic value.

Due Process

The term "due" means an entitlement or right, and the term "process" adds to it a regularity or institutionalized formality of legalistic nature. It reflects the social need for some regular form of procedure to apply the laws as a means of social control. In the U.S., the Due Process Clause in the Fifth Amendment imposes limitations upon both federal and state governments in civil, criminal, and administrative proceedings, as well as upon acts through their three branches.

In other words, due process, whether in the general area of human conduct, or the particular one of law, connotes a procedure or method that includes regularity, fairness, equality, and a degree of justice. The idea of due process is also applicable to internal disciplinary or other procedures of a wide variety of social groups and institutions, from social clubs to major business firms.

Common Law

Common law is a category of the jurisprudence of every legal system that has reached a certain level of complexity; its body of rules applies generally, not just in some particular court or group of people, and its content stands in contrast to particular laws, such as tribal law. Common law is thus a relative notion with no fixed content. The most sophisticated are laws common to all mankind. Today, common law, especially as practiced in the Anglo-American cultural domain, indicates the form of uncodified law, i.e., case-by-case method of building up the law through judicial decisions as opposed to systematic legislative enactments. The strength of modern common law lies in this treatment of concrete disputes, rather than in focusing on logical development of general principles, and in the U.S., in the power of the courts to declare legislations invalid.[35]

Civil Law

This term covers the second major group of laws, applied mostly in Europe and Latin America, which developed as a combination of Roman and Germanic traditions influenced by local political and ecclesiastical powers. It is difficult to define the real differences between common and civil laws; the key may be in the different procedures. In civil-law countries, in official theory, courts are not strictly bound by precedents and are free to consider any legal question anew, and the task of changes in law is performed not by judges, but usually by professors who deal more with hypothetical than actual cases.

In the future, the traditional difference may diminish because of the gradual assimilation of each other's techniques.

Natural Law

Natural law seems to be a group of principles that transcend the law of different historical epochs, i.e., the law that outlives the times of its conception. Attempts to define it in an objective manner, by disengaging it from its environment, are doomed to failure.[36]

The idea of natural law is tied to the concept of an organized universe and may be considered its spaciotemporal representation. In many ways it is as ambiguous as the idea of "natural right," the subjective rights that man possesses as a human being. Natural rights thus appear as a manifestation of individualism, independence of political allegiance, and the dignity of the human person as such. According to the theory of natural rights, the dignity of the human person is supposed to take precedence over any social order. The idea of natural law, therefore, can play a metalegal role by validating a new political system intended to replace the old one.

It is obvious that law is a major instrument of social control, with two recognizable aspects: substantive, which defines the norms to be enforced, and adjective, describing how the norms are to be enforced and by whom. Even though the content of the law varies immensely, the greatest historical differences are found among legal procedures. In primitive systems, we see the power of self-appointed leaders; in advanced societies, only the due process is acceptable. In modern times, the influence of ideology preferred by the state, and lately, the potential controls imposed by the international laws being formulated, may bring many unexpected changes.

But for the majority of the population, judicial systems' controversies are most painfully visible in their resulting poor performance. We may consider the U.S. system, perceived to be one of the best in the world, where only a very low percentage of burglaries result in imprisonment, criminals serve usually only a part of their sentence, and many criminals placed on parole are on the streets without serious probation or police supervision. The victims of crimes are treated as an afterthought: they are frequently barred from the courtroom, denied the opportunity to address the court, and forgotten when their convicted attackers are released or paroled. In simple words, those whom society has failed to protect are at risk to be victimized a second time by our society's distorted, biased, and often unjust legal system.

CONCLUSIONS

Conclusions reached about social studies and studies of man seem applicable for the issues related to ethics and morality as well. Both philosophical and practical aspects suggest a judgment by cultural anthropologists that there seems to be nothing common, nothing acceptable to all mankind, besides the old wisdom: "Don't do to anybody what you would not like anybody to do to you." The reality of present-day society, with the widely known facts of the extent of social pathology—crime, drugs, illegitimacy, terrorism, revenge, corruption, ethnic cleansing, etc.—indicates that even this simple and obvious maxim is not considered binding anymore, and has lost its appeal.[37]

The critical time when moral philosophers forfeited all their respect was the first half of the twentieth century with its wars, totalitarian regimes, concentration camps, gulags, death marches, and so on. What did the majority of philosophers do amidst this madness and mayhem? Many joined the fascist, communist, and national socialist parties of their native countries. Elsewhere in Europe, intellectuals argued about the relative merits of the alternative totalitarian regimes. And in the Anglo-American world, had they been aware of what was going on in the world, they would have probably wondered what Hitler meant by "The Final Solution."[38]

Maybe because law is dealing with the negative aspects and tendencies of human behavior, it presents a more realistic picture of man and society, without the Enlightenment's bias about man's general goodness. Jurisprudence, especially, provides some insights into the problem of evil and justice, in spite of theorists' desire to decouple law from morality. Another commendable aspect of legal theories and systems is their open admission of the influence of locally prevailing ideologies. But even these observations cannot change the obvious fact that our hopes to find the desired answers in a man-made ethical system have been left unfulfilled again.

SUCCESSFUL INDIVIDUALS

6

The disappointment caused by the inability of the theoretical knowledge in ethics and of practical rules of law to answer our questions stimulates curiosity about what kinds of personal empirical understanding of life direction and modes of behavior are possessed by those individuals who are widely admired, envied, and copied. What is the secret of their influence, of their success in controlling their own life situation, and of their easily achieved dominance over others? Is there anything substantial we can learn from them? Every discussion of these topics—be it theoretical or practical, advanced or elemental— encounters almost immediately the problem of power and authority because they make a person's success best visible.

"Power" is the term used to define the capacity or ability of an individual, or a group of individuals, to determine and control the behavior of other individuals or groups in accordance of his or the group's wishes. Power is always the same despite the variety of its means of expression, such as wealth, authority, armament, influence on opinions, etc. This becomes apparent in conflict situations where, at one extreme, physical dominance is needed, and on the other end of the scale, a rational argument or leader's charisma are sufficient. Power is one of the most important and decisive phenomena of human relations. It has been observed, experienced, and studied throughout history.

POWER

The meanings of words such as "power," "influence," "control," and "dominance," are uncertain, frequently changing, and also overlapping. This shifting accounts for most of the difficulties associated with the attempts to explain power's nature.

An analytical approach to the problem of power identified five important features recognizable in the concept: (1) a relationship between at least two persons, (2) exercise of power is always a manifestation of an intention, (3) a conflict of interests or wishes the initiator desires to overcome, (4) intentional initiation of that exercise, and (5) success (or failure) in achievement of the initial intention. Of course, not every feature is present in every instance.

Studies of power can concentrate on its diverse uses and different variants, or on the analysis of its concept favored by theoreticians.

Power as a Human Desire and Social Necessity

Many regard power as a dirty subject, and desire for its possession a naughty emotion. The general Western attitude toward power is that of distrust and dislike accompanied by reluctant and rationalized appetites for it. This reflects the prevailing and natural conviction that power is an evil thing in the hands of others, but beneficial in one's own. It also points to the known facts of its essentiality for human development, and of its predisposition to be abused. Power, though always personal, attains its most dramatic form when it becomes intensely political. Political power easily masks the personal dramas in its wake. Nevertheless, appeals for and to power are continuous. The reasons for power are not as obvious as the fact itself, but the two being pointed to most frequently are individual man's instinct for power and the society's need for order.

Power as desire. The instinct for power, stronger in some and weaker in others, is always present. Most men want some measure of power. The fundamental drives behind this are essentially personal and emotional, and result in many dramatic life episodes, as epic poetry and literature well document. But probably the greatest single study of power ever written is Niccolò Machiavelli's *Prince,*[1] which deals with the qualities a prince ought to possess, with virtues free of morality. His prince could be expected to keep his promises, commitments, and alliances only as long as they correspond to his interests and strengthen his power. In present times, Machiavelli's ideas are evidenced by authoritarian statesmen, by totalitarian dictators, in psychological control of the masses, and by political opportunists. A mix of Machiavelli's ideas with Social Darwinism represents their most dangerous mutation.

Personal power is a universal human experience. All have the opportunity to exercise it, even if in its minimal degree, and all are subject to one or another form of it during most of their lives. Some see in fear and power the primary determinants of human personality. Nietzsche[2] even suggested that all psychological phenomena might be reduced to the "will to power" and proposed that human actions are to be evaluated in terms of their conduciveness to power, or in terms of the power they manifest, as the principal moral standard. For him, power is the standard of value. Nietzsche claims not only that the feeling of pleasure is a secondary symptom of the possession of power, but also that the striving for pleasure is, similarly, a secondary symptom of the will to power, which in turn is independent of consciousness. Power is the only thing men often want for its own sake.

In Nietzsche's view, the man who achieves fusion of power and joy achieves ultimate happiness. The man who lives such a life is the powerful man, while the man who does not is weak. He admits that worldly power may cover the most abysmal personal weaknesses because success is not the appropriate measure for value; a successful dictator is apt to actually be the slave of his passions.

Since power is made effective through individuals, the personality of the power holder is also a factor. Holding power is, in itself, also an emotional experience. The greater the power, the greater the impact; it may indeed be a shattering experience, especially when acquired suddenly. The effect of power on its holder is unpredictable. One known impact is his discovery that acts of power, or directing events, have surprising consequences, both positive and adverse. This causation of consequences cannot be controlled.

Power as a means of social control. The Renaissance drew a contrast between the conception of power personally embodied in a ruler and power as abstract force capable of being given or withdrawn. In that general aspect, power is a continuing phenomenon of history, politics, and human organization; actually, power is an essential ingredient at every level of human organization.

In a society, the evident need for order, for survival, subsistence, and general livelihood has always been used as the justification of all levels of coercive governments, including the most obvious tyrannies. Considering some more general observations, power comes to existence when three elements are present: assertive men, some idea system to justify the desire (or need) for it, and a group of people capable and willing to establish some form of power organization. These three elements must not be in conflict with the group's existing culture: the body of habits, thoughts, and expressions accumulated from tradition and heredity. Emergence of power may be a short and explosive event.

A power organization, be it country or corporation, government or school, cannot long maintain itself unless it is supported by a more or less accepted and respected system of values. If not supported, the head of any organization will lose touch with reality, become irrational, and in the end, his power will vanish.

The laws of power. Power is governed by the same laws in any situation and whenever found. They hold in a pluralist as well as a centralized society. Observations of power, as applied in history, led to the formulation of five natural laws of power:[3]

1. Power invariably fills any vacuum in human organization. This law is a direct consequence of the discussed second reason for power and confirms that in competition between chaos and power-based order the latter always triumphs. Despite power's prevalence, chaos is never too far away. Power impacts the environment both tangibly (forts, roads, . . .) and intangibly (laws, art, . . .).

2. Power is invariably personal, even though human organizations or society's stratification may assist the processes of concentration of power in individuals. Statements about the power of the state, party,

class, etc., are only compressed shorthand expressions behind which is acknowledgment that power does not exist in abstract, but always as an attribute of its holder. There are two classes of power holders: those considering themselves subject to no control, except by external circumstances, and those who claim to exercise their power or authority on behalf of some organized group and aiming for goals desired by that group. Holding power impacts the holder's personality through the related emotional experience. Similarly, sometimes even stronger emotions are associated with involuntary separation from power. The personal aspect of power is one cause for its limitation. Power ends with the holder's death, resignation, term expiration, or expulsion.

3. Power is always based on a system of ideas. Without any underlying philosophy, ideology, or social program the essential institutions of the power structure cease to be effective and reliable. This system of ideas also limits the exercise of power by the ruler of the organization based on it. Therefore, some tension always exists between the power holder and the members of his organization. The power holder can, of course, violate the idea system for some time, namely for as long as the violations are hidden. Concealment of the actual organizational objectives is a frequent strategy of revolutionaries.

4. Power is exercised through institutions, which are used as instruments of its delegation. The fact that power is personal, and the power structure institutional, is a source of continuous conflict that is never resolved. These internal frictions must be kept in balance because, if left unchecked, they lead to anarchy. Institutions are created to transmit the will and accomplish the plans of the power holder, and to concentrate its use for defined ends. For these reasons taking care of power institutions is a major task of all power holders.

5. Power always confronts its field of responsibility and influence, and interacts with it, in hostility or cooperation, in an organized or unorganized way, in dialogue or struggle, or any other form. Recognition of the importance of this field of responsibility is a normal condition in exercising power, and is accomplished by dialogue aiming to extract information essential to the success of policies at any level. Paradoxically, information and feedback from the power organism is essential especially for the most absolute power holders, the dictators, who do not recognize or admit need for it. Because the field of responsibility is actually a network of many

power organisms, it may challenge and deny support to the chairman by allowing cliques to emerge. Sometimes the challenges are of external origins and represent attempts to weaken the power structure, e.g., by unfriendly propaganda.

These five natural laws are observable wherever power appears, on any level from a family up to a dictator of an empire. Due to their universality they also provide a natural basis for its critique and may be applied as a means of analysis of any power-related controversy. In the twentieth century, most controversies have centered around political, economic, and international power, and in the power of seemingly powerless elements of the human society.

Power as a relation. Power may not always be a relation between people, but between a person and a thing, which manifests itself as the result of power-holder action. Power is, of course, relational in a logical sense in that it requires more than one term for a complete statement. The power seeker must find human beings who value the things he controls sufficiently to obey his orders in return. Here the character of the relationship is between power and consent. In cases where power depends on threats or physical coercion, the subject's acquiescence reflects not the values of the power holder, but the subject's own values protected by this imposed consent.

The expansionist character of power shows itself in many concrete ways, but two are most common: the increase of the budget it disposes, and the creation of new regulations to be imposed on its subjects and of new bureaucrats enforcing their implementation. This impulse to grow is present in every power whatsoever, but is not always successful. It is nourished by egoism, great and small, noble or sordid, which taken together make up the egoistic character of power in general.

To raise contributions needed to cover their demands for new resources, the power holders must invoke public interest as the means of their social justification. This demonstrates the inherent dualism of power: being ambitious, it tends to grow, and being egoistic, it primarily covers its own immediate interests. The social justification of growth is often used to mask the associated encroachment on private individuals' liberties, making it look like the individual's benefit.[4]

Types of Power

Power is organized and transmitted through institutions. Power may be personally won, but the power holder must work through existing institutions, extending or modifying them or creating new ones. The original purposes of the institution, its field of influence, and character of enforcement mechanisms, provide an obvious perspective for classification or typology of power.

Political power is the most visible form of power associated with the state.[5] It forces people to live in a rank system, assigning them a position on a vertical scale above or below each other, with priorities and associated privileges established by the state. The political system is constituted out of two types of institutions: one is designed to govern, the other is charged with selection of those who will govern. Governmental institutions have their primary function outlined by the task of defining power-holding positions with assigned power associated with them. The selection institutions search for guardians and expositors of the system ideas that should be carried out by the government, and identify principles that should guide the execution of assigned powers. The problems of consent vs. dissent, conformity vs. nonconformity, support vs. opposition, which must be addressed by both types of institutions, reflect the natural sociopolitical differences attached to various power levels. This status quo hinders realization of humanity's longing for equality and ideals of social justice. History provides a proof that permanent and total equality, social stability, and full satisfaction are out of man's reach.

Judicial power. In some societies, most visibly in the U.S., statist power is nominally divided between three branches of government: the executive, the legislative, and the judicial. They are theoretically coordinated and provide a power balance, with the legislative as the supposedly paramount institution. The actual interplay among these branches only very seldom follows the script. The president is quite often the true initiator of legislations and actions, up to the point of being accused of practicing "imperial presidency."

In the second half of the twentieth century, the most surprising development placed the members of the Supreme Court into a power position clearly senior to both the executive and the legislative branches, often perceived as the "judicial usurpation of power."[6] This started with liberal ideology-based rulings in domains of public morality, namely about abortion, school integration, affirmative action, and separation of the church and the state. In some cases—for example, in the domain of special rights and protection of groups practicing "alternate lifestyles"—courts ruled sometimes actually in opposition to the results of popular vote. Here we may see another example of the intellectual chaos caused by the failure of philosophy and ethics, confusion of common laws, and legalistic dogmatization of rationally indefensible ideological positions.

It is not surprising that similar development is observable in the international arena in the creation of "international tribunals," courts with vested power exceeding that of individual states and negating their sovereignty. To avoid dominance of ideology in such intrinsically controversial institutions is impossible, considering the ideological division of today's world. Not a "philosopher on the throne," as the old world dreamed, but the "lawyer on the throne" is what has become reality in the Western world, especially in the U.S. of the twentieth century.

Economic power projects itself in ability to cause or refuse economic activities such as production, purchase, sale, and delivery of goods, or rendering of services. It encompasses capacity to impose conditions and prices on entrepreneurs desiring to employ labor or perform the mentioned activities. Most individuals have some fragment of this power and may combine it with others in forms of labor strikes, boycotts, etc. Economic power holders are not competing with individuals but concentrate on influencing the direction, time, scale, and nature of economic and industrial development which, of course, has consequences in impacted neighborhoods, communities, regions, and even entire countries. Social philosophers developed arguments for all three views: That political and economic systems are the same, that they are two independent and competing systems, and that one is a system assuring the power and benefits of the other. Empirically it can be observed that both systems interact at all times, but they usually don't merge. Unquestionable dominance of either one presents a high risk of a major social disaster.

International power is a new form of power associated with developments in the last hundred years. Presently, it is derived from a combination of elements giving each nation-state a degree of ability to enforce its will or influence events outside of its borders. International power today is actually, though with difficulties, applicable to the entire planet by means of military intervention, economic sanctions, organized intensive propaganda or, positively, through power holders' moral and cultural standing. The unpredictability of direction of historical developments will continue to frustrate the quest for a system of world order, but already visible accomplishments are indicating adverse consequences that are probably graver than currently admitted. The major difficulties of international power stem from its interface with a quite amorphous field of responsibility, namely the disorderly, confused, and poorly informed "world opinion," and from lack of a system of ideas acceptable and supportable worldwide.

Absolute power. A short note is due to the illusion of absolute power in which dictators or business tycoons often indulge. The cases of Stalin's and Henry Ford's despotic rules over their domains are spectacular, but they are less dramatically and endlessly duplicated at various levels and organizations, including families. Despots often turn paranoid, and geniuses' actions may become impulsive, arbitrary, irrational, and irresponsible. They forget that they all are as bound to die as anybody else.

Power of the powerless is another form of power that became visible in the twentieth century.[7] It demonstrated itself, probably the first time, in Mahatma Gandhi's militant nonviolence[8] which started in South Africa in the year 1907.[9] Gandhi's strategy has been emulated in many instances of civil disobedience[10] and, in a new form, by the dissidents in countries of the former Soviet Bloc and recently in mainland China. They differ from the traditional opposition which, in both parliamentary systems and classical dictatorship, represent a political force fundamentally on the same level of actual power, only presenting an alternative political program. In the majority of cases, civil disobedience movements and dissidents express elementary revolt against government manipulation. Their focus is on the dignity of the individual, truth in reporting, freedom of thinking and expression, etc., and have a purely defensive character. This makes them significantly different from the traditional violent and aggressive expressions of opposition through assassinations, terrorism, hostage taking, and so on, as observed in the Balkan region, the Middle East, India, Latin America, and, regretfully, the United States as well.

Critique and Decline of Power

Inadequacies in the field of responsibility invite a variety of critiques because they are indirectly offering to the participants ways to exercise the limited power they have. The complaints can be aimed at the system imperfections visible, for example, in continuing disorder, they may point to the personal weaknesses of the power holder, or they may reflect poor performance of governing institutions. Potential for major difficulties is encountered when objections are brought up against the ideas or goals underlying the power structure and institutions. In such situations, risks are at least twofold: Power may become divorced from the world reality characterized by new ideas, and the obvious temptation may cause new candidates for power to emerge. The importance of substantive dialogue cannot be overemphasized.

The emergence of the international power, the power of the powerless, and the overall balance of political currents in the past century are undermining the possibility of concentrated power. This fragmentation of power is accompanied by a major change in the role of key power holders from rulers to administrators. Current thinking considers power an instrument, rather than an end. Modern sciences have been unable to develop idea systems that have the same hold on the hearts and minds of people as the past systems. This overall decline of visible powers may well result in new chaos and new calls for reestablishment of centers of power to which appeals can be made, and which will be capable of assuring beneficial changes in the course of events.

It is prudent also to acknowledge that the power of any man, or men, invariably ends in time. There is, of course, death of the power holder or his voluntary renunciation of power before death as strength ebbs. *C'est la vie.*

Death aside, men leave their position of power in one of three ways. One, they voluntarily resign or abdicate it when suggested by the institution conferring their power; two, when their term of office expires; or three, being expelled by means not genuine to the institution, e.g., by conquest.

During the early post-power period, it is easy for former power holders to become bitter that their hour of greatness has ended, or to develop irrational hostility to their successors—in other words, to make fools of themselves. In most cases, the post-power syndrome is a passing problem. A surprising number of former power holders have actually made their greatest contribution after their days in power.

AUTHORITY

The focus of our study is the individual, so the power-related issues of the state, sovereignty, civil disobedience, democracy, etc.,[11] do not call for a closer examination. On the other hand, the concept of "authority," because of its intuitive and popular connotation with some outstanding person, must be addressed to obtain insights into its historically demonstrated, chameleonic characteristics when compared with power.

Concept

The idea of authority has no single historical definition. Originally, its dominant meaning was the capacity to evoke voluntary compliance, or assent, on grounds distinct from coercive power or rational argument. Currently, its dominant meaning is the capacity to evoke compliance, or assent, whether voluntarily or not, on grounds that bestow an official right to exercise coercive power and a compulsory force, if rationally justified. In both perspectives the concept seems to point to authority as legitimate power.

Relation between power and authority is complicated because of the vagueness of both terms. Jouvenel (see note 4) insisted that power is something very different from authority. Power has no master and aims toward a social order. Authority justifies itself and its dues by pointing to its ability to provide social services. But the difference is obvious: someone who has authority to act may be unable to make his will effective; he may command respectful attention and influence beliefs but have no impact on men's behavior. This difference becomes a disguise for many power seekers who parade in front of the electorate as servants of the people, but frequently do serious mischief by clothing old, failed dreams with the language of new ideas, or promising achievement of unachievable goals. Nor is authority necessarily legitimate, when taking into account authority based on tradition or charisma, or when considering an innovative leader who impresses his will by the appeal of his personality, by generating a faith in his mission, or by belief that he can free his followers from their predicament.

Modern views of authority seem to focus on political authority and have crystallized into two opposing attitudes. There is the liberal attitude, which reduced political authority to the status of a necessary evil, inevitably opposed and declared normatively inferior to the individual's freedom. The antiauthoritarian cast of liberal idealism used the idea of men's equality to reject any natural authority and invalidated the exercise of power by anyone claiming such authority. Empiricists also associated authority with power and remained chronically suspicious, even hostile to it. Then there is the conservative attitude that accepts only extrapolitical authority, and stresses the voluntary and spontaneous commitment of subordinates to their authorities. Politically conservative scientism insisted both upon the immunity of social superiors from political power and upon their capacity to employ political power.

Principal political thinkers of the modern era expressed a wide variety of perspectives. Comte's innovative suggestion of a nonpolitical "intellectual authority" tried to attach morality to politics as the latter's point of departure. For Marx, authority was a simple rationalization of oppressive power and material exploitation; for Mill, it was a principle of control contradictory to the notion of uncoercive power. Hitler endorsed the authority of personality and the authority of leadership; Marcuse asserted the desirability of the combination of centralized authority and direct democracy; Freud recognized the coercive content of the idea of authority as a reflection of the fantasies of individual child about the "Primal Father"; and so on.

There is no doubt that the actual content of modern ideas of authority came from a long succession of empirical, idealist, and scientific modes of thinking. It is also clear that, despite their overt conflicts over the value of authority, liberals and conservatives share mirror images of the proportionate relation between authority and liberty. In postmodern times, it looks as if the neoconservatives and neoliberals switched their positions.

Modern and postmodern developments did not diminish the need to distinguish between *de facto* and *de jure* uses of the word "authority."

- *De jure* authority is a rule-created competence that logically precedes the practice of delegating limited authority from one person to another. In other words, some persons are authorized to do certain things, but no other things. True authority, in contrast to power, is derived from rules and, therefore, must be limited and restrained by rules.

- *De facto* authority exists whenever a man recognizes another man as entitled to command him. To have *de facto* authority is to stand in such relation to other people that one can, as a matter of fact, induce them to do what one tells them because, for whatever reason, they are convinced that they ought to do so.

In the real world, both types of authority are often mixed together. It is widely recognized that while the qualities characterizing authority may vary between societies, the less a leader's authority is firmly rooted *de jure* in accepted institution or tradition, the more it will depend *de facto* on his continuing success, on his faith in his own mission or destiny, and on his ability to communicate this faith to others.

Justification of Authority

The problem of justification of authority emerged after the Renaissance and Reformation. Before, all authority had been assumed as of suprahuman origin, and the key concerns were who should exercise it, under what conditions, and within what limits.

With the growth of early liberalism, and its exploration of the relations among authority, reason, and freedom, the problem of justifying human authority in secular terms became urgent. A few solutions emerged:

- Natural justification reflected the fact of a father's tutelage of his children and, therefore, assumed as necessary that members of a society must forgo acting on their own judgment and must submit instead to the instructions and leadership of others, either because they are wiser and better, or simply because they ethnically or socially belong to them.

- Justified authority is self-imposed and derived from a contract, or covenant, whereby each member of the society agrees with all the rest to submit to one or few of their number, or to the "general will" of the whole people.

- Authority can be justified by the consent that it is essential to social survival and by voluntarily surrendering individual rights to act against this achieved consent.

- Authority may be justified by its generally positive consequences, while consistently negative consequences would condemn it.

All justifications of authority are based on the assumption of a moral duty to submit to authority as of higher importance and value when compared to a moral duty to act on one's own judgment and conscience. But the idea that one could give up this fundamental right, or suffer its extinction, is incompatible with the common view of a rational and morally responsible person.

ELITES

In the past, authority—the capacity to evoke respect, admiration, and voluntary compliance—has been endowed to hereditary nobility, or aristocracy. In the time of its Greek origin, the term "aristocracy" did not have any connotation with social classes; it simply denoted a small group of people in a city leadership, a group that considered itself, and usually considered by their fellow citizens as well, "the best." The characteristics that defined the good and the best were, of course, different from one city to another, from culture to culture, but in all situations they pointed to the few who ruled.

This rule of the few has been recurrently associated with all political regimes: monarchy, communism, democracy, and so on. In monarchy, a prince must secure a supportive group of people who will not only assist in governing, but who will also provide a broader and respected base for his legitimacy and authority. A democracy must find "the best" to wield temporary power and rule in accordance with people's wishes. This observation leads to the proposition that, in principle, all governments are aristocratic, and the concept of ruling class has served to emphasize this insight.

The virtues assumed associated with "the best" can be easily and credibly reduced to the capacity to succeed, instead of searching for a list of some transcendental qualities of goodness. While expounding this perspective, it is necessary to keep in mind that to say, "Those few who succeed always rule," is little more than a tautology of the same nature as the evolutionist's "Those who are the fittest always survive."

Modern Perspective

In contemporary language, the terms "aristocracy" and "nobility" have acquired a somewhat antiquated flavor, and the preferred notions in social studies are "ruling class" and "elite," which are now considered synonymous.

Vilfredo Pareto (1848–1923)[12] distinguished formally between "a governing, political elite" and "a non-governing, non-political elite" within the generic class of "elite." He defined membership in this generic class by a superior capacity in any social activity whatsoever, and proceeded to work out the authority of this elite in terms of its relations with political power. In the context of its authority over nonelite, the political elite became simply the higher stratum of society, which usually contains the rulers. Their superior skills were seen in the ability to stay in power, exercise the functions of the government, and use force if necessary.

Pareto also described the circulation of elites as a process of lower-class nonelites moving into the governing elite accompanied by elitists dropping out of the governing class. This process demonstrates the inevitable triumph of political skills over any skill carrying the label "social."

Since the Enlightenment, the superiority of intelligence has always been invoked as an argument by those who happened to have the upper hand, despite the simultaneous moralization about human equality. So the unpopular doctrine of inequality was recast into the doctrine of elites, which, in some of its versions, teaches not only that all governments have always been of the few, but also that the few who govern deserve to do so because of their special gifts and prowess.

The trouble with the elitist doctrine is that it is inadequate by itself to provide a ground for political obligation. In fact, it suggests two alternatives:

- The elite is "imposed." Clearly, this is not a reflection of the merits or the intrinsic superiority of the elite that matter, but of the capacity to seize power, if necessary, by force.

• The elite is "proposed," which is the case in modern societies, since those merits and that superiority call for recognition and acceptance on the part of those on whom the elite is to exert its power.

In neither case does the elitist doctrine offer a third solution, in addition to the old alternatives: force or consent, might or right.

In summary, the elite cannot be truly thought of as men who are merely doing their duty. They are the ones who determine their own duties, as well as the duties of those underneath them. They are not just following orders; they issue orders. They are not just bureaucrats; they command bureaucracies. They may try to disguise their power and imagine themselves as mere instruments or servants, but because of their dominant position in dominant institutions of a dominant nation, they do make decisions with enormous, sometimes terrible, consequences for the whole of mankind.

Diversity of Elites

In modern Western societies, major power now resides in the economic, political, and military domains.[13] Other institutions, such as systems of education and religious organizations, are not autonomous; on the contrary, they are increasingly being shaped by the dominant three. At the top of each of these three, a layer of higher social stratum has formed that makes up the economic, the political, and the military elites. These groups devise a more or less compact, self-conscious, social and psychological entity. The most interesting and historically unique feature of modern elites is that they exercise their power virtually unopposed, restricted only internally by ideological differences. The common perspective seems to recognize a few different groups, such as:

The celebrities, people with names that need no further identification; they are recognized with some excitement and awe. Whatever they do is automatically assumed to have publicity value; therefore, they are the material for communication media and entertainment industries.

The very rich stimulate, in public eyes, two contrasting, but not contradictory images: that of robber and that of innovator. The key fact is that their wealth allows accumulation of advantages important for further wealth and influence.

The chief executives are the organizers of major private property systems. They are usually born to upper-middle-class parents and are well educated, often with some college degree. Even though some started as entrepreneurs, the majority's career paths went through corporate hierarchies.

The leisure class consists, usually, of members of clannish families withdrawn from productive enterprise for whom spending is synonymous with high social status and prestige.[14] They protect their economic privileges by shrewd exploitation of loopholes in existing tax laws and by various investment strategies—in short, by prudent management of their money. They often translate their economic power into political power through support of political parties and enhance their public image through extraordinary gifts to charities.

The politicians, the men who more or less regularly enact roles in political institutions, do not constitute any psychological type. They cannot be classified and understood in terms of a definite standard set of motives. They may be driven by the desire for power for its own sake, prestige, love of campaigning and conspiring, etc. Their career paths lead either through a party machinery or the machinery of the state—the bureaucracy.

Power elites. The ultimate political layer belongs to the power elite composed of political, economic, and military men who come together only at certain occasions, each conveniently labeled "crisis." Despite their social similarity and psychological affinities, they do not constitute a club with permanent membership and formal boundaries. Personal friendship, sometimes pretended by people of similar ideological convictions, is not the primary relationship within power elites. The unity rests, in most situations, upon the coincidence of personal and institutional interests, upon the similarity of origin and outlook, and mutually beneficial exploitation of existing power structures. There usually is a recognizable inner core (inner circle) whose members may interchange commanding roles as required by the character of the crisis faced. There is also an outer fringe, people who count but are very seldom invited to participate on decisions. Power elites display also the risks they are bringing into the governing of society, namely risk of semiorganized stalemate, increased secrecy, purposeful absence of unbiased expertise, and conspiratory potential as well.

In contrast to elites, the individuals who attempt to transcend themselves and, therefore, are more noble and made of "better stuff," are nonelites, the population that sluggishly relaxes into comfortable mediocrity under the elite's protection. This is, of course, an unrealistic and naïve description of the current status of affairs, but it contains a hint about potential future dangers.

Current world societies often fit into one of two major categories: public and mass society. The public is characterized by its willingness to express and consider opinions that are formed in discussion and often result in actions against the prevailing system of authority. In a mass society, public has become an abstract collection of individuals who passively receive opinions from mass media and the controlled education system. Feedback on received impressions is with no effect, and individual autonomy is curtailed by agents of authorized institutions who penetrate this mass. The mentioned dangers are related to certain structural changes taking place in modern society which began to cut off the public's active participation in decisions, and to create an ever-widening gap between the public and the power elite—i.e., the transformation of public into mass has began.[15] The most noticeable dangers are trends toward unification of the top echelons of power, while continuing fragmentation of the public renders it more and more impotent. This transformation of public into mass provides one of the most important clues to the meaning of power elites. They are all what we are not.[16]

INTELLECTUALS

During the twentieth century many power elites, most visibly in Europe and the U.S., have become a breed of men entirely different from those who, in the past, have been recognized as a cultural elite as well. For that matter, they actually ceased to be cultivated men, some even lacking basic human sensitivity. Today's power elites, and other celebrities, often do not have even a passing acquaintance with culture, knowledge, and morality, and have lost touch with them. The characteristic member of the higher circles today is an intellectual mediocrity as revealed in continuous delegation of his tasks to committees, to speech writers, to media advisers, etc., and in public utterances empty of content in their universal generality, in abbreviated one-liners, and in their reliance on opinion polls.

That is why the elites are not alone on the top of visible institutional hierarchies. They are supplemented by agents, legal technicians, public-relations experts, spinmasters, advisers, and other people who influence and modify their self-conceptions and create their public images, as well as shape many of their decisions. In short, they are surrounded by intellectuals.

Knowledge and Power

Originally, intellectuals were perceived as possessors of cultural capital, as a group moving toward self-representation, as a social force on the basis of knowledge that does not require any additional external reference. Knowledge is legitimized by its own methods and procedures, so intellectuals don't need to be subordinated to the economic status of the society nor to the prevailing forms of political rule. This autonomy may be illustrated by the statement, "The intellectual is someone who concerns himself with what is none of his business," attributed to Jean-Paul Sartre.

Marxism, on the other hand, did not accept the idea of autonomous intellectuals due to its conviction that the world of ideas is strongly dependent on the prevailing form of production and distribution of goods. It even criticized those who were absorbed in academization, specialization, and professional-ization because they reneged on their public role and duty as potent critics of political regimes. Marxists also predicted the demise of the independent intellectual.

Industrial developments, which led to the adoption of both intellectual and practical knowledge as productive forces, refuted the autonomy hypothesis as well. Lately, intellectual labor by knowledge workers replaced manual labor as the primary force in the reproduction of capital. Intellectuals, scientists, and engineers, by being subject to managers, lost their autonomy and turned into servants. Being not a full partner in the system of power, their social and political influence remained minimal.

This changed during the revolutionary episodes of the twentieth century. In these situations intellectuals linked themselves with political movements, helped articulate their goals, devised strategies and programs, organized propaganda networks, took control over state apparatuses, etc. In this reprise, intellectuals ceased to be the functionaries of power and attached themselves to the power core.[17] Their utopias formed the political images of social transformation; their organizational skills provided the backbone of administration and, in some instances, even monopolized both the means of legitimate violence and the means of ideology production. They turned Descartes's dictum, "I think, therefore I am," into "I am, therefore I think." They began to constitute a state oligarchy with power to determine what counts as science and, more broadly, as legitimate knowledge.[18] As Machiavelli observed, they committed the error of not knowing when to limit their hopes.

Some students of post–World War II society contended that intellectuals were rapidly constituting themselves as a new class capable of competing for political power corresponding to their already formidable economic and cultural positions.[19] But this situation changed significantly after the collapse of the Soviet Union and revelations of the poverty in communist countries. The dream of Marxist intellectuals that they would reform, if not rule, the society, vanished. Many of them have retreated to academia and other professional enclaves and hideouts. Their unwillingness to admit the defeat of their ideological position invited critiques from postmodernists and conservatives, resulting in the spread of popular anti-intellectualism.[20]

The environmentalist movement, and the growing power of lawyers and financial experts in shaping the agenda of international politics, point to the fact that not all intellectuals are abstaining from their public role and support the plausibility of the emerging new class hypothesis. By insisting that they are self-legitimating, they anticipate their power to come to full fruition in the postindustrial society where the old capital-labor relation will no longer dominate, and where cultural capital is expected to be the leading force.

Since the twentieth century, knowledge is no longer seen as an ideal providing men with satisfaction of its own; it is seen as an instrument of power and wealth. The problem of knowledge and power is, therefore, actually the problem of the relations of men of knowledge with men of power. In the future, because there are no new ideologies on the horizon, it may well become the problem of power of men of knowledge against the power of men in power.

Failure of the Intellectuals

Looking at the described developments, it is possible to recognize a few causes behind the induced changes—for example, the imposition of political interest on all men without exception, the desire of intellectuals to play a part in the game of politics, the view of the future through the eyes of political romanticism associated with the decline of the knowledge of the past, the diminishing discipline in intellectual work, etc. This changing environment carries with it the seeds of failure of intellectuals as respected arbiters of things cultural and moral. The defeat of intellectuals starts at the very moment when they claim to be practical. This claim turns them into political laymen, demands them to support arbitrary authorities, and elevates self-interests, such as career and social status, to the major driving force.

The intellectuals have most violently broken with their tradition by their doctrines, and by the scale of values, scorning any existence which, in any respect, raises itself above or beyond the material. They started to praise the efforts of men to feel conscious of themselves. They placed the possession of concrete advantages, of material and political power, and the means by which they are procured at the top of the scale of moral values. Modern intellectuals finished the transformation of Plato's "Morality decides politics," through Machiavelli's "Politics has nothing to do with morality," to today's "Politics decides what is moral."[21]

Modern-age intellectuals have introduced two novelties into the theorizing of politics by which political passions have been remarkably intensified: (1) claims that advocated political movements are in line with the evolution of man and some profound unrolling of history and (2) claims by all political ideologies that they are founded on science and reflect precise scientific observations of social facts. It is not difficult to recognize the level of self-assurance, rigidity, and inhumanity that can be associated with such convictions. The modern age is indeed the age of intellectual organization of political hatred. This may be one of modernity's chief contributions to the moral history of humanity.

These trends, which began at the end of the nineteenth century, have been observable even lately, especially during the Cold War era. Those years—the times of the Western world's people tasting real affluence for the first time—contain powerful evidence of the resistance of the ideological mind-set of the intellectuals to obvious empirical evidence.[22] Western prosperity had no impact on left-leaning intellectual orthodoxy overoccupied with residual pockets of economic backwardness. If noticed, it was accused of being a result of neocolonialism and neoimperialism, or attacked as crass materialism, vulgarity, and dependence on the creation of spurious wants. While Western democracy has been under communist ideological attacks, academics subjected it to a behaviorist analysis, stripping most of its idealism, denying the validity of the notion of common purpose, and stressing the self-serving preoccupation of competing interest groups. This betrayal provided a favorable environment for adversary cultures to emerge, and for disruptions of democratic institutions and mediated procedures of government.

The attitudes toward atomic weapons are one of the examples how wrong the left was in the assessment of the world situation. While intellectuals maintained that the world was at the edge of an imminent disaster (consider, for example, slogans such as "Nuclear winter," "Better red than dead," or "Ban the bomb" aimed at unilateral disarmament of the West), the Cold War was in fact an era of the most limited conflicts in history.

In a similar way to the uncritical embrace of communism by the left, the conservative intellectuals were frightening themselves by studies of its generalization as totalitarianism, total terror, total domination, unmitigated evil, and government with a totally different character to be fought at all cost.[23] To it were attributed a vast and terrifying capacity to discipline, mobilize, and transform individuals and societies.

The collapse of communism, in a very brief period of time and without serious resistance, is the most striking historical irony demonstrating the vanity, blindness, and fundamental errors in ideological thinking, even when conducted by the brightest intellects.

Some historians[24] render a harsh judgment also on the college-educated professional and managerial elites in America and other advanced countries, accusing them of having abandoned the common life, subverting democracy, and becoming dangerously isolated from the rest of the country. In an increasingly global and information-based economy, the economic, cognitive, and moral gaps between the lives of intellectuals—the knowledge elite—and nonelite, are growing inexorably. The denationalization of business causes a shift in the elite's loyalty away from nation, to loyalty to themselves only. This brings into dominance self-indulging agendas of cultural and moral radicalism, further alienating the public with its own views of civil virtues. The evidence of intellectuals' desire to have an impact on culture may also be seen in ridiculous simple demands, such as defining the correct minibehavior of college students, or defining correct expressions by demands to change from simple "he" to "he or she," "mankind" to be replaced by "humankind," and so on, in the famous tradition of communist governments which, after coming to power, renamed all the streets, all holidays, even some cities.

But what really points to the "treason of the intellectuals," using Benda's characterization, is the abdication of their image of contemporary nobility, and of the traditional leadership role in domains of culture and morality. In words of an anonymous poet:

Who the hell's yer leader anyhow?
Who's yer leader anyhow?
We ain't got no leader
We're all leaders.

With the exhaustion of political and ideological ideas, [25] the public opinion polls have been substituted for political leadership; public opinion pollsters with statistical analysts are now the only remaining social scientists who really count, and politicians' spinmasters with mass-media reporters have become the opinion leaders. Lack of longer-term goals is providing openings for opportunists, for fraud and corruption, for short-term beneficial deceit, and for executive sloppiness inviting social parasites and speculators, etc.

Adjectives such as "mundane," "profane," "violent," "obscene," "offensive," "indecent," or "worldly" are now used to characterize the products of men of letters and art who are defining the cultural image of the successful entertainment industry. Profitability and popularity of forms of amusement based on the lowest common denominator are guaranteed and unquestionable. What is questionable is their longer-term impact and consequences. It is alarming when well-respected sociologist Daniel Bell names a chapter in his influential book, "Crime as an American Way of Life."[26]

In the domain of personal morality, we see intellectuals and other elites sharing life with the frivolous or the sultry members of the world of celebrities. By their actual lives they often display the absence of any firm moral order or belief which, as a consequence, makes the whole society more open to moral manipulation by celebrities' laughing, erotic, and glamorous alternative lifestyles. Intellectuals are presenting to the public a strange set of idols, some of them resembling frivolous clowns in disguise. Browsing through the almost unimaginable wealth of biographies and autobiographies of the famous and infamous, and reading critical studies of personalities of leading intellectuals,[27] may actually lead to even less favorable conclusions.

CONCLUSIONS

Defeat of ideologists by the historical developments in the twentieth century, and abdication of ethical leadership and moral responsibility by intellectuals, made law—the lowest common denominator in man's social behavior control systems—the dominant power institution with unpleasant consequences, e.g.:

1. Crime, the caricature of a society's morals and manners, starts to play, both directly and indirectly, an important functional role as an alternative strategy for upward social mobility.

2. The "Lawyer on the Throne" replaces the grassroots politicians' favored environment of compromise with a conflict-based courtroom environment that allows only winners and losers.

3. Mass media, with their focus on everything controversial and sensational, favor and promote these changes for their own profit, strengthening their self-appointed role as the final referee.

All these detrimental developments are reconfirming power as the clearly dominant goal of, and reward for, worldly success. Those who lead men to the conquest, and those who support them in this endeavor, have no need for justice and charity. That is the essential difference between elites and common folks, whose lives without justice and charity will be a continuous misery. In other words, elites do not resemble the common man in any way. They are not composed of representatives whose conduct and character constitute good role models for imitation and aspiration. Their fabulous success is not a result of moral virtues, nor is it firmly connected with meritorious abilities. This is reflected in public's morally cynical, and politically unspecified, distrust of elites.

The real tragedy of the postmodern society is that, in the world of most successful people, there is no set of men with whom the general public can rightfully and gladly identify. In this fundamental sense, current society is without leadership.

LESSONS LEARNED

7

There is no other way to start a discussion of conclusions to be drawn from the previous chapters than with an apology for such a quick and limited treatment of the deep and fundamental topics that have occupied the minds of the most knowledgeable people throughout history. Justification for this restricted approach may be found in the fact that the goal has not been to teach those ideas, but only to provide a review sufficient for the development of a big picture, of a framework, of the domains reviewed. Readers desiring more details may consult books referenced in the endnotes.

Visits to the various bodies of knowledge, created and accumulated by the best and brightest individuals over many millennia, would be of limited value and of no benefit without serious reflection upon them, and without assessing their relevance and importance vis-à-vis the overall objective of our search for answers fundamental to man's life questions outlined in the Introduction.

When attempting to draw appropriate conclusions, it is necessary to constantly fight the temptation of sliding into a critique of individual or particular opinions, and into subjective personal valuations. Another risk is to claim observance of some major general trends, either of progress or decline, so popular in the intellectual world of the twentieth century. Because in reaching conclusions and spelling out lessons learned some generalizations are unavoidable, it pays to keep in mind the risks associated with making them.

Considering the immensity of talent, intelligence, erudition, experience, even genius behind the visited bodies of knowledge; the quality of generated insights; the precision of arguments; the creativity in developing of new fields of investigation and knowledge, etc., the author's effort to reach some conclusions may look foolish. So, the best defense, and the surest way to avoid the mentioned temptations and risks in this venture, is to let the experts in the particular branches of knowledge make the assessments and report upon their findings, a strategy already adopted in previous chapters.

PHILOSOPHY

Because the initially posed questions about man, the world, and the meaning of life intuitively seem to have the character of ultimate questions, it is no surprise that the first visit has been paid to philosophy. For a long time, philosophy has been perceived as "that department of knowledge which deals with ultimate reality, or with the most general causes and principles of things."

The fundamental problem philosophers encountered relates to the question whether there are such things as ultimate reality and general causes and principles. Doubtless, philosophers searched for ultimate explanation, ultimate foundation of knowledge, ultimate reference point for meaning, etc., but others also pointed to facts indicating that this whole project is a mistaken one.

Ludwig Wittgenstein and other logical positivists declared that such philosophical problems are actually pseudoproblems, illusions stemming from misuse of language.[1] On the other hand, Colin McGinn thinks that such problems are real, but their resolution lies beyond man's cognitive ability. Man can formulate them but cannot solve them.[2] Man is constrained by his cognitive limits.

Once upon a time, history of philosophy was conceived as a repository of timeless wisdom, higher truths, fundamental concepts, and perennial problems. Today it looks more like history of "brilliant errors"[3] with skepticism as the only valuable heritage.

Of course, philosophy will never really end. It will simply continue in a more overtly ironic, literary mode, as already demonstrated by Nietzsche, Jean-Paul Sartre, and Albert Camus. It can be carried on as a part of the humanities responsive to changing values, or even as an art form.[4] In our times, the respectability of philosophy, especially of metaphysics, disappeared, and its previous speculative results became highly suspect. Therefore, philosophy cannot serve as a body of knowledge pertinent for our search.

When speculations about ultimates failed, the allure of involvement in improving man's social conditions become irresistible—especially under the spell of the Enlightenment's optimism—and philosophy mutated into ideology. Because all ideologies deal with issues related to some desired social change, or change in the power structure, they have become attractive social icons of modern culture.[5]

The effectiveness of rational critique helped to uncover the distortion of truth in the critiqued social condition. Because the critiqued social conditions themselves have been based on some system of ideological thought, ideology must be seen as a truth-distorting perspective.[6] But distortion of truth does not diminish ideology's reality or reality of its effects. Ideology was part of the complex processes whereby modernity gently subjugated man's thought. Ideology became a central, if often underestimated, characteristic of modern man's identity, especially of his social identity. Ideology's proclamations about intentions to critique itself, to point only to repression in current culture, are evidence of its duplicity. To accept ideologies at their face value is a sure way to self-deception.

The key facts most ideologists forget to take into account is that no philosophical explanation, no philosophical system, no socioeconomic system, no political regime is able to satisfy all men in all places and at all times. This fact is clearly illustrated by the modern history of the French nation, whose writers have been very open about their troubles, failed intellectual programs, and confusion about their politicoeconomic system. Stanley Hoffman, in his article "France: Keeping the Demons at Bay" in the *New York Review of Books,* (March 3, 1994, pp. 10–16), describes the attempts to implement a succession of myths starting with Jean-Jacques Rousseau, revolution, Bonapartism, disillusionment with the Third Republic values and deeds (pacifism, compromises during the Spanish Civil War, improper responses to both fascism and communism), downfall in 1940 and, after World War II, state planning, decolonization of Vietnam and Algeria, DeGaulleism, inability to deal with the first oil crisis in 1973, union of the left (between communists and socialists) with aggressive nationalization and public spending, followed by unemployment, austerity, deregulation, privatization and, recently, by opposition to globalization. What is even more enlightening is the inability of French intellectuals to help, wavering from existentialism to communism, anticommunism, American neoconservatism, liberalism, and in the 1990s back to an old-fashioned nationalism.

Some of the ideologies turned into a political system, declaring their concept of truth and views of social structures and processes of social change as absolutes beyond critique. Absolutizing some finite and conditioned part of social reality—such as political power, state, nation, history, morality, personality, etc.—turns such realities into an idol, and forces the members of the given society into uncritical idolators. Any system of thought that elevates some object or event to a quasidivine status transformed itself into quasireligion, and entered a one-way path toward totalitarianism.[7]

Today, however, it is necessary to consider ideology differently because the world has changed. But despite the fading away of modernity and ideology's strong link to it, ideology will not disappear. Experiencing the intellectual, as well as historical, failure of major utopian ideological systems, politicians began to deconstruct such systems into the language of individual political issues and practical social problems selected to match the prevalent public opinion. For example, socialist doctrines are being deconstructed into saving Medicare, improving Social Security, proposing patients' bill of rights, hate-crime legislation, and covert taxation of selected industries through various anti-industry campaigns. On the other side of the ideological spectrum, *laissez-faire* conservatism is presented in the form of lowering taxes, school vouchers, family values, and pro-life campaigns. Such developments only confirm that ideological distortions of the social truth remain effective thought-influencing tools, and point to the importance of staying in touch with postmodern philosophical developments, which usually predate intellectual trends in power politics and its methods.

In one important area of the human knowledge enterprise, in history, the truth-distorting ideologies actually fabricated lies.[8] To repeat the reasoning behind this attitude, as stated in George Orwell's *1984,* is not necessary. E. H. Carr of Cambridge University, in his 1962 Trevelyan lectures, warned that the belief in a hard core of historical facts existing independently of the interpretation of the historian is a preposterous fallacy, but one that is hard to eradicate. History proceeds by revisions and counterrevisions; in other words, history is an argument without end.[9] These continuing revisions do not represent a people's movement in any sense. They are raised by a few well-established intellectuals, professors, and writers.[10]

American history did not escape the effects of prevailing ideologies either. In recent decades, it has been rewritten and transformed by a handful of publishers who are more concerned with meeting business demands of ideologists of both the multicultural left and conservative right. Over the years, constant business and ideological pressures took a form of a "conspiracy of good intentions" that resulted in dumbed-down products. Textbooks are not written for students, but for textbook committees looking for recognizable buzzwords and politically correct ethnic balance.[11] The growing infatuation with CD-ROMs and other high-tech gadgetry favors even more the publisher, and strengthens the dominance of image over text, at the expense of history.

Such assessment of their field of interest by historians themselves does not create too much confidence in attempts to learn from history more than from literature. Because philosophy of history showed it impossible to separate human behavior from its historical circumstances, historians are asking the same questions as those that initiated our study. As long as man remains the unknown or unknowable entity, there is no prospect for discovery of any credible meaning in history, or for history-based underpinning of nature of man and society.[12] No philosophical or ideological concepts of history can adequately appreciate the silence of human sorrow that settles down after a social catastrophe.

Considering the admission of truth distortion as an unavoidable characteristic of all ideologies, it would be foolish to look at them as a knowledge source credible enough to help in our task. Attempts to distill out of them a generic, common-foundation knowledge will be futile in a way similar to the futility of philosophies.

SCIENCES

The futility of expectations that philosophy would provide the ultimate understanding of nature and man was made clear by David Hume more than two hundred years ago. However, the parallel impressive developments in natural sciences since Copernicus, later supported by the Industrial Revolution and the Enlightenment's worldview, kept optimism not only alive, but actually strengthened it by the vision of an all-encompassing exact science. This optimism created two new myths: that science is the only way to achieving unity of all knowledge, and that science is indispensable for freeing man from the dominance of nature.

The scientific method of collecting and analyzing by observation and measurement-obtained data is an excellent tool when there is unanimity about those observations. In the case of different interpretations of the same data, even the best scientists are very close, if not already in, the domain of metaphysics. So, there we go again.

Science is on safe ground when it describes in its special language natural objects, when it categorizes them according to some measurable characteristic, and when it deals with repetitive events and processes bound by cause-effect relations. When science attempts to design explanations requiring reasoning with concepts outside its own laws-bound territory—i.e., by reasoning in metalanguage—it encounters all the problems known from philosophy.[13]

Even while contemporary science is asserting ever-greater success in in-depth descriptions of natural phenomena and their links to established laws of nature, scientific knowledge obviously has never represented the totality of man's knowledge. Scientific knowledge cannot know, nor make known, that it is the true knowledge without resorting to other, narrative kinds of knowledge, which, from the scientific point of view, are not knowledge at all.[14] The Big Bang hypothesis is nothing more than a narrative based on mathematical solutions of equations describing Einstein's General Theory of Relativity. Theories of evolution are nothing more than narratives based on similarities in anatomy of a variety of animals and organisms displaying different levels of complexity, and on time-stamped findings of paleontology. This contradiction makes it clear that the principal issue of legitimacy of the sciences is still unresolved. In the words of Sir Walter Raleigh, scientists are confusing the state of science with the state of the universe.

The Sokal's Hoax[15] illustrated that this confusion is not some insignificant, peripheral problem, artificially created by some contemporary "enemies of science," but a fundamental concern. In his article[16] Sokal published a fictitious narrative, but with many quotes supporting it, dealing with current topics in mathematics and physics, and drawing various cultural, philosophical, and political conclusions that, he felt, would appeal to fashionable academic commentators who question the claims of science to objectivity. This article is, by Sokal's admission, nonsense, but had been accepted for publication because it flattered the editor's ideological preconceptions. Another similarly humorous situation was created in 1968 by Carlos Castaneda who published his novel, *The Teachings of Don Juan: A Yaqui Way of Knowledge,* in the form of an ethnographic field study. His novel was accepted by many as a serious scientific anthropological study because it was a perfect fit to the popular drug culture's preference for hallucinatory experience-based apprehension of reality over Aristotelian logic.[17] This humorous episode points to the irrationality of scientists' claim to legitimacy when they speak on matters of history, philosophy, and sociology of science. They are mistaking social studies for leisure activity, displaying the prevalent ignorance and lack of appreciation of the amount of craft, knowledge, and practice that is required to be an even minimally competent historian or philosopher. They are also missing the degree to which prior ideological commitments govern what scientists do or say about the real world, even though they are readily observable in, for example, the lack of weapons scientists in the disarmament movement, or fetal tissue researchers at antiabortion rallies.

It is a serious issue to consider that scientific research and its results, or even laws, are flexible enough to be affected by the social setting of their discovery, that scientists may under pressure, or willingly for some reward, discover laws suitable to the powers that be. There is more at stake than just the health of science. The case history of "junk or impure" science in Nazi Germany, in Communist U.S.S.R., and the democratic U.S., unfortunately indicate that ideologically based scientific research work is not an artificial problem.

Social sciences, studies of social phenomena in general, and sociology in particular, are even more controversial than theories in the natural sciences. Historically speaking, the idea of social science is inherently contradictory. This contradiction is that when man makes himself the object of his subjective thoughts, the relation between subject and object cannot be made clean. There is always an element of conflict to be resolved by ideological belief. Marx did in fact make this conflict the basis for his theory of social change. This subjectivity and closeness to ideology made sociology a science whose peculiar feature is the difficulty it has of becoming a science like the others.

From its beginning as storytelling by a tribe's sages, sociology has been an imaginative effort to re-create the present and establish characteristics of a desired future out of the dreamy residues of a frequently assumed perfect past. Confused about the past and about what was actually lost, sociologists dreamt of possible new societies that would bring a perfect peace, a healthy division of labor, a classless society, or a rehumanized rational society. With the collapse of ideologies, such dreaming is not fashionable anymore. The current history-based doubts about the world's wholeness, its peace and integrity, are reflected in the crisis of sociology.[18] Sociology and other social studies seem to be unable to survive in the real world, outside of their own concept of "society," and outside the selected preferable ideological framework. The negative public opinion of, and disinterest in, social sciences, namely the most visible sociology and economics, is not without reason.

When scientists and philosophers turned toward the study of man and tried to define "who and what man is," they invited very hard questions. Robert Nozick,[19] after close to one hundred pages of arguments about the identity of the Self, personal identity through time, reflexivity, and the Self-Conception of the Self, observed that his conclusion of the Self as a property of man is not sufficiently illuminating, clarifying, and fruitful in its consequences. He pronounced his own view as too much froth and too little substance, with a little bit of philosophical chicanery.

Anthropology, failing so far to deliver more than narratives, sometimes formulated as a hypothesis, began to drift—as did other social and human sciences, especially in the U.S.—toward its practical applications in the domain of politics and ethnography. This brought into the field of view the well-known dilemma of ceasing to pretend to be a strictly scientific, objective, and disinterested study of society.[20] Anthropologists found themselves embarrassed by the excessive confidence of their employer—the government—that they have the key to all problems. But these are dilemmas already well known with the favored solution in abandonment of the "disinterested scientist" position. It is hard to imagine a philosopher, whatever he may say, or a man of science, whose conclusions will run counter to the dearest wishes of his heart, who will work against them or condemn his hopes to death. There is a real danger to all of man's reason and logic when his deepest desires of self-interest are disturbed.

The history of the quest for human nature[21] confirms what many critics have said all along: findings of studies are often ideologically biased, but presented with a pretense of impartiality. It points to the fact that ideology also underpinned the repudiation of biology in social and human studies, and the related preference of explaining human behavior through cultural influences, up to the point of taking away man's responsibility for antisocial behavior and self-destructive addictions. But we all know from experience that to be a human being is to be continually confronted with personal decisions, especially in situations characterized by encounters with other persons and unexpected circumstances.

Without too much additional investigation, it seems to be obvious that in domains of social and human studies we are encountering well-known phenomena of pseudoscience and scientism. We are facing domains lacking well-defined scientific problems and experiencing a lack of legitimate methodologies, in want of a common, widely accepted paradigm, and characterized by the inability to deliver credible predictions of events in their domains, but, at the same time, displaying a strong belief that methods of exact sciences are appropriate in their fields of interest and capable of delivering true knowledge about man and society.

Considering the linguistic and postmodern discussions about the fundamentals of science, stimulated by the flood of exotic theories spun with no way to test them, by the admitted dominance of ideology and dependence on government favors, and by the signs of questionable professional ethics of some practicing scientists, it is no surprise that suggestions reemerged recently about the end of science.[22] The reasoning behind this view is reflecting the belief that all great questions in science, as related to nature, have already been answered, and additional theoretical research will be too expensive and with questionable return on investment. Questions related to man and mankind are simply unanswerable. The time has come to accept, in the field of sciences, that there are unknowables substantively distinct from knowns and unknowns.

The arguments against this "end of science" perspective are coming from both camps. The traditionalists see it as another cyclic reoccurrence of the nineteenth-century romantic movement, best visible in Oswald Spengler's work, which assumed science's internal tendency to degenerate into a kind of mathematical formulas-based mysticism. Arguments about the fundamental importance of science, and predictions that science will provide a synthesis of all knowledge from all fields of inquiry (including philosophy, ethics, art, and literature) through evolutionary biology and cognitive science, will continue to be presented without acknowledgment of any other alternative, and without a rational response to critique.[23] The situation is similar to the optimistic dreams about "perennial philosophy" (a permanently significant philosophy providing universal and inclusive, internally coherent and fruitful insights, reasoned so conclusively as to be beyond refutation, and presented so convincingly that reasonable minds cannot resist it) spanning history since Plato to Aldous Huxley's work in the 1940s. The postmodernists agree that science will continue because it is nothing more than a linguistic game. But even this observation is, actually, nothing new. Thucydides (c. 460–c. 399 B.C.) noted that play with the meaning of words is one of the first discourse strategies in times of discord. But, of course, newly modified Marxism sees in postmodernism nothing more than a cultural variant of late capitalism that will lead to the emergence of a new international proletariat.[24]

Contemporary developments in the sciences and philosophy of science strongly suggest that, in the domain of science, answers to our questions belong to the scientifically unknowable class.

ETHICS

From the beginning, the contemplation of issues and opinions in the domain of ethics confirms the enormity of difficulties stemming from the lack of some intuitively obvious link of ethics to the natural world. Ethics does not deal whatsoever with inanimate objects or their qualities; all its concepts relate to the human mind, to consciousness, beliefs, judgments, and so on. It is not, therefore, surprising to encounter a very rich variety of ethical attitudes displayed by individuals, especially from society to society, and between different periods of history. Furthermore, their differences often seem to involve deep matters of principal beliefs that have no common ground for resolution. A common language statement, "man of principle," can serve as an illustration of the problem. At face value, a positive evaluation of a person is sometimes viewed as a characterization of someone who acts in accordance with a fixed set of rules, ignoring the uniqueness or complexity of the situation and failing to adapt his behavior to changing circumstances. The morality of principles and rules is put in contrast with the morality of sensibility and empathy. In very general terms, this is the conflict between the demands of objectivity and autonomy, a fundamental problem of philosophy pointing to the conflict between ultimate principles that can never be rationally resolved. In other words, neither logic nor science can derive an "ought" from an "is," meaning that in those matters which concern man most vitally, man is left to some dogma, such as a Darwinist declaration that morality is nothing more than a reflection of fear, or an unconscious strategy for reproductive success of close relatives,[25] or whim. Once man has been declared "the measure of all things," there is no longer a true, or a good, or a just, but only opinions of equal validity, whose clash cannot be resolved by argument, but only by force. Man's yearning for some objective ethical guidance of his life cannot be satisfied.

The study of jurisprudence started with an optimism that legal systems, concerned with behaviors that are in conflict with society-sanctioned patterns, might provide indirect clues leading to those that are preferred and beneficial. We have been rewarded by man's insight into the ever-present problem of evil, and into man's desire for justice. But the original optimism became clouded by the positivist attempt to decouple legality from morality, by open admission of ideological influences, and by the ubiquity of the common law, especially as practiced in the U.S.

The hard truth of the matter is that American courts have no intelligible, generally accepted, and consistently applied theory of statutory interpretation. This fact allows viewing the primary legal documents, such as the Constitution, as untidy and complex charters of governance that cannot be reduced to the purposes and prescriptions of any single interpretative method, and opens the door to ideological interpretations changing with the times and personalities of justices.[26] Common man has his own views of morality attenuated to the institutionalized immorality of the political system and blunted moral sensitivity of the public. He is left again without clear direction for his own life and how to raise his children. What is unacceptable today may become preferable tomorrow and vice versa.

ROLE MODELS

When trying to learn from successful individuals, the need to understand the concept of power, as the most obvious reward for worldly success, presents itself as an immediate challenge because the optimism of intellectuals about the victory of reason over authority came to an end in the cruelties of World War I at the beginning of the twentieth century. The only potentially successful alternative strategy, known for a long time, has been to turn knowledge into power, and the intellectuals into competitors with the existing powers that be. The ideological environments of the first half of the twentieth century in the West were conducive to this change, and many intellectuals were attracted to participate in it. Early successes of dogmatic ideology-based states also brought success to intellectuals willing to abandon the world of ideas and join the struggles of the world of power politics. Many started to dream about reforming, if not ruling, the world. This dream vanished with the collapse of the totalitarian regimes, and of the intellectuals' image as modern-day nobility, as moral and cultural leaders of their societies, as well. Czech philosopher Nicholas Lobkowitz saw the catastrophe and its cause clearly: "Almost everything that has gone wrong in the recent history of our culture originated in the minds of people such as ourselves, people who are university graduates and intellectuals."[27]

The heritage left by modern power elites is visible in these few unappealing behavioral options:

- Narcissistic *"carpe diem"* or "after us, the deluge" attitudes, as an extreme variant of consumerism, may provide some satisfaction, especially when some major social catastrophe is expected in the near future.

- Joining some protocommunistic commune organized for the protection and promotion of local interests with minimum links to the rest of the society.

- Assuming a position of a disinterested critic and observer.

- Joining, or forming, a new political party with the ideal to reform the current power system.

- Escaping the world reality by employing "elevated states of consciousness" achieved through cultic or mystic ecstasies or, simply, by drugs.

The success of the majority of members of existing elites does not seem to be a result of moral virtues, nor linked with laudable abilities and work habits. Actual lives of worldly successful people, as individuals or members of high social circles, often show that their conduct and character do not constitute a good role model worth being imitated and aspired to. They are not men with whom the general public can rightfully and gladly identify.

Does this mean that the current age did not produce any worthwhile role models? Not at all! We may point to Dr. Albert Schweitzer (1875–1965), Mother Teresa of Calcutta (1910–1997), Dr. Billy Graham (1918–), or Pope

John Paul II (1920–). But the lives of these people, obviously, are not reflections of science-based modernity.

SUMMARY AND CONCLUSIONS

For over six hundred years, West European humanism—presenting itself under impressive and exalted labels of Renaissance, Enlightenment, Age of Reason, Modern Age, and Age of Science—has been downgrading all other views of the world and man as myths, superstitions, and prejudices characterized by narrowmindness, dogmatism, intolerance, and so on. This trend intensified in the last 150 years, the era that may be called the Age of Ideologies. In its prideful, exuberant optimism (i.e., optimism capable of belief that everything is beautiful, including what is ugly), it promised not only final answers to all man's fundamental questions, but also to lead humanity into a man-designed paradise. These ill-fated dreams came to an end in the ideology-based terrors and social disasters jolting twentieth-century Europe and, later, other continents as well. Recent philosophical developments revealed also the conceptual naïveté, ethical emptiness, and atrophied moral imagination called "objectivity" of modern humanism. Due to (1) humanistic ideology undermining public education, (2) simplistic acceptance of scientism, multiculturalism, and ethical relativism, combined with (3) disrespect for truth, history, cultural traditions, and common sense, even well-educated contemporary man stands facing life's fundamental questions poorly equipped, equipped probably worse than his medieval counterpart. It seems that Tom Wolfe's radical assessment of humans as "Masters of the Universe," in the go-go 1970s was, at least, a little bit off the mark.

The unquestionably enormous progress in man's ability to create wealth and significantly improve the living standard and conditions in many parts of the world have almost nothing to do with humanism, in spite of the claims of intellectuals and politicians, as witnessed by improvements even in autocratic and totalitarian regimes. With some exceptions, not even science can claim to be the source of this progress which, actually, is the result of the creative work, skills, and experience of ordinary people, specialists, entrepreneurs and investors. Not scientists with their theories, but inventors of the clock, printing press, telescope, steam engine, light bulb, telephone, wireless communication, automobile, computer, World Wide Web, etc.—with entrepreneurs and investors making their inventions available society-wide, all working quite independently, and sometimes against the ideological trends and economic framework—are the real driving force behind all this advancement.

We can conclude that, after more than a half of the last millennia, humanism is leaving modern man with a chaotic multiplicity of opinions, narrow perspective regarding where to look for sources of credible knowledge, Copernican preferences for simplicity and distaste for the complex, and moral relativism of the individual elevated to the godlike position of being the ultimate measure of all things. Our walk through the bodies of human knowledge available to the contemporary person is leaving us unsatisfied in our desire to find clear answers to the original questions. We have encountered many excellent proposals and initiatives, often contradicting each other, but all of them seriously criticized or even refuted. None of them escaped the postmodern view that they are nothing more than highly sophisticated word games. We have also found that both Dante and Goethe, as quoted in the Introduction, missed the crucial point that T. S. Eliot[28] had seen quite clearly:

> *We shall not cease from exploration*
> *And the end of all our exploring*
> *Will be to arrive where we started*
> *And know the place for the first time.*

The true starting point is the Bible, and the source of answers to the questions posed is God's wisdom revealed in the Bible. Our conclusion is the same as that of the seventeenth-century hero of J. A. Comenius's book, who—after returning from the confusing and disappointing tour through the labyrinth of the world—looked to God as the only person who is able to give the desired paradise of the heart.

PART TWO:
GOD'S TRUTH

God chose the foolish things of the world to shame the wise; God chose the weak things of the world to shame the strong.

1 Corinthians 1:27

THE BIBLE

8

Obviously, any serious discussion of biblical Christianity must start with the discussion of the Bible because of the role it plays as its fundamental and indubitable reference document. For biblical Christianity, the Bible is the Word of God in human words, showing God's willingness to bend Himself down to meet human beings at their own level.

The variety of books on the market carrying the word "bible" in their title, and the scope of perspectives from which their reading can be approached, leads to the first question, "What is a bible?" This question is completely natural to the majority of modern readers, to whom the Bible appears both familiar and strange. They may know about its central importance in the history of Western culture, and surely they are acquainted with humanistic denials of its importance for the current world. Over the past few decades, there has been some revival of interest reflecting the demise of utopian ideologies, disputes surrounding new cosmogonical hypotheses—mainly Darwinism and the Big Bang—and by new controversial changes in legislated morality. This renewed attraction has been strengthened by recent discoveries of well-preserved ancient texts, such as the Dead Sea Scrolls, and archeological confirmation of persons and events described in the biblical narrative. In general, biblical texts are proving again their role as a valuable resource for devising personal responses to unfavorable tendencies and failures of modern humanism and secularism, and for answers in the search for life's fundamental values and directions.

The recognized importance of the Bible stimulates questions about authorship and time of origin of its individual books, how the laws presented in it were formulated, and how accurately the historical events and personalities are described. Another, more detailed group of questions then relates to the authors themselves. Did the author witness the events described? If not, where did he get the idea of what happened? Did the author write his work with the intent that it should become a sacred, authoritative text? And so on.

More than 600 years of textual research—the last 100 years under the strong influence of Julius Wellhausen (1844–1918)—generated many insights, critiques, and speculations,[1] unfortunately, mostly for the purpose of discrediting Christianity as a superstition, unjustifiable when judged according to humanistic standards. This research continues and provides many entertaining discussions. In our time, therefore, many views of the Bible are being pursued. The two most dominant are: the Bible as a work of general literature, and the Bible accepted as God's recorded message to man.

CONTENTS AND ORIGINS

The word "bible" is derived through Latin from the Greek word *biblia,* meaning simply "books." The earliest Christian use of *ta biblia* ("the books") emerged about 150 A.D. Before, the terms "the Writings" and "the Scriptures" had been used, which keep their role as synonyms even today. The word "testament" also goes back to Greek through Latin, where it originally meant "covenant." The terms "Old Testament" and "New Testament" for the two main collections of biblical books came into general Christian use in the later part of the second century, somewhat unfortunately, because the Bible does not represent "testaments" in the ordinary sense of the term, only in its loosely associated meaning of "bearing witness."

The Old Testament

The books of the Old Testament, a.k.a. the Hebrew Bible, had been written during the one-thousand-year period between ca. 1400 and 400 B.C. The most popular Greek translation, the Septuagint, then followed in the third century B.C., in the years ca. 250 to 200.

Most of the books in the Old Testament are anthologies of authoritative utterances. The Ten Commandments had been written in stone by God. Moses then assured that all the laws and covenants had been put in writing, and later expanded by oracles, new utterances, and descriptions of important historical events as well. Other books of the Bible began also as authoritative sayings or speeches by respected people. In the middle of the second century B.C., the contents of the Old Testament had been fixed around three major divisions: the Law, the Prophets, and the Writings. The origin of this arrangement of books in the Old Testament cannot be traced; it is believed to correspond to the three stages in which the books received canonical recognition: Pentateuch (The Law, Torah, or The Five Books of Moses) was both complete and canonized in the fifth century B.C., and the Prophets and the Writings probably in the middle of the second century B.C. These are the Scriptures referred to by Jesus, accepted by the apostles, and used by the early Christian church. At the beginning of the second century A.D., the council of Jamnia confirmed the original Hebrew canon (i.e., the catalogue of accepted books), but later other (deuterocanonical) books (the Apocrypha) were added, and are a part the Roman Catholic Bible. In today's Bibles, the Old Testament is arranged into four sections: law, history, wisdom and lyrical books, and the prophets.

For Israel, the Hebrew Bible contains authoritative statements of covenants, law, warnings and promises associated with Israel's historical conduct in the framework of her relation to God, and prophecies about her future. For Christians, most fundamental are the Old Testament's prophesies about the Messiah (Savior), now perceived as fulfilled in the person of Jesus Christ, as well as those about the end of times.

The New Testament

Books of the New Testament, written originally in common Greek, were addressed to the audience living in the eastern parts of the Roman Empire, and have literary forms familiar and popular there. They form four groups: The Gospels, The Acts of the Apostles, Letters, and The Book of Revelation.

What is a gospel? The Greek word for "gospel," *to evangelion,* means "the good news," and was used for imperial proclamations. Before the Gospels were written, the gospel was presumably an oral proclamation of the teachings, life, and resurrection of Jesus. The first writings assembled and distributed as a collection were, in fact, early Christian letters. And the Gospels? The first one gaining official status, but probably not the first one written, was Luke's. Their number grew, but in the second half of the second century Irenaeus proposed the order and number we are familiar with now: Matthew, Mark, Luke, and John.

The whole group of books forming the New Testament grew from an early collection of Marcion (ca. 140 A.D.) to the consensus-based collection (canon) of the twenty-seven books of Athanasius (367 A.D.). Athanasius's list did not settle the matter for everybody, but since Jerome's time (the early part of the fifth century), the canon of our New Testament has been stable, and approved by history, tradition, and worship.

For the Jews, both leaning toward the original Hebrew Bible–based tradition and law, as well as for those who joined the humanistic tradition of the Greeks and the Romans, the books of the New Testament were, and still are, mostly irrelevant, representing just another literary work coming from the ancient world. But for Christians, they are the Word of God presented in the form of a principal collection of memories and a witness of people living in, or close to, the times of Jesus. They include Christ's biography, a description of the impact that His life, work, death, and resurrection had in the framework of Hebrew prophesies, of opening the door to God's forgiveness to the Gentiles, of freeing man from the burden of the Law, and of future expectations related to God's plan of salvation. The power of the good news about forgiveness through faith in Jesus Christ, presented in the New Testament, is well documented in its impact on personal lives of believers and moral developments in the realm of historical Christendom.

In the majority of contemporary Christian environments, the modern English titles *The Bible* or *Holy Bible* are confessional descriptors, usually accompanied with the name of a particular version or translation, of the traditional twofold contents, The Old Testament and The New Testament. Only some versions are supplemented by Apocrypha and simple explanatory aids. These titles also suggest treatment of the text as the revealed Word of God. But even here, at closer examination, it is easy to find variations in contents when comparing, e.g., the Catholic, Protestant, Orthodox (Russian and Greek), Ethiopic, Coptic, and Syrian Bibles.

Manuscripts

Manuscripts are written texts copied individually by hand, the only versions of the Bible in every language existing before the invention of the printing press in about the mid-fifteenth century. Because of the obvious possibility of human errors, or intentional changes of the text, the first aspect of the Bible's reliability rests in comparisons with the earliest manuscripts available. Currently, there exist thousands of ancient manuscripts and fragments making the Bible the best authenticated historical document.

The earliest known biblical manuscripts are those discovered in 1947, and following years, in the caves of Qumran, the "Dead Sea Scrolls,"[2] which go back to the closing centuries B.C. This discovery confirmed the integrity of the Old Testament's text rather than supporting highly fashionable speculations about its documentary disunity.

The oldest surviving manuscripts of the New Testament, written on papyrus, are codices in the Chester Beatty collection dating from the second to mid-third century, fragments in the John Ryland's Library dated before the middle of the second century, and codices in the Bodmer Library dated from the late part of the second century. But the most important seem to be the Vatican and Sinaitic codices of the fourth and fifth centuries.

No single manuscript is clearly the best; so, the evidence of each must be weighed very carefully. Over the last three centuries many have worked hard to assure that the Bible of today is as close as possible to what its authors originally wrote.

Translations

Since the middle of the twentieth century, many new complete translations of the Bible, as well as of its individual books, were introduced mainly in the English-speaking West. The popular 1611 Authorized Version of the "King James Bible," and the official Roman Catholic 1722 version of the Douai Bible, found competitive translations, compressed versions, and paraphrases.[3] A similar explosion occurred in translations into the majority of the 5445 languages known to be used in the world, thanks to the work of missionary

Bible translators and Bible societies. In purely quantitative terms, this is the greatest age of Bible expansion, although it goes mostly unrecognized by the general population because, intentionally, the Bible is never included in the lists of bestsellers.

At least two groups of experts are involved in the translation task, Bible scholars who worry about translation accuracy, and stylists concerned with issues of its effectiveness. Difficulty enters with the recognition that every translation is actually an interpretation, as the old cliché, "to translate is to betray," indicates. A conviction that translation should help to explain rather than simply represent the original text is an unacknowledged heresy underlying many of the modern versions of the Bible. This is clearly seen in gender-free language, feminist interpretation, or in the vocabulary of Latin American liberation theology. These are, of course, not philological, but ideological goals imposed on the translation. Indeed, similar attitudes have been displayed also by many literary critics who have engaged in "deconstructing" the biblical text with two obvious agendas: bringing suspicion about the actual motivation of the biblical authors, while simultaneously masking their own, not very well hidden, sociological or ideological goals. On purpose, literary critics place authority outside the Bible, into the human authors and their social environment and circumstances, which makes it possible to elevate themselves above the authors on accord of the sophisticated analytical skills they posses and, by that, above the Bible. Such critical attitudes are nothing more than arrogant postures demonstrating that the key point has been missed. Ironically, critical attitudes—for example, denials of authenticity of selected biblical statements—contain a flavor of censorship, something literary critics themselves claim to oppose.

Despite the veil of intellectual sophistication and pretended scholarly objectivity, translators' actual objectives are usually self-evident and, therefore, defense strategy against introduced biases is also obvious. Prudent students of the Bible, especially when not familiar with the original languages, will use literal translations (e.g., the New Revised Standard Version Bible) for their conceptual studies, and, for enjoyment, the rhetorical brilliance of classical versions, such as The New King James Version.

Views of the Original Authorship

In terms of the actual authorship, there are two major perspectives: a purely human origin of the Bible is assumed by non-Christians, while Christians believe in either God's inspiration, or God's direct dictation, of the biblical texts. Among the most extreme believers in God's literal guidance are Orthodox Jews, who hold the view that not only every word of the Torah, but its every single letter was dictated directly by God to Moses in a precise and unerring sequence. According to Orthodox Jewish tradition based on this view, the Torah contains all knowledge, including the knowledge that transcends the limitation of time.

In 1988, a paper was published in a highly respected professional journal[4] claiming discovery of words and phrases encoded into the Hebrew text of the Torah that could not have been accidental, nor placed there by human hand, because of their predictive nature, some of them linked to twentieth-century wars and assassinations. For some people, such discovered coded phrases are perceived as evidence of God's hand not only in the writings of the Torah, but in all human history. Public fascination with such "bible codes" grew during the 1990s, with involvement of statisticians, cryptoanalysts, and linguists. Peer reviews by mathematicians equipped by powerful computers, and additional analyses and checks done by the authors, confirmed that the observed effect persisted. As a control, a Hebrew translation of Tolstoy's *War and Peace* was tested for similar data using identical procedure. The result? Only very few similar discoveries of names or events were reported. There is no shortage of skepticism, ridicule, and mockery—assigning such work to the category of word search puzzles, or even to mistranslation and false interpretation—but interestingly enough, the openly published challenge to find a flaw in the method has not produced anything.[5]

The discovered phenomenon might be real, but what to do with it and its results is up to the individual. Christian belief in the Bible as the Word of God rests on much higher authority than a computer program, or a sophisticated statistical analysis.

Lost and Forgotten Books

Throughout the Bible, there are scattered mysterious references to unknown books, such as the Book of Jashar and Book of the Wars of Yahweh. In total, there are about twenty potential candidates for the title "lost book" because no copies are known to exist. Although we have no actual texts, their general content and character can be assessed from situations in, and the purpose for, which they are referenced in the Bible, and from additional references found in noncanonical literature and legends.[6]

Another extensive set of books consists of those that are known but have not been accepted into the biblical canon. The majority of these, in an attempt to give them sanctity, were ascribed to various biblical personalities far more ancient than the books themselves. Because of this falsely ascribed authorship, these writings are called Pseudoepigrapha.[7] Their literary form makes precise dating difficult, but they all reflect aspects of Jewish history associated with events several hundred years after the Babylonian exile, thus written mostly between the years 200 B.C. and 100 A.D. Even though these books failed to achieve permanency in the framework of biblical heritage, they do enrich our insights into Jewish thought after the close of the Hebrew Bible and our knowledge of early Christianity.

INTERPRETATIONS

In terms of reading approaches, we can recognize perceptions of the Bible purely as an ancient human work of literature or a collection of mythical stories and narratives; on the opposite side of the spectrum, we can view the Bible as a verbally inspired book containing the Word of God, or even as a liturgically sacred object. In addition, individual translations may also be based on different sources, usually of Hebrew, Aramaic, Greek, or Latin origin.[8]

This rich variety makes biblical texts an interesting subject of study for scholars, and for serious Bible students in the domain of the Christian church as well. For readers who see in the Bible the Word of God directly applicable in their daily lives, the selection of the version to adopt may well be a function of the quality of the translation, of the type of language used, or of an accepted tradition, because in the majority of the versions now available the biblical message and its meaning are almost identical. But a word of caution is needed for reading paraphrased versions, or versions that are not real translations but covert interpretations fostering some ideological viewpoint.[9]

Bible Study and Biblical Studies

General reading and study of the Bible is characterized by a plurality of interests. Members of the church, synagogue, or academia must decide what kind of a study is most useful for their stated purpose. Customary use of the current English language distinguishes between two major approaches: Bible study and biblical studies.

Bible study is what church members do privately, or in their communities, to reach a better understanding of the Scripture as it directly relates to their lives. This study considers the biblical message as authoritative, and its interpretation is usually related to some doctrinal definitions of the Bible and its role in the context of their faith. It may be supported by a search for additional information about the Bible, its original languages, its history, authorships of individual books, archeological findings, etc., but these activities are ancillary and by themselves bring no deeper religious understanding. Despite their potential to create a high level of intellectual interest, these studies are an incidental accessory to church teachings and church members' education.

Biblical studies, on the other hand, is the name for an academic discipline that is, in contrast, focused on how and when biblical literature came into existence in the environment and constraints of the original language and social situation, and how it was transformed into the text in contemporary language, form, and social interests. Academic studies should not get involved in questions of the text's authority and inspiration for the simple reason of having no tools for addressing and resolving such matters; at best, such issues can only be described and analyzed.

Confessionary and Nonconfessionary Studies

Despite the fact that an overwhelming majority of biblical studies are humanistic, i.e., nontheological and nonconfessionary, in their nature, theological biblical studies are being conducted also, especially under the auspices of theological faculties. While confessionary and nonconfessionary approaches to the academic studies of biblical literature may both be considered important and even critical, they are nevertheless quite different and ought not to be confused in theory or practice. The choice between the two involves ethical and methodological decisions related to all agents involved: the authors, readers, and the institutions sponsoring the study. These two approaches imply two different definitions of the object to be studied and result in two different and frequently diverging discourses; they actually form two separate disciplines.

Additional facts complicate the situation. Academic theology exists largely outside the church and, therefore, it often houses scholars who are much closer to a humanistic position than to Christianity. On the other hand, some scholars also write devotional books. This mixture of personal theological perspectives may cause in the believing Christian community a false perception that competence in scholarship results in a higher authority in pastoral matters and questions of Christian belief.

Similar confusion exists in the humanistic nonconfessional biblical studies as well. Some scholars hold that Christian faith is not compatible with proper academic standards, nor with academically required openness to alternative perspectives. They also hold that proclamations are inappropriate in an academic environment not just because of the continuing quest for truth, assumed to be the primary function of the university, but also due to conjecture that academic discourse must be open to all opinions in order to lead to their later convergence toward some future unified theory of universal explanation. But there are also scholars adhering to postmodern epistemology, which emphasizes the impossibility of reading any text without some prior ideological commitment that originated in the reader's unavoidable factual, social, and cultural circumstances; in short, Christian faith is covertly substituted by faith in a humanistic ideological system. In the most extreme version of this postmodern view, the claim is made that the meaning of all texts is actually generated by the reader, whose interpretative perspective is ideologically predefined. This refusal of objectivity leads to interpretative strategies called political allegory, and justifies interpretations actually contradictory to the text author's original intention and motive.[10] Such an approach to the Bible, in reality, dismisses the underlying biblical text and engages in a cultural subversion for the purposes of modern secularism.[11] Hostility of those studies toward confessional Christian approaches is sometimes masked by using the language of deconstruction, and justified by the view that all languages are unstable and, therefore, the meaning of texts fundamentally indeterminate.[12]

Even when disregarding the goal of interpreting the Bible, serious general scholarship issues are at stake in this approach. For example, political allegory might become unethical because it simply permits domestication of the text to the reader's perspective, so that the text merely reinforces opinions and conclusions already achieved, or authorizes ideological positions already held, instead of providing ground for creative cultural exchange. Another ethical concern is in elevating readers above the authors, who should be a regulative ideal for any interpretation, and denying them respect by manipulating their work for the reader's own purpose. This approach also allows uncontrolled proliferation of meanings and interpretations without providing the means for distinguishing between valid and invalid correlation of the proposed interpretation with the author's original referential intent. Last, but not least, it neglects the fact that in most situations the problem is not the Christian or other belief, but its role in discourse, its acceptability as working assumption, and its exclusivity in assertions about the truth in the text. The previous experience with biblical texts indicates that whether or not the interpreter has "faith" does not prevent him or her from seeing the difference between alternatives of the textual research. In summary, the tyranny of humanistic academic criticism, and imposition of the monopoly of acquired academic norms, is no improvement over the rejected medieval hegemony of ecclesiastical authoritarianism. Criticism of the Bible is inevitable, but it should not be declared normative, especially not by freedom of research proclaiming academia. Professional status of scholars is probably good, but not *summum bonum;* it may turn harmful when not accompanied by self-criticism.

Church and the Bible

Despite the fact that biblical texts have readers outside the church, the Christian religious community obviously has a unique claim on their Bible.[13] In the history of the church, it is possible to identify three basic approaches to Scripture. The first regards Scripture as the primary channel or medium of God's revelation, of His communication with man, with the writers being the instruments of God.[14] The second view (scholastic) perceives revelation as the disclosure of higher truth that, nonetheless, stands in continuity with rational or natural truth.[15] The Bible and its humanity are regarded as representing aspects of divinity and, therefore, contains no errors in any respect. The third perspective is associated with the liberal-modernist view of revelation as a means to self-discovery and inner enlightenment.[16] The most recent discussions among the leading church intellectuals are characterized by the dislike of the idea of inerrancy, and by fear of the conclusions possibly drawn from the modernist view denying the Bible any authority. Such attitudes result, for example, in viewing homosexuality as an alternative lifestyle acceptable to God, or accepting knowledge gained in the social sciences as superseding revelation.[17] It is actually very sad that the church intelligentsia is so much interested in impressing the world and its humanistic colleagues, while at the same time and despite apostolic warning (1 Tim. 6:3–5) being unable or unwilling to stop creating arguments and controversies about such a fundamental issue.[18]

THE BIBLE THROUGH THE EYES OF BELIEVERS

Where do these debates leave ordinary Christian believers? The first proper attitude in respect to this question is a genuine thankfulness to God that His truth does not depend on confirmation by any scholar, be he a humanist or a theologian. Therefore, academic discussions may be interesting, but remain essentially irrelevant to the individual Christian's faith. The second proper attitude reflects understanding that denying God's authority revealed according to His will through the Bible puts man outside the domain of Christianity; as there is no Christianity without the lordship of Jesus Christ, there is no Christianity without the authoritative Bible either. The third attitude is based on God's and man's rationality and practicality: if God chose to inspire people to write down His revealed word, He provides inspirational help in reading this word to those who ask for it as well. Such views lead to these evaluations of the work of scholars:

- When scholars study issues of factual origin, original languages, time and circumstances of writing, etc., of the biblical texts, their nonspeculative work is laudable and, despite its secondary importance, may be supportive of the interests of biblical Christianity.

- When scholars start to address issues of biblical text authority and inspiration, they are engaged in speculations outside of the domain of their expertise and accepted methodologies and, therefore, should be subject to the critique by other scholars.

- When scholars or theologians are inventing and propagating interpretations, opinions, assumptions, hypotheses, conclusions, etc., in conflict with the as-literal-as-possible reading of the Bible, they are putting themselves in a dangerous position of false teachers by setting aside, or even nullifying, the Word of God in order to comply with human academic tradition (Matt. 7:9, 13). The theologians are especially at risk of joining the group about which Jesus Himself said, "These people honor me with their lips, but their hearts are far from me. They worship me in vain; their teachings are but rules taught by men" (Matt. 15:8–9).

The believers' final conclusion (naturally disputed by the unbelievers) is, therefore, straightforward: the authority and credibility of the Bible, the Word of God, is based on the authority and credibility of God Himself, as revealed and witnessed by the writers of the biblical books and letters. Confirmation of this view is then traced to God's own revealing words. Consider, for example, these direct commands:

- "Then the LORD said to Moses, 'Write down these words, for in accordance with these words I have made a covenant with you and with Israel'" (Exod. 34:27).
- " Look at the scroll of the LORD and read . . ." (Isa. 34:16).
- " . . . this word came to Jeremiah from the LORD: 'Take a scroll and write on it all the words I have spoken to you concerning Israel, Judah and all the other nations from the time I began speaking to you in the reign of Josiah till now'" (Jer. 36:1–2).
- "Write, therefore, what you have seen, what is now and what will take place later" (Rev. 1:19).
- "To the angel of the church in Ephesus (Smyrna, Pergamum, Thyatira, Sardis, Philadelphia, Laodicea) write . . . " (Rev. 2:1, 8, 12, 18; 3:1, 7, 14).

Similar witness of God's origin of the biblical text may be found in the many statements by Jeremiah, "This is what the LORD says," or by Ezekiel, "The word of the LORD came to me 'Son of man, say to. . . .'" Jesus Himself confirmed the absoluteness and truth of the Old Testament and of His own words:

- "Do not think that I [Jesus] have come to abolish the Law or the Prophets; I have not come to abolish them but to fulfill them. I tell you the truth, until heaven and earth disappear, not the smallest letter, not the least stroke of pen, will by any means disappear from the Law until everything is accomplished" (Matt. 5:17–18).
- "Heaven and earth will pass away, but my words will never pass away" (Mark 13:31).
- ". . . [T]he Scripture cannot be broken" (John 10:35).
- "I [Jesus] gave them [disciples] the words You [Father] gave me and they accepted them" (John 17:8).
- "[Father] Your word is truth" (John 17:17).
- "But these [Jesus' miraculous signs] are written that you may believe that Jesus is the Christ, the Son of God, and that by believing you may have life in his name" (John 20:31).

- "[T]he Gospel he [God] promised beforehand through his prophets in the Holy Scriptures regarding his Son . . . Jesus Christ our Lord" (Rom. 1:2–4).

- "[T]he word of God is living and active. . . . It judges the thoughts and attitudes of the heart" (Heb. 4:12).

And in sharpest contrast to the scholarly and intellectual debates that only create controversies, arguments, quarreling, malicious talk, strife, and constant friction (1 Tim. 6:4), God's word in the Bible is revealed for man's benefit and peace. In the book of Amos we may find a clear assurance that God does nothing important for man without communicating His intentions to His people. By such revelation, God also clarifies man's responsibility for his acts and for his attitude toward God Himself, and his fellow men:

- "Surely the Sovereign LORD does nothing without revealing His plan to His servants the prophets" (Amos 3:7).

- "For everything that was written in the past was written to teach us, so that through endurance and the encouragement of the Scriptures we might have hope" (Rom. 15:4).

- "All Scripture is God-breathed and is useful for teaching, rebuking, correcting and training in righteousness, so that the man of God may be thoroughly equipped for every good work" (2 Tim. 3:16–17).

- " . . . the holy Scriptures, which are able to make you wise for salvation through faith in Jesus Christ" (2 Tim. 3:15).

- "These things [episodes from Israel's history] happened to them as examples and were written down as warnings for us, on whom the fulfillment of the ages has come" (1 Cor. 10:11).

Christians' understanding of the Scripture is based on the help of the Holy Spirit and accompanied by promised blessings and issued warnings to both listeners and preachers.

- "This is what we [the apostles] speak, not in words taught us by human wisdom but in words taught by the Spirit, expressing spiritual truths in spiritual words" (1 Cor. 2:13).

- "Blessed rather are those who hear the word of God and obey it" (Luke 11:28).

- "Blessed is the one who reads the words of this prophecy, and blessed are those who hear it and take to heart what is written in it, because the time is near" (Rev. 1:3).

- "For the time will come when men will not put up with sound doctrine. Instead, to suit their own desires, they will gather around them a great number of teachers to say what their itching ears want to hear" (2 Tim. 4:3).

- "If anybody is preaching to you a gospel other than what you accepted, let him be eternally condemned!" (Gal. 1:9).

For believing Christians the answers to the Bible-related questions are simple, easy, and based on faith. On Jesus' authority it is known that the Bible is the Word of God written by men moved by the Spirit (2 Pet. 1:21). Jesus appealed to the Old Testament as the final authority with His frequent phrase, "It is written." For the New Testament He promised " . . . the Counselor, the Holy Spirit, whom the Father will send in my name, will teach you all things and remind you of everything I have said to you" (John 14:26), and assured that, " . . . when he, the Spirit of truth comes, he will guide you into all truth" (John 16:13).[19] The power of God behind the word is witnessed by the millions of changed lives when the biblical message penetrated human hearts and led them to accepting Jesus Christ as the personal Savior and Lord. Biblical view of human sin and associated limits of understanding render the debate about inerrancy false and abstract. Holy Scripture is, indeed, infallible when it sets forth unmistakable teaching about God, man, and the world. But human interpretations and applications, especially those devoid of the leadership of the Holy Spirit, are not.[20] To confuse spiritual infallibility of the Bible with human fallibility hinders the work of the Holy Spirit in the world.

When the Bible is read in a believing and worshipping community, the Spirit bears witness that it is the Word of God, God's chosen medium of communication with contemporary man. For the believers the most important issue is to read the Bible and obey God's will reflected in it, rather than be engaged in interpretations.

The importance of the Bible for a believer's growth in knowledge of his Lord and Savior, and of His will for his own individual life, is supreme and unquestionable, even though prayers, meditations, and communal worship are of high value as well. For the unbeliever, the Bible may be irrelevant, or be actually a closed book with no understandable message, or it may play only an indirect role through some of the aspects of the overall cultural environment. This is obvious from resurrected Jesus' command (Mark 16:15) who sent His disciples to proclaim the good news to the whole creation, not to distribute Bibles to them, irrespectively that this, in some cultural situations, may be the second best service to man as well. This truth has been historically demonstrated by the legions of people coming to Christ without any biblical knowledge, many times without access to it, some even illiterate, and also by the number of Bibles left unread in many homes across the whole world.

CONCLUSIONS

The Bible is neither a direct, unmediated speech of God, nor an indirect historical witness to divine revelation. For the believer, the Bible is God's personal message to him, the Word of God in human language, God's revelation through human concepts, images, and historical events and personalities.

When we say that the Bible is the Word of God, we mean (1) that all the words had been selected by the Holy Spirit guiding human authors, (2) that the truth is enshrined in these words, and is mediated to the believer through these words by the Holy Spirit. The principal participation of the Holy Spirit in the disclosure of the personal meaning of the biblical message makes all attempts of rationalistic, human-only approaches to determine the truth-content of the Bible misguided.

In other words, the Bible is the Word of God in all that it teaches, though this teaching is not self-evident, but must be unveiled by the Holy Spirit. What is infallible and inerrant in the Bible is the meaning given through the Holy Spirit–led human testimony. There is an overarching fundamental unity between the written Word of God in the Bible and the Word of God that became flesh and historically lived among us in the person of Jesus Christ (John 1:14).

GOD OF THE BIBLE

9

What can be said about God of the Bible, the God of Abraham, Isaac, and Jacob? Philosophers, and even some theologians, are convinced that it is impossible to really talk about any god, that what may be said is inadequate, that it is possible to describe only what God is not, and that the very nature of such attempts is misguided. But how can Christians credibly communicate their God's message if the above statements are valid? A few explanatory comments are evidently due.

Philosophers are unquestionably right in their own metaphysical domain. They cannot realistically describe their god, who is nothing more than an abstract projection of an idealized human being into eternity and infinity. The philosopher's god, and gods of natural religions, are made in the image of man. These gods have nothing to do with Yahweh (Jehovah) of the Bible, God who disclosed Himself and His name to Moses in the episode of the burning bush (Exod. 3:13–15).[1] The majority of such limiting opinions simply omit information revealed by God Himself and made available in the Bible, and attempt to form insights by philosophical speculations about, or investigations of, created nature and man only. Such perspectives repeat the fundamental mistake of social and human sciences approaching man from the outside as an object. Common experience recognizes that to know a person requires that given individual to disclose himself, to voluntary open personality normally hidden behind the barrier of his will.

Both philosophers and theologians are also right in recognizing the limitations of the human mind. The Bible admits it as well: "Now we see but a poor reflection as in a mirror; then we shall see face to face. Now I know in part; then I shall know fully, even as I am fully known" (1 Cor. 13:12). Even the most philosophically inclined theologians recognize that people can talk to God.

GOD AS PURE SPIRIT

For Christians the knowledge of God as the Lord, and of His relationship to man, is certain because it is based on God's voluntary disclosures of Himself. This knowledge is personal and confirmed by biblical witness. The Bible makes it clear that man cannot know God objectively or approach Him as an object of direct observation. The Bible makes it also clear that God reveals Himself to man according to His own free will and wisdom, as sovereign divine authority. In the history of mankind, not only human sovereigns, but all men, used and are using a similar privilege of revealing themselves only partially and according to their own will and timing.

The sizable number of biblical statements about God, attributed either to God Himself, or presented by His chosen witnesses, provides enough information for construction of a reasonable and valid glimpse of God's nature and character.

In His nature, biblical God is pure Spirit, as documented in His self-disclosure as the Creator of the universe, when He is represented as the Spirit who brought light out of darkness (Gen. 1:2–3). Jesus Christ confirmed this fact in His conversation with the Samaritan woman, "God is spirit, and his worshipers must worship in spirit and in truth" (John 4:24). He is Spirit without form or parts and, for this reason, He has no physical presence. It is necessary to distinguish between God, the pure Spirit, and angels, His spiritual creatures.

When the Bible speaks about God as having eyes, ears, hands, etc., it attempts to communicate that God has abilities comparable to senses associated with those parts of human body. Contemplation of disclosed attributes of God's nature leads immediately beyond human experience and comprehension, but that does not have any influence on their actual existence. Consider His:

Infinity—Jeremiah 23:24

Eternity—Deuteronomy 32:40; Isaiah 40:28

Transcendence—Isaiah 66:1

Self-Existence—Exodus 3:14; Acts 17:25

Sovereignty—Exodus 15:18

Holiness—Psalm 19:1; 57:5

Glory—Revelation 4:8, 11

Omnipresence—Psalm 139:7–12

Omnipotence—Matthew 19:26

Strength and Power—Isaiah 40:26, 29; Jeremiah 32:17

Unapproachability—1 Timothy 6:16

Unsearchability—Psalm 145:3; Romans 11:33

Omniscience—1 Samuel 2:3; Matthew 10:29–30

Wisdom—Job 9:4; Psalm 33:11

Understanding—Isaiah 40:14, 28

Incomprehensibility—Job 12:17, 19, 20; Isaiah 55:8–9

This provision of a structured, even partial list of God's attributes leads to at least two dangers:

1. In the current world of inflated value of abstract ideological terms and deflated value of personal moral characteristics, there is always a temptation to see these attributes on a relative scale only. Because God does not make human mistakes, He may be wrongly perceived just a little better, little more powerful, little more loving, etc., than some good men.

2. The environment of modern technology forces man to deal with extremes, with very big and very small numbers and objects, which may contribute to the risk of overlooking the absoluteness[2] of these attributes, and cause man to remain unimpressed.

GOD THE CREATOR

By faith in God as the Creator of heaven and earth Christians attain understanding of the source of their own personal existence, and that their lives are at the Creator's disposal. For biblical Christians to "know" God as the Creator is not to have some intellectual concept of Him, but to acknowledge His distinctive difference, accept Him as the Lord, and submit to His will. This reverence is well described in the Book of Job, which documents a dialogue between God and man, a dialogue without precedence and without sequel. The genius of this great book is in stating openly to man, "You poor fool, by what right have you started to believe that you can comprehend Me and My thought? I am God, and forever inaccessible, and My designs are impenetrable." God's proclamations are neither answers to Job's questions, nor a defense and justification of His actions to Job. They are proclamations of God as the absolutely supreme and different person, as divine authority.

The reflections of Christians on God the Creator, when considering His revealed attributes, lead immediately from an investigative position to an inescapable personal relationship, with dependency and fear as the naturally first aspects of it. The Bible mentions even terror of God as a reasonable response (Gen. 35:5). In the framework of the Christian view of God, this fear is a healthy attitude because it is the foundation of wisdom (Prov. 1:7) and of life (Prov. 14:27). Christians don't cringe in terror, but live before God the Creator in reverence and awe. A beautiful expression of this respect, with a simple summary of God's attributes, may be found in 1 Timothy 1:17, "Now to the King eternal, immortal, invisible, the only God, be honor and glory for ever and ever. Amen."

Despite characteristics of God's personality that point to His transcendence,[3] the Bible stresses His local and temporal manifestations in the world of humans. God manifested Himself through the work and messages of prophets, apostles, and other biblical witnesses, and continues to be present in our world as the person of the Holy Spirit. This God, whom many know by the name Yahweh, made Himself known personally through Jesus Christ, the Word of God that became flesh (John 1:14). The introductory part of the Johannine gospel testifies that in Jesus Christ we are meeting our Creator. Thus faith in Jesus Christ contains within itself faith in God the Creator.

GOD THE JUDGE

Both the Old and the New Testaments emphasize that judging belongs to God's essential activity, and justice to His nature. God's justice forms what the philosophers may call a dialectic unity with God's mercy and love. If God would not be the judge whose holiness demands justice, elimination of sin and punishment of sinners, but a permissive bargaining judge we know from our world, there would be no need for Christ's substitutionary death on the cross, no need for the Savior. The whole world of God's creation would lose its absolute standards for behavior, its perception of God's will would be blurred, and men's moral lives would be lived in an atmosphere of an ethical variant of the institution of an oriental bazaar. It is beneficial to compare the rationality of God's teaching about the need to repent by the trespasser, and the encouragement of the victim to forgive, against common worldly judicial systems, where the guilty criminal may plead "not guilty"; is not encouraged to apologize, but encouraged and supported to use all means to escape responsibility for his or her act by bargaining about the legal definition of the committed crime, by blaming society, neglect by parents, or abuse in early childhood, or by exploiting technicalities of the judicial process; and where the right to forgive has been taken away from the victim and given to the judges, or arbitrarily selected juries.

Man will be judged according to his response to the revealed will of God. This judgment will include the entire spectrum of human deeds, words, and thoughts. God will take into account all the secrets of man's mind (Rom. 2:16) and, especially, the real motivation behind man's actions (1 Cor. 4:5). He will also take into account the different degrees of the knowledge of God's will, as witnessed by the apostle Paul in his letter to Romans (2:12–15),[4] and the verdict will be completely convincing and just. God's just judgment can bring both deliverance for the righteous (Ps. 24:4, 5) and damnation for the wicked (Deut. 32:41).

God's judgment does not imply a detached impartial judge weighing good and evil against some abstract, complicated, and often incomprehensible and contradictory system of laws. Because man's sin is always against God, God Himself is the victim, and therefore His judgment will be a part of His vigorous, highly personal actions against both sin and evil. Because all men fall short according to the will of God and all have sinned, all will be judged in all aspects of life. This judgment will include Christians (Heb. 10:30). Even the angels will go through judgment (2 Pet. 2:4). The fact that nobody can escape God's judgment[5] is made very clear in Jesus' parables of the weeds, of the net, of the tenants, of the wedding banquet, of the ten virgins, and of the sheep and goats, in the Evangelium according to Matthew.

Even though both Old and New Testaments verbally emphasize the final judgment associated with Christ's second coming, the spirit of the Bible makes it clear that God's judgment is at work during man's whole life (John 3:18). The gathering of evidence and, therefore, the process of humanity's judgment is already in progress.

The Bible's revelation of God's role as the judge of the world provides an additional view on the set of attributes of His person and character. The most dominant traits seem to be:

Impartiality to Persons—1 Peter 1:17
Righteousness—Psalm 96:13
Truth—Romans 2:2
Purity—1 John 3:3
Justice—Luke 18:7
Jealousy—Deuteronomy 5:8
Ability to Be Angry—Hebrews 3:11
Vengeance—Hebrews 10:30
Delivering Wrath—Romans 1:18
Patience—Romans 9:22
Mercy—Luke 1:50
Forgiveness—Matthew 6:14
Compassion—James 5:11
Loving Kindness—Titus 3:4
Peace Loving—Romans 15:33

From these and other previously listed revealed attributes we can assert that God is a supreme mind, a self-determining moral agent, and the source of all rationality in the universe. Out of this plenitude and richness of God's personality one attribute must be recognized as all-pervading: His holiness. This holiness is the foundation and predicate for His justice, love, and wisdom. This holiness makes God's will an absolute measure of all actions in the created world, both decretive will, which is always accomplished (e.g. "You will crawl on your belly and you will eat the dust all the days of your life" —Gen. 3:14), and preceptive will, by which He admonishes His creatures, and assigns to them special duties (e.g., "Honor your father and your mother" —Exod. 20:12). This will is often disobeyed, as demonstrated by the request in the Lord's Prayer: "Your will be done on earth as it is in heaven" (Matt. 6:10).

Considering these active and permissive aspects of God's will, we may attribute the entrance of sin into His created world to the permissive will, giving man and some other creatures the liberty to act independently of God's preferences.

Because the judgment of mankind has been given to the Son of man (Matt. 25:31–34), everybody will face Christ's judgment (2 Cor. 5:10), including Christians, because all mankind is under sin. As it is written (Rom. 3:10–18): there is no one righteous, not even one; there is no one who understands, no one who seeks God; there is no one who does good, not even one; there is no fear of God before their eyes, all have turned away, they have together become worthless.

Unfortunately, modern man has a tendency to dismiss God's future judgment. Modern man readily rejects the idea of giving account for his decisions and actions to anybody, probably because of the loss of conviction about the life after death.[6]

The universal judgment spells out the distinctive difference between God's glory and the proud, boastful, narcissistic, think-positive mankind. How can we then escape from God's wrath? Only through faith in Jesus Christ whom God delivered over to death for our sins, and raised Him from the dead for our justification (Rom. 4:24–25). Because of this salvation and justification through faith, which is credited to Christians as righteousness, they will be judged by their Lord Jesus only in respect to their use and stewardship of God-given talents, gifts, responsibilities, opportunities taken, etc., through their lives. In this judgment[7] Christians rationally expect a fatherly approach full of understanding for the weakness of the flesh and temptations of the world (Mark 14:38). The image of judging a sporting event, evoked by Paul in 1 Corinthians 9:24–27, seems to be a fitting comparison. But even the least person in God's kingdom will be greater than John the Baptist, the greatest man ever born of a woman (Luke 7:28).

As the head of His church, Jesus also continuously evaluates the characteristics of individual congregations. Sometimes His assessments are very unfavorable, and may result in hard sentence, as the example in the letter to the Church in Thyatira (Rev. 2:18–27) points out clearly.

When the new era will be initiated by the second coming of Jesus Christ to the earth, Christians will be called upon to exercise judgment with respect to the world and angels (1 Cor. 6:2–3).

Human desire for justice is understandable, but expectation of justice in human terms borders on foolishness. Jesus never called for justice in this world, or showed any expectation of it. Actually, he never mentioned the word "justice." If man were capable of rendering or receiving justice, then there would be no need for laws, parliaments, lawyers, police, prisons, as well as no business for revolutionaries and reformists continuously advocating new systems of law and order.

Because just judgment requires understanding motives for peoples' behavior and actions, an understanding not available to man in the current age, Christians are being advised to abstain from passing human judgment on others. Even the best discrimination and discernment in moral matters are provisional in the light of God's coming judgment. A similar advice relates to abstaining from cursing and revenge against personal enemies and wrongdoers. In Deut. 32:35, God Himself assumes the role of avenger: "It is mine to avenge; I will repay."

GOD THE SAVIOR

The person of Jesus Christ is the heart of the Christian confession of faith: "He is the Lord and Savior." Therefore, attempts have been made, in the past, to deny His historicity and, by that, assign Christianity into the sphere of mythology. Archeological findings and ancient non-Christian literary sources resolved this issue, and historical authenticity of Jesus of Nazareth is now accepted by all first-rank scholars.[8] No serious scholar will venture to postulate His nonhistoricity.

Jesus' life has always attracted a high level of attention, as demonstrated by people who have been writing stories of His life for a very long time. There have been more of them than of any other person in history. Over sixty thousand were written in the nineteenth century alone.[9] As usual, unable to dissociate themselves from their own age and environment, all of them superimposed Jesus' times with something that properly belongs to their own century. We need to read only Albert Schweitzer's work[10] to realize in it the dominant images of the Enlightenment, German idealism and socialism, the romantic concept of a religious genius, champion of the proletariat, etc. More recent attempts are, of course, similarly biased, despite the noble goal of providing benefits from additional information about the most important person who has ever lived. Their problem is again in the writer's personal judgment and rules used to decide which parts of the New Testament should be accepted or rejected and which other biblical and nonbiblical sources to include. Resulting deformations, and false searches for the "real" Jesus, are well described and summarized, for example, by Malachi Martin[11] and are visible even in the most recent literature.[12]

Christian writers, relying completely on the biblical account of Jesus' life and work, seem to provide a personal witness or commentary of a man who still lives and is to come to our world again. A masterpiece of eloquence of this approach has been written by Malcolm Muggeridge.[13] A scholarly counterpart for that book may be found in the work of Jaroslav Pelikan,[14] examining also Jesus' impact on the culture and history of the last two millennia.

Rationality of the acceptance of the biblical picture of Jesus as the primary source reflects the common Christian belief that the Bible is the word of God. The biblical witness about Jesus must, therefore, be considered the most accurate characterization of His person, role in God's plan, actual work, and impact on other people's life. The Bible testifies that Jesus is the image of the invisible God, the head of the church, and the firstborn from among the dead. For God was pleased to have His fullness dwell in Him, and through Him to reconcile to Himself all things, whether on earth or in heaven, by making peace through His blood, shed on the cross (Col. 1:15–20).

For people living in the current age, accepting the uniqueness of Jesus should be relatively easy because of His well-documented influence throughout history and in the present as well. The current generation may also benefit from the work of the past students of the Bible, who prepared many helpful tools and teaching aids, for example, the summary of the fulfilled prophecies concerning the life, personal traits, and work of Jesus Christ.[15]

For the Jews of Jesus' times, including John the Baptist (Luke 7:20), it was much more difficult. Living for a long time under foreign rulers, their desire to achieve national sovereignty and independence skewed their picture of the expected Messiah toward a true, but incomplete image of a victorious military liberator and king. These expectations masked the other important biblical characterizations of the Messiah as a suffering servant. In their religious history, the Jews had already observed a variety of sects and persons with false messianic claims, also a possible explanation of their skepticism. Even though Jesus taught with authority, He often spoke in parables,[16] so the initial knowledge of the secrets of the kingdom of God had been given only to a few chosen disciples (Luke 8:10). God exercised His sovereignty in revealing His Son only according to His will and purpose. God was fulfilling the prophecies given, e.g., through Isaiah in 6:10, about blinding the spiritual eyes and hardening of hearts of Israel's religious leaders (John 12:37–41). Israel's crucial mistake, with terrible and long-lasting consequences, has been her rejection of Jesus as her Messiah—the central figure of the Old Testament's expectations, of a man of God's choice appointed to accomplish a redemptive purpose toward God's people.[17]

But the most difficult was to accept Jesus' divinity, despite His teaching with full authority and the many miracles He performed. The divine power He demonstrated by forgiving sins was perceived as blasphemy. They also missed His divinity reflected in His death; Jesus being without sin, and death being wages of sin, He could not have died except voluntarily laying down His life (John 10:17–18). No man could have killed Him because He is life.

There are five distinct features associated with the person of the Messiah: He is God's choice, He is the appointed redeemer of God's people, He is the judge of God's adversaries, He is given the final and ultimate dominion over the nations, and He is the best conduit of God's actions. It is quite clear that these five characteristics are true of Jesus Christ. Other Old Testament characterizations apply to Him as well. He is the obedient and suffering servant[18] with marks of a prophet, who extends God's ministry to the Gentiles, and is the agent of worldwide revelation and salvation, the conqueror bringing all the redeemed under David's rule,[19] a branch of the family of king David,[20] the seed of a woman,[21] and the Son of man.[22]

In modern times, worldly Messiahs, in biblical view false Messiahs—be they politicians, reformers, revolutionaries, leaders of popular movements, or even religious leaders—are introducing themselves with statements about their programs leading to a society without the currently pressing difficulties and solving problems of crime, drugs, homelessness, poverty, unfairness, etc., and about claims how the society will plunge into a disaster without them personally, or with the opposing candidate at the helm. It is quite enlightening to compare those "visions" to Jesus' own simple "mission statement" found in Luke 4:18–19: "The Spirit of the Lord is on me, because He has anointed me to preach good news to the poor. He has sent me to proclaim freedom for the prisoners and recovery of sight for the blind, to release the oppressed, to proclaim the year of the Lord's favor."

This quote related to Isaiah 61:1–2 indicates the solid foundation of Jesus' mission in God's will and approval; avoids dealing with abstract social concepts, such as poverty, justice, etc.; addresses real needs of individuals without any discrimination whoever they are; and by using terms with both physical and spiritual connotation (poor in spirit, spiritually blind, prisoner of sin) shows concern for the total man, not just the physical man of politicians. There are no opponents to disagree or fight with, no personal attacks on anyone, no request for contributions, as we know too well from our experience with worldly leaders. And still, a few minutes later after hearing these words, the people around Jesus, His own neighbors, attempted to kill Him by throwing Him down the cliff (Luke 4:28, 29). This Jesus, now resurrected and sitting on the right hand of His Father in heaven, almost two thousand years later is still being verbally abused and mocked.

Clearly the Messiah was needed because mankind is completely unable to reconcile itself with God. Despite the few persons who were pronounced by God as righteous,[23] the need for God to provide reconciliation by Himself through His own sacrifice is obvious. Even when the best people tried, they discovered that no human deed is able to satisfy God's holy justice that requires judgment and punishment for disobedience and rebellion against the Creator and source of life. That is why God, who loves this world, gave His one and only Son that whoever believes in Him shall not perish but have eternal life. He did not send His Son into the world to condemn it, but save it through Him. Therefore, whoever believes in Him is not condemned, but whoever does not believe stands condemned already (John 3:16–18).

God the Son's willingness to obey His Father's will up to the death on the cross, to accept punishment for rebellious humanity, is a demonstration of supreme love. It demonstrates the contrast between man continuously seeking increasing power and the almighty God voluntarily giving up His power, His might, His omnipotence, and showing His wisdom through weakness, meekness, and humility. It also opened the deep mysteries of the Creator becoming a creature, of God becoming man.

In His earthly life, Jesus Christ,[24] God the Savior, revealed additional attributes of God:

Love—John 10:14–15

Obedience—Mark 14:36

Meekness—John 12:15

Humility—Matthew 11:28–30

Authority—Mark 4:41

Forgiveness—Luke 5:20–21

Faithfulness—John 17:6–26

Dependability—John 17:12

Subject to Temptations—Matthew 4:1–11

Subject to Suffering—Luke 22:63

In the person of Jesus Christ we see all the previously listed attributes of God demonstrated, because He is all:

God the Creator—Colossians 1:16

God the Judge—John 5:27 or 2 Timothy 4:1

God the Savior—Luke 2:11

Jesus is the way and the truth and the life (John 14:6).

The biblical witness indicates that for the community of believers Jesus plays four major roles: Savior,[25] who took on Himself the sins of the world and, by that, freed His disciples from God's wrath and punishment; Lord, to whom lives of believers are dedicated; head of the church, which is His mystical body (Eph. 5:23); and a role model and example of perfect life and attitudes toward God and fellow men.

But during His lifetime believers were only a small group of people. The majority of the Jews had different opinions, consisting of both positive and negative perceptions that Jesus is:

- A rabbi (a teacher), a good title considering the characteristics of His activities. This title was used also by His disciples—e.g., Mark 9:38 or John 20:16—because it conveyed high respect.

- A prophet, indicating recognition that Jesus was regarded as more than an ordinary teacher (Matt. 21:11), a teacher with authority (Matt. 7:28–29) distinct from the other religious leaders.

- Elijah, the prophet Jewish thought expected to return to usher in the end (Mal. 4:5–6).

- A blasphemer, a label reflecting the opinion of the high priest and the whole Sanhedrin (Mark 14:64), and others as well (John 10:33).

- Possessed by a demon (John 8:48, 52) and empowered by the Beelzebub, the prince of demons (Luke 11:15).

During the subsequent history of Christianity and Christendom, the name of Jesus was used and misused many times for a variety of purposes, as Malachi Martin and Jaroslav Pelikan have well documented. We can see Jesus as the Light of the Gentiles, King of Kings, Prince of peace, inspiration for artists,[26] as well as inspiration for dictators, generals, inquisitors, politicians, philosophers, and even for officials of the organized church. There are also many portraits of Jesus designed to fit the variety of Christian denominations, to fit the modern perception of Jewish heritage and justify resistance or support of anti-Semitism,[27] to fit needs to fight the influence of modern mass media,[28] to respond to the personal needs of the modern man, or simply to curse.[29] All this only confirms the greatness of Jesus Christ, and richness and importance of His life and heritage, as the apostle John had recognized many years ago (John 21:25).

THE TRINITY

Because the Bible's primary concern is bringing the fallen man to the most beneficial relationship with God, it emphasizes the whys and hows of the way back to God. Therefore, the Bible's main focus is on God's functions in the plan He prepared to make both reasonable and easy. In His role as God the Judge, He points to the eternal, extremely adverse consequences of being judged only according to man's own deeds without being first reconciled with Him through Jesus Christ. Knowing this is unachievable by man's own means, in His role as God the Savior He provides this reconciliation and salvation as a gift to those who ask for it. In both roles He demonstrates His holiness, justice, and love for man.

Besides these two roles, the Bible presents also both revelation and mystery of God as man's personal partner by using analogies from earthly life in a family, such as of father, son, bride, bridegroom, etc. All this information offered has again its primary importance in man's practical day-to-day life. God's attributes listed above then are a reflection of the experience of those with whom God dealt directly.

God remains silent about His nature, with the disclosure of His name being the most noticeable exception. But there are biblical passages that provide a few hints about the mystery involved.

The first point is found right at the beginning, in the first chapter of Genesis, where we find Spirit of God mentioned and the statement "let *us* make man in *our* image, in *our* likeness . . ." (emphasis added) where the plural, used with singular in other statements, is suggesting plurality in unity. Similar plurality may be seen in the personalized Wisdom in the Book of Proverbs. Indications that Israel's Messiah has divinity ascribed to Him can be found in Isaiah 7:14 and 9:6.

The New Testament provides similar clues in the angelic annunciation to Mary, in the baptism of Jesus, in Jesus' teaching addressing the Father and, most directly, in His declared commission (Matt. 28:19) of making disciples of all nations, baptizing them in *the name of the Father and of the Son and of the Holy Spirit* (emphasis added). What has seemed to become later a great conceptual mystery to many Christians was a practical life experience for the disciples living with Jesus. They encountered:

• God the Father as the recipient of Jesus' prayers, the source of revelation of His will, and God who was residing in heaven while Christ dwelled on earth;

• God the Son in the person of Jesus Christ, whom they recognized as God and Lord (John 20:28); and

• God the Holy Spirit, during and after the Pentecost.

And recognized them all as one Spirit, as one God in three different persons.[30]

These are the primary sources of the church's doctrine of the Trinity. This word "Trinity" is not found in the Bible, but it has been used since the end of the second century and formally accepted as representing the highly distinctive and all-comprehensive doctrine of the Christian faith. It makes three affirmations: (1) that there is but one God; (2) that the Father, the Son, and the Holy Spirit are each God; and (3) that the Father, the Son, and the Holy Spirit are distinct persons.[31] It is human and incomplete understanding that in God in three persons there is equality in dignity, diversity in operation, and unity in diversity.

The Holy Spirit is the divine person with whom man has to deal in the current age.[32] Christians are baptized with the Spirit, are filled with the Holy Spirit, led through their lives and protected from the evil one by Him, and receive gifts of the Spirit that qualitatively enrich their lives. His importance even for non-Christians is hard to overemphasize considering Jesus' warning that "anyone who speaks against the Holy Spirit will not be forgiven, either in this age or in the age to come" (Matt. 12:32). This statement is frighteningly different from the general invitation to accept in faith God's forgiveness as a free gift.

It is not surprising that the mystery of Trinity, as well as other mysteries of God, man, and God's plan of salvation, attracted many philosophers and theologians who tried in human words and ideas of contemporary interest[33] to express what is actually inexpressible. These human attempts of a rational or logical explanation of God's mysteries are in danger of serious error. The simplest statements expressing mostly awe and amazement are the best and most appropriate. Man, who does not understand himself, is surely incapable of comprehending God.

CONCLUSIONS

The Bible provided the two affirmatives essential for the foundation and inspiration of Christianity: that God is and makes Himself known to man. The complete rejection of validity of any attempt to come to the knowledge of this God through human means, and the claim that He may be known only through His self-revelation, makes Christianity distinctive from other religions. Biblical Christianity, believing that God's dealings with man are not institutional but direct, unmediated, and strictly person-to-person puts itself almost out of the traditional concept of religion.

Yahweh, the God revealed in the Bible, is a pure Spirit[34] who presents Himself as the Creator of heaven and earth, including man; as the future Judge of all mankind; and as God the Savior desiring to help man to avoid the adverse consequences of that judgment. He revealed Himself through His Word, written in the Bible and made flesh in the historical person of Jesus Christ. For today's man, this one God is known through three persons, God the Father (who lives in heaven and is the receiver and grantor of prayers), God the Son (the resurrected Jesus Christ, Lord and Savior, who is now in heaven with God the Father and will return to earth), and the Holy Spirit (who now dwells in believers as their protector and counselor).

Personal knowledge of the biblical God brings man to proper understanding of the source of his existence and dependence, of God's desire for mutually respectful and loving relation with man, of risks stemming from the actuality of man's alienation from God, and of the plan God has for bringing this rebellious man back to this desired relation.

GOD'S CREATION

10

The biblical account of creation should not be considered a variant of a theory of origin in the scientific sense. Its purpose is not to satisfy man's curiosity about details and timing of the creation process; it actually suggests the vanity of any search for them. If they would be important, God would have revealed them.

The core rests with the simple factual sentence, "In the beginning God created the heavens and the earth" (Genesis 1:1), with its significance shown by being widely referred to in both the Old and the New Testaments. The principal purposes of this statement are to display God's eternal glory, power, wisdom, and goodness, and to let man know, from the beginning, what is the only true, fundamental, direct, and unmediated relationship between God and man: the relation between the Creator and, by Him, created being. It also clarifies to whom man is responsible for his acts, attitudes, and thoughts toward God, his fellow men, and nature. Accepting this creation statement made by the actual Creator is a matter of faith and of trust in the truth and power of God's word.

In contrast to scientific and humanistic cosmogonies focused on the universe or man, the biblical message is unquestionably God-centered. The brevity, simplicity, clarity, and authority of the biblical account make it distinct also from all other creation stories coming from nonbiblical sources, such as the early cosmogonies discussed in chapter 2.

BEFORE CREATION

God, being the Creator, can and does communicate to us about the activities that led to creation as well. The Bible is using here the common word "before" not in the sense of time-ordered relations, but as a description of intent-action or hierarchical order, in the sense that God is before creation, before all things (Col. 1:17). In addition, it reflects the rationality of God's free decision to create by the existence of a plan for creation. This is documented in the Bible by the usage of the word "wisdom," as found in the personalized allegorical statement in Proverbs 3:19, 20: "By wisdom the LORD laid the earth's foundations, by understanding he set the heavens in place; by his knowledge the deeps were divided, and the clouds let drop the dew." The priority of wisdom, indicated again by the word "before" in Proverbs 8:22 and 23, confirms the idea of a plan also: "The LORD brought me forth as the first of his works, before his deeds of old; I was appointed from eternity, from the beginning, before the world began."

Ten verses (Prov. 8:22–31) indicate both the well-defined purpose and rationality behind the plan of creation, and the pleasure from its implementation.

Our life as employees, managers, and especially as professionals is full of analogical, human-scale situations. We plan our activities or projects not just in terms of time and resources needed, but also by emphasizing the motivation behind, with the objectives and value to be achieved by their implementation, as well as by the benefits desired for all project participants and users of final results. The information about God's plan for creation provided by the Bible can be structured according to this project analogy as well:

God's Project: Creation

Motivation—Love (John 3:16)

Objective—Mutual Loving Relation (Revelation 21:3)

Implementation Concept—Man created in God's image (Genesis 1:27)

Principal Value—God's will done (Matthew 6:10)

God's Benefits—Glory (Habakkuk 2:14)

Man's Benefits—Honor and joy (John 15:11)

It is impossible to overemphasize the importance of understanding this "before creation" phase for these reasons:

1. Considering God's wisdom and power, it points to the inevitability that God's final purpose will be achieved.

2. It indicates the absolute uniqueness, value, and irreplaceability of each and every single human being, as defined by the framework of God's love.

3. It points to God's lasting desire for mutually beneficial relation with all individuals.

4. It provides a basis for assessing the rationality and value of God's actions in this world, from the perspective of both God's glory and man's benefit.

This understanding then allows man to contemplate the facts of God's assignment of the highest possible absolute value and dignity to every single person, and compare them with the paucity and the degrading assessment of humanity as a meaningless product of random variations of physical, chemical, and biological processes, favored by evolutionary models—models that contradict the commonly recognized human desire for personal self-esteem and social acceptance.

CREATION OF HEAVEN AND EARTH

The frequent and continuous attacks on the biblical doctrine of creation are underscoring its fundamental importance. Rejection of this doctrine is identical with a complete rejection of Christianity as a whole. If God did not create this world and man, the concept of sin is meaningless, and the life, crucifixion, and resurrection of Jesus Christ, as God's dealing with sin, irrelevant. The close relation between Christian doctrines of creation and reconciliation points to the misunderstanding perpetuated by people, who, often with good intentions, are trying to find a compromise for Christian belief with the variety of cosmogonical theories proposed by physicists and philosophers. The principal purpose of the biblical belief in creation is spiritual and, on the periphery, ethical. The spiritual aspect, and its decisiveness, is observable in the frequency and spread of references to it through the whole Bible. The key to resolution of any real or potential controversy is found in the New Testament Epistle to the Hebrews 11:3: "By faith we understand that the universe was formed at God's command, so that what is seen was not made out of what is visible."

Biblical belief in creation is founded on information revealed to us by God, and accepted as such. The actual details of God's creative work remain unrevealed, hidden from us, a mystery that cannot be solved by human speculations, even when supported by the most sophisticated physical and mathematical models. The most imaginative human mental processes based on observations cannot explain creation out of nothing (*creatio ex nihilo*),[1] an event or action that has been communicated to man to point to the substantive difference between God and His creation. The act of creation must be understood as an act of God's free will. He chose to do so and needs nothing from His creation (Acts 17:25). This confirms the superiority of God the Creator, His self-existence and self-sufficiency, in contrast to the dependency of the world and man on Him. Connoisseurs of the spoken and printed word may recognize God's grandeur in the power and linguistic beauty of the Bible's opening statement: "In the beginning God created the heavens and the earth" (Gen. 1:1). Considering the importance of its content and the majesty of its author, this direct introduction has no comparable literary sequel.

Creation of earth, sea, sky, sun, moon, stars, animals, etc., and man—the so-called secondary creation—is God's creative activity making use of already created materials. In view of the objective to create a target for God's love, the creation of man must be accepted as the culmination of the secondary work sequence. This confirms the breathtaking recognition of man's value seen in the real possibility that not just the earth, but the whole universe, was prepared for him. This man-related universe does not include heaven, the abode of God and those closely associated with Him and, only later, the final destination of His earthly saints. The books of the Bible don't pay too much attention to the description of heaven. The apostle Paul, in 2 Corinthians 12:3–4, talks about his experience as a man who was caught up to heaven, where he heard inexpressible things, but was forbidden to tell about them. The apostle John, on the other hand, describes in the Book of Revelation (e.g., in chapter 4) heaven as he saw it. But even his eyewitness account points more toward the inadequacy of human language than to the actual splendor of God's throne and the living creatures present around it.

In contrast to Near Eastern myths—which never explicitly refer to the creation of the universe out of nothing, prefer to talk about "birth," and are marked by open polytheism—or the contemporary impersonal cosmogonies ascribing to the universe no purpose or value, the biblical account in the first two chapters of the Book of Genesis is dignified, void of coarse details, and concerned more with the value of God's individual acts than with the sequential steps of the creation process. This simple narrative, written from the viewpoint of an observer, is focused primarily on things visible to the naked eye, even though it mentions the creation of the spiritual world of heaven also. That is why it starts with the creation of light as the obvious necessity for any kind of visual observation. The emphasis is on God's handiwork, not on the fine distinctions or classifications of various species of animals. It frankly answers the fundamental question, "Where did the multitude of creatures we know come from?" by "God made them." The correctness of this eyewitness narrative is confirmed by God Himself when He challenged Job (see Job 38:4) or spoke to the prophet Isaiah (44:24).

Another significant difference from other creation stories is in biblical statements about the transient character of major parts of this creation, clearly indicating the coming new heaven and new earth.

Among deeply believing Christians, it is possible to find those for whom evolutionary sequences proposed by scientists are a proof of the power, rationality, and subtlety of God the Creator.[2] The scope, scale, complexity, and results of evolution only enhance their admiration of God's wisdom and confirmation of His power. God might not have written down each and every DNA base in the human genome, but His demonstrated architectural skills are admirable indeed. The logic of this position rests on so-called "intelligent design theory," which states that living organisms reveal details of structure and physiology so exquisite and intricate that they cannot be explained by the random workings of evolution, but must be a product of careful and conscious design.[3] Of all the creationists' arguments advanced against evolution, intelligent design theory is the most appealing and effective due to its simplicity. But it displays philosophical weaknesses that are already being used as an argument by the proponents of evolution.[4] Primary arguments against the belief in evolution, used by scientists in their debates, usually point to missing links that the evolutionists are unable to produce, and to the fact that no development of new species is being observed today. Christian rejection of evolution is based on its contradiction to God's word revealed in Scriptures.

A total of eight creative acts are introduced by the words "God said" and compressed into six time periods called "days." The problem of their strict chronology may very well be artificial, considering that other parts of the Bible also give more emphasis to great facts and pay less attention to chronological accuracy.[5] Even though the whole creation story describes actual events, it is a highly poetic description, which makes critiques of its lack of close correlation with evolutionary models unreasonable. For example, the fact that Genesis talks about light existing before the appearance of sun and stars is actually an evidence of the divine authorship of the biblical creation story. Even though the contemporary Big Bang theory may accept the existence of light in general before any cosmic object had been formed, it is simply inconceivable to natural thinking that any life on earth could exist without the sun and its light, as witnessed by pagan religions, which, in times of Moses, worshipped the sun as the source of life.[6] This biblical account needs to be put in the context of biblical expectation related to the New Jerusalem, where sun and moon will not be needed, because the glory of God will give the life-supporting light (Rev. 21:23). In other words, God's personal presence on earth during the acts of the secondary creation provided the necessary life support.

In a similar way, it is not reasonable to interpret the word "day" as a twenty-four-hour period known to us. The word "day" has several meanings in the Bible, including an indefinite period.[7] It is, therefore, possible to consider the periodization of God's creative activities in the way of periodization of human projects with their sometimes overlapping activities, phases, or stages. In this perspective the words "evening and morning" may refer to the starting point and the terminus of a given activity.

Other perspectives should be considered also. For example, ancient Middle Eastern languages did not have grammatical nor syntactic tools to express sophisticated nuances in timing of events as known in Greek or modern English. Local cultural environments, as well as languages, also put more emphasis on the time-value of events (e.g., event relevant in the past, but unimportant in the present; event eternally relevant, etc.) than on their accurate historical sequences, and on the content of messages than on the time of their utterance.

In the same framework it is possible to reflect on the repeated statement "and God saw that it was good" as a simple confirmation of accomplishment according to the plan's intent, not as a statement of achieved absolute perfection in the terms of human abstract generalization.[8] Man's industrial environment provides many examples of similar statements of satisfaction based, for example, on an observed match of a new product with the designer's ideas. Another interpretation of the word "good" follows Thomas Aquinas's line of reasoning: If God chooses to create a world, it must be a good (not evil) world. He adds: The created universe is the best, considering present postulates, but not considering what God could have done.

While reading and contemplating the biblical story of creation, major emphasis should be placed on what God has said. The word "said" carries more spiritual weight than operative words, such as "made" or "created," because all these activities spring from the word of God, which brings order from chaos, light out of darkness, and life out of inanimate matter. But whatever approach is taken, the central assertion is always that it is God who made all that constitutes the universe we live in. The clear purpose and, therefore, the uncompounded meaning of creation is to make possible God's relationship with man.

BIBLICAL VIEW OF MAN

A biblical search for the nature of man starts with a call to God: "[W]hat is man that you are mindful of him, the son of man that you care for him?" (Ps. 8:4), and continues with acknowledgment of the revealed information:

You made him a little lower than the heavenly beings and crowned him with glory and honor.

You made him ruler over the works of your hands; you put everything under his feet: all flocks and herds, and the beasts of the field, the birds of the air, and the fish of the sea, all that swim the paths of the seas (Ps. 8:5–8).

The verses of this psalm outline the biblical doctrine of man, which sees him primarily in relation to God, who has created him to hold a special, almost supreme position in the whole universe, and in God's plan to be the target and object of His love and a partner in mutual fellowship. Man displays both uniqueness and difference from the world by being created in God's image and likeness (Gen. 1:26), and physical and biological similarity with other creatures populating this earth by being formed from the dust of the ground (Gen. 2:7).

This should not be interpreted as dualism between the material body and the immaterial soul, which is a Greek, not a biblical idea, nor as an indication of distinction between good and evil projected into distinction between spirit and matter (matter is not intrinsically evil, while some spirits are). More realistic is the recognition that even being able to make nature to serve him, man has to serve nature as well, tend it, and bring it to fruition (Gen. 2:15). Man is subject to the forces of the natural world, a position that can easily overwhelm him, due to both nature's power and grandeur.

An analogy of this "dependence-versus-free-will dilemma" is known in both classical and quantum physics as the autonomy and consistency principles. Man can arrange his immediate environment into any configuration the laws of physics permit locally, without reference to what is going on in the rest of universe (autonomy principle). The consistency principle demands that the only configurations that are locally permissible are those that are globally self-consistent.

Yet, in spite of all these dependencies and limitations associated with man's physical and biological nature, the fact of carrying God's likeness outweighs them all. This applies to all men at all times, because man's rebellion does not nullify the faithfulness of God (Rom. 3:3). On the other hand, the true and full image of God in man has been realized only twice: in Adam and Eve (Gen. 1:27) before their fall, and in Jesus Christ. Therefore, Jesus Christ being the true image of God is also the true man[9] and, therefore, the key to understanding human nature. It is impossible to know the real man until he is known through Jesus' life, His crucifixion and resurrection, and the consequences stemming from these events. In any search for the true nature of man, the beginning and end are in the information found in the Bible, in the revealed word of God.

Human existence is always historical. Man should not be viewed as an object of nature. In the biblical faith, man is understood as a being with personal past requiring atonement for the sin in it, and facing the challenges and promises of the future to which he can respond in the framework of his God-given freedom and, preferably, in consonance with God's will.

Human existence is also always individual. Man never exists "in general," but only as an individual, concrete, and historical man. For this fundamental reason, true positive relationship with God can be described only in terms of a witness and servant as "my relationship," never in general terms of a group alliance or a species affinity. Even God's relationships with Israel and the Christian church are, in their essence, relationships with individual Israelites and Christians. Only God's commandments and covenants address topics of His concerns about wider strata of the human population.

Sin

Man's uniqueness in being the image of God has been distorted by another difference from the rest of the living creatures populating earth: man sins. In general, sin may be viewed as a deviation from the moral norm, breach of relationship, rebellion, deliberate wrongdoing, perversion, etc. In the biblical view, sin, in all its aspects, is always directed against God. It is a violation of that which God's glory and holiness demands and is, therefore, in its essence the contradiction to God.

Sin was obviously present in the universe before the fall of Adam and Eve. However, the Bible's focus is not on its origin, but on sin in human life. This orientation is understandable when sin is recognized as the epitome of man's blasphemous ambition to achieve not only autonomy, but also equality with his Creator and Lord.

Sin is one-sided, but its consequences are not, for God in His holiness cannot be complacent to it. Sin elicits God's displeasure and wrath, and in man it leads to shame and fear; it resulted also in God's curse upon that over which man was given dominion, and introduced death to man—the separation of integral elements of human being (body, soul, and spirit)—and man's separation from God as well. Therefore, sin never consists merely of a voluntary act of transgression, but is a reflection of total impurity: of heart, mind, disposition, and will. For this reason, the depravity of sin implicates man's solidarity with Adam, as witnessed in Psalm 51:5: "Surely I have been a sinner from birth, sinful from the time my mother conceived me."

Despite the gravity of sin, the Bible never completely loses hope and optimism because everything in it points to Jesus Christ, the Savior, who from the beginning has been foreordained to deliver the required redemption. At the final stage of the current age, Christ will visibly triumph over sin. In Christ, God has conquered sin, which will be banished from God's creation when the current heaven and earth will be consumed by fire, and the new heaven and the new earth will be brought into existence.

It is necessary to point out that evil has a broader meaning than sin because it binds together the evil deed and its consequences. Sin is a violation of God's will, of that which God's lordship and glory demands, while evil, both physical and ethical, is general in its hurtful effects and influence. As already mentioned, sin is always oriented against God. In His sovereignty God tolerates evil in the created universe and uses it as punishment for individuals and nations. God is separated from all evil and is in no way responsible for it; evil can be attributed to the abuse of free will by created human and angelic beings.

The Meaning of Life

The Bible also provides a clear and succinct description of what constitutes the meaning of man's life and points to ways that lead to its fulfillment and resulting satisfaction, joy, and eternal rewards. Because human behavior is significantly influenced by man's sinful nature and world situation, visible and humanly measurable results cannot be the right indicators of life's value. God's focus on inner motivation is the only wise, rational, and valid approach to its evaluation because it avoids human pitfalls of considering personal appearance, ethnic origin, level of academic education, social status, etc., as of crucial importance. The apostle Paul's ethic of freedom, a witness that in Christ there is neither Jew nor Greek, slave nor free, male nor female, but all are one (Gal. 3:28), rejected these traps as well. This criticality of motivation is reflected in the Ten Commandments (Exod. 20:1–17), Jesus' own summary of the greatest commandments (Matt. 22:37–40), the Golden Rule (Matt. 7:12), and in Paul's praise of love (1 Cor. 13:1–13). This preeminence of motivation, which is outside human observational capability, confirms that the actual value of man's life can be assigned to it only by God.

The Bible is uncompromising in its teaching that all evaluations of our fellow men must be done in the spirit of meekness and humility. There is a lot for Christians to appreciate in humanistic world cultures, their arts, architecture, technology, medicine, etc. Christians must admit that unbelievers are capable of extraordinary excellence, virtue, creativity, knowledge, and also altruism shown, e.g., in the extent of humanitarian aid given to the poor, victims of natural disasters, war refugees, or in the help many Jews received during time of the Holocaust.[10] Therefore, Christians, as Daniel of the Old Testament, should always seek to be best in their fields of work for the glory of God, and for the benefits of their fellow men, especially their closest neighbors.

The outwardly observable behavior of Christians should reflect the love Christ demanded (1 John 4:7–21), but it must be understood that the actual behavior reflects also the persistent conflict of the old sinful human nature with the influence of the in-dwelling Holy Spirit (Rom. 7:14–25). Positive aspects of Christians' behavior come only as fruit of the work of the Holy Spirit (Gal. 5:22–23). Again, it is the inner motivation to do the will of God that is the principal distinction between a Christian and a culturally motivated moral man.

The biblical search for the meaning of man's life may be concluded by accepting Solomon's final verdict presented in two simple sentences (Eccl. 12:13–14) which provide life's final goal and its explanation: "Fear God and keep his commandments, for this is the whole duty of man. For God will bring every deed into judgment, including every hidden thing, whether it is good or evil."

HEAVENLY BEINGS

Even though the Bible does not go into a detailed description of heaven, it pays attention to spiritual heavenly beings, known as angels. That this is not an insignificant subject may be deduced from the recently increased popular interest visible in general news media and exploited commercially in angels-related products. Then there is the ages-long interest in paranormal and the occult, and in demonic cults. The spirit world, and the idea of the supernatural, are not only taken seriously, but accepted as a fact by many. In the Bible there are close to three hundred references to angels and their existence.

Angels are created spiritual beings called to perform many functions.[11] They minister to people, protect them, bring God's warnings of judgment, and have the power to destroy armies, kings, first-born, etc. They also ministered to Jesus during his life and supported the Gospel by special pronouncements. In the future, according to biblical prophecies, angels will accompany Jesus as He returns in glory, will gather God's elect, and, at the time of the final judgment, will separate the righteous from the unrighteous. They will be God's emissaries carrying out His judgment against those who deliberately rejected Jesus Christ and the salvation God offered through Him.

But the Bible also talks about the bitter conflict between angels faithful to God and those who allied themselves with Satan[12] in rebellion against God. When this rebellion started the Bible does not say, but it may be concluded that it happened sometime after God's creation of man, because God pronounced His creation "good," i.e., not evil. Some prophets rationally concluded that, in some way, God is the ultimate cause of evil (Isa. 45:7). But, in reality, the actual origin of evil is part of the mystery of lawlessness (2 Thess. 2:7).

On the other hand, it is clear who started this rebellion: Lucifer (Ezek. 28:12–17) whose pride in his by-God-created beauty corrupted his wisdom by covetousness up to the point of desiring supreme authority and replacing God as ruler of the universe. This Lucifer became known later as Satan, the Devil, and called also the Adversary, the Father of Lies, the Dragon, the Evil One, the Tempter, the Accuser, the Murderer, the Serpent, the Prince (god) of this World, the Prince of the Power of the Air, Apollyon, Belial, and Beelzebub.

Along with Lucifer, many angels also chose to deny God's authority and, as a result, are reserved unto judgment and everlasting punishment with him in hell prepared for them (Matt. 25:41 and 2 Pet. 2:4).

This conflict rages also here on earth. While God controls all, He permits Satan to deceive many in the world. Satan seems to be winning important battles in his war against God through deception of the powerful, of the leaders of nations, and of ordinary men through stimulating human pride and covetousness, traits he himself is known by. Satan and his fallen angels (demons) demonstrate great power in corrupting moral standards and society's order, creating havoc through natural disasters, and through their mastery in presenting themselves as "agents of light," or even as Christs, in order to deceive (Matt. 24:5).

While Satan is defeated in principle, God has not yet eliminated him from the world scene. His presence is visible in continuing wars and power struggles plaguing humanity throughout history. His power has been enhanced by his ability to work covertly, thanks to the widespread denial of his existence. In the future, Satan's power will be manifested even by miracles and great signs. Currently, Satan's power is restrained by the presence of the Holy Spirit in the world. Holy Spirit protects believers from the evil one and from deceptions by false gospels and false teachers, and assures that they are not ignorant about Satan's devices (2 Cor. 2:11).

THE SEVENTH DAY

The sixth day, or stage, of creation ends with statements of completion and satisfaction: "Thus the heavens and the earth were completed in all their vast array" (Gen. 2:1), and "God saw all that he had made, and it was very good"

(Gen. 1:31). The seventh day (or stage or epoch) emerges as completely different from the previous six. God has finished the work He had been doing, has rested from all His work of creating (Gen. 2:2), and has blessed the seventh day and made it special, made it holy (Gen. 2:3). This difference is emphasized by the absence of previous repetitive statements; there are neither pronouncements about how good it is what God saw on this seventh day, nor about the "evening and morning." The significance of these differences may be assessed by reflection on conclusions that can be drawn from them.

The first, and probably the most significant, is recognition that the seventh day is not over yet, that it is still in progress. Our lives, our current age, and for the same reasons, all human history is taking place in the framework of this seventh day.[13] It is actually quite surprising that this simple and obvious conclusion, with its many important conceptual consequences, is not emphasized in the current Christian thought. This recognition completes the "big picture" of God's plan in its scheduling aspects, and is in agreement with the biblical symbolism presenting the number seven as an image of completion.

The second is a set of conclusions derived from the meaning of God's rest. This rest is not divine leisure time or recreation. God decided to stop creating, but He did not stop being who He is: the almighty Creator deeply interested in His creation. The primary conclusion is the recognition that by choosing to rest God indicated that He did not want to impinge on the freedom He had given to His creatures. Man was created free, because he was made in God's image. In God's decision to rest, we can see confirmation of the high level of respect God has for man, leaving the field free for him up to the point of freedom to reject Him and His love. But man's freedom is not absolute; man cannot freely select consequences of his decisions and actions. His freedom is not an expression of God's abandonment either. The simple and easy-to-understand warning, " . . . you will surely die . . ." (Gen. 2:17), indicates God's sincere desire for an unbroken relationship with man, and concern for his well-being. Man's willful breaking of this original relationship with God brought to man the indicated death, resulted in God's grief, but it did not cancel the freedom given to man. However, it changed man's real and pure freedom in the environment of God's partnership and love into a false perception of autonomy and independence from God.

Because of continuing respect and love for this "autonomous" fallen man, God leaves the flow of history mostly under man's control, intentions, and possibilities. Laws and warnings in His word, and occasional interventions into human affairs, document that He did not abandon His creation, but shows divine patience with it (Ps. 145:8). Being love, God cannot remain indifferent even to self-inflicted difficulties of His creation. In the present age, God's main agent in this world is the person of the Holy Spirit, who dwells in the physical bodies of His chosen people (1 Cor. 6:19).

This conclusion points to the falsity of the unbiblical idea of providence. God does not make history, God does not direct individual historical events, but does not cease to be interested in man, to keep His covenants and promises, or to be concerned about what is becoming of His created world. The word "providence," or another Hebrew or Greek word expressing the idea, is not found in the Bible. It is of Greek origin (e.g., Philo wrote a book *On Providence*). In the world of some Christian theologians "providence" is used to describe the assumed, unceasing activity of the Creator who guides and governs all events, circumstances, and the free acts of man, as well as of angels. It is expected to convey recognition of God's divine sovereignty, but in reality it is in conflict with the fact of man created in God's image, i.e., with his freedom. The concept of providence deductively assigns to God the role of a totalitarian autocrat, which is in conflict with His openly revealed roles as loving father, just judge, and suffering Savior.

Considering the many tragic reports in the Bible, we can clearly see that God's rest is not a full rest, but a rest disrupted by need for interventions into His created world, for modification of His plan's implementation details due to consequences of human disobedience and neglect of warnings. Human history troubles God because it causes human suffering, and God's suffering with it.

The third conclusion relates to God's blessing of the seventh day. All human history is set in the framework of this blessing. Curses and woes, pronounced by God after the fall of Adam and Eve, are all oriented toward some particular elements of His creation, such as the serpent, or the ground, or people displaying distinct patterns of behavior that are in conflict with His commandments (Luke 6:24–26), but never toward creation as a whole.

Acceptance of the fact of God's rest helps to explain what some people perceive as God's silence, feel as personal abandonment, or classify as God's inaction. The realism of these perceptions of God as hidden is confirmed by many statements found in the Bible. In the times before the selection of Israel, it can be recognized in Job's call: "If only I knew where to find Him!" (Job 23:3). During His last visit with Moses, when predicting Israel's rebellion, God issued a warning, "I will hide my face from them . . ." (Deut. 31:17); that came true as documented by the call, "Awake, O Lord! . . . Why do you hide your face?" (Psalm 44:23–24). But the overall biblical message is also confirming that, in actuality, this hidden God is always close to His people and fulfilling His promise, "I will not forget you" (Isa. 49:15), or "I will be with you always, to the very end of the age" (Matt. 28:20). He is continually seeking reconciliation with all humanity, as openly indicated in John 3:17, or in 1 Timothy 2:4.

The last conclusion leads to the acceptance of the seventh day's finality because there is no "eighth day" mentioned anywhere in the Bible.

NEW CREATION

One of the completely unique characteristics of the biblical cosmogony is the New Testament's clear statements about the final end of this current world.[14] Even though there are passages with millennial content in the Old Testament as well, in their majority they frequently consider the millennium and the eternal state together, the destiny of the righteous and the wicked merged, and focus mostly on the New Jerusalem, allowing contradictory conclusions about the time of its creation.

The New Testament makes it unmistakable that the present earth and heaven will not be restored, nor the earth destroyed by another flood, but that the earth is reserved for fire. The heavens will pass away with a loud noise, the elements will be destroyed by fire, and the earth and everything in it will be burned up (2 Pet. 3:10–12). God will resume His work of creating and forming new heaven and new earth as announced by the prophet Isaiah (65:17) and confirmed by the apostle John in the Book of Revelation (21:1). The twenty-first and twenty-second chapters of Revelation provide the most comprehensive description of this new creation by statements about the size and structural characteristics of New Jerusalem and its general environment.

As in other important revelations, God outlines there a real explanatory cosmogony by disclosing why He is making everything new. He wants to make sure that the former things will not be remembered, people will be relieved of suffering and toil, there will be peaceful coexistence among the animals and man (Isa. 65:17–25), there will be no more death or mourning or crying, death and Hades[15] will be in the lake of fire (Rev. 20:11–15 and 21:1–8), all confirming that the old order of things has passed away. This final revelation points to God's ultimate purpose of Jesus Christ's involvement on this earth, His new position in the new heaven and new earth, the final destination of man and, by that, the final objective of God's plan, i.e., accomplished restoration of the original relation of mutual love between God and man.

It is probably worthwhile to note that the promise of new heaven and new earth does not mention anything about "new hell." After God's final victory over Satan, the old one will continue as is in the proverbial "lake of fire," and a new one will not be needed.

In a true display of God's love, His revealed word documented in the Bible ends with another, but this time final, invitation to whoever wishes to partake in this free gift of a glorious future (Rev. 22:17).

CONCLUSIONS

Biblical cosmogony, if we venture to use this term, avoids all the familiar controversies by the recognition of the severe limitations of the human mind and shortcomings of human judgment, especially in comparison to the superiority of God's word. We can accept the biblical account of creation without speculative skepticism because of God's assurance through the prophet Amos (3:7) that He does not hide from man anything important.

The biblical creation story also clarifies to whom man is responsible for his attitudes and behavior, especially those related to God and man's neighbor.

For man, the most precious is the biblical confirmation of his unique and privileged status: being created in God's image, made only a little lower than heavenly beings and being a candidate for glory and honor. Man remains the focus of God's love even now in his current fallen and sinful state up to the incomprehensible point of giving His only begotten Son as sacrifice, that whoever believes in Him will have everlasting life (John 3:16). Man's simple question to God about "Who is this Man?" has been overwhelmingly answered not only by words in the Bible, but most importantly for us sinners by the love and sacrifice made by Jesus Christ on the cross of Calvary.

GOD'S DEALING WITH MANKIND

11

God's act of creation provided the stage on which His plan for the relation of mutual love and respect with man is to be executed. History, then, is the time dimension in which this drama is unfolding, and God's plan is being brought to fruition. Therefore, the historicity of God's dealing with His creation and associated observable events, especially prophecies and their fulfillment, is fundamental as the demonstrated validity of Christianity. In addition, Christian faith is inseparably related to the historic person of Jesus Christ and, for that reason, every other historical event is assessed for its significance according to its relation to His life, mission, and message. The words and acts of Jesus Christ are the foundation of everything in a Christian's life, including the development of a sound biblical understanding and interpretation of the historical ways of God's dealing with individuals and mankind, and evaluation of their differences from other past and current, natural and humanistic interpretations.

Biblical descriptions of historical events invite three possible periodizations of man's past, offering insights into God's plan and its implementation:

1. The self-evident, but potentially misleading, is periodization based on year count. The highest risk here is associated with the already mentioned difference between God's and man's perception of time.

2. Periodization based on the different dominant modes of God's dealing with man (dispensations), namely: the Edenic age of innocence, the age of conscience between the fall of Adam and Eve and the call of Abraham, the age of promise fulfilled in Exodus, the age of law ending with Jesus' crucifixion, the present age of grace, and God's future millennial kingdom between Christ's second coming and the final judgment of mankind.

3. The most natural periodization, which takes into account major disasters caused by man's rebellion against God, disasters requiring change in God's plan implementation tactics and reflected in covenant change. These major past disasters are man's expulsion from paradise, the Flood, the confusion of languages during the construction of the Tower of Babel, and the crucifixion of the

Messiah. When this list is supplemented by the establishment of Israel and of the church, we have a periodization similar to the one based on dispensations.

COVENANTS

The relation between God and man started in the Garden of Eden with a period of man's innocence during which God established patterns of revealing His will and commitments through covenants, promises, warnings, and communication with man either directly or by selected messengers. We find two types of covenants in the Bible: general or universal, covering all mankind, and theocratic, describing conditions of God's rule over Israel. Both depend solely on God's grace, indicated by frequent unconditional declarations, "I will . . . ," and contain statements about both rewards and punishment.

For modern man, whose human rights are frequently violated by governments and fellow men, and who knows about governments and powerful people who are putting themselves frequently above the law, it is amazing to see the respect God the Creator pays to man by covenant partnership and unilateral voluntary commitments.

The first universal covenant, the Edenic covenant, established the role, goals, authority, boundary, and conditions for Adam's life. It also specified God's commitment to act if the terms of this covenant would not be honored.

> Then the Lord God took the man and put him in the garden of Eden to tend and keep it. And the Lord God commanded the man, saying, "Of every tree of the garden you may freely eat; but of the tree of knowledge of good and evil you shall not eat, for in the day that you eat of it you shall surely die" (Gen. 2:15–17, NKJV).

The Edenic covenant was terminated by man's disobedience when Adam and Eve ate the forbidden fruit. This disobedience initiated an era of human conscience (mental sense of right and wrong) and caused God to fulfill His part of the covenant by introduction of death to man. God also recognized the change in man:

> Then the Lord God said, "Behold, the man has become like one of Us, to know good and evil. And now, lest he put out his hand and take also of the tree of life, and eat, and live forever"—therefore, the Lord sent him out of the garden of Eden to till the ground from which he was taken (Gen. 3:22–23, NKJV).

The change in man has been double-edged: it brought him closer to God (like one of Us) and, by loosing his eternal life (cannot eat from the tree of life), the distance between eternal God and mortal man had increased dramatically. God's continuing love for this fallen man is visible in the new alternative in

God's plan: availability of salvation from the consequences of man's disobedience through repentance, and of eternal life as God's gift to repentant sinners.

The violation of the Edenic covenant necessitated establishment of a new one, the Adamic covenant (Gen. 3:14–21), in which Satan is judged, the serpent and the ground cursed,[1] woman's social status changed, pain of childbirth increased, man's physical body changed, and work for food introduced. But the original assignments about increasing in numbers and filling and subduing the earth (Gen. 1:28) had not been canceled nor changed. In this covenant God committed Himself to ultimately judge and punish Satan because he was instrumental in man's fall. This major event also started the part of God's "Seventh Day," characterized by the appearance of God's silence and inaction, and man's assumption of autonomy.

The explosion of wickedness, evil thoughts and desires, and violence in Noah's time, with only a few men deserving favor in God's eyes, resulted in God's grief and announced decision to wipe out all mankind and animals, and creatures that move along the ground, and birds of the air (Gen. 6:7) by a flood. Only Noah respected God's warning and was saved with his family by Lord's grace. The changes caused by the Flood required changes in the covenant also. God has established His third universal covenant with man through Noah, in which He reaffirmed man's responsibility to populate the earth and his dominance over the animal kingdom, allowed man to eat the flesh of animals but not their blood, established the sacredness of human life[2] and related death penalty, committed Himself never to destroy the earth again by a universal flood, and established the rainbow as a testimony to this covenant (Gen. 9:1–17).

Even this arrangement led to conflict with God's will by men building a city and tower with the goal of disregarding God's commandment to populate the earth by staying together at one location and, by that, glorifying themselves (Gen. 11:4). Here Satan's original Edenic temptation of an innocent individual, "you will be like God," has been transformed into a temptation of sinful human social pride emulating Satan's desire to be equal to God by one's own power and intelligence, "let *us* reach heaven" (emphasis added). This particular attempt ended by God causing confusion of human language, leading to man's inability to communicate and dispersion. But human pride challenging God and His kingdom is still present even in our age, as demonstrated by Hitler's Thousand-Year Reich, Marxist-Leninist communist society, Lyndon Johnson's Great Society, the variety of "peace processes," or by Stephen W. Hawking's quite blasphemous, " . . . then we would know the mind of God."[3]

Historically, God's next major goodwill interventions were the call of Abraham leading to the establishment of Israel as the chosen nation, making visible His will through commandments with related rewards and punishments, and the earthly birth of His own Son. This again resulted in disasters: the first—exiles—due to Israel's rebellion, the second due to the cooperation between Israel's religious leaders and the gentile government of Rome that led to the crucifixion of Jesus Christ, the Son of God, and Israel's Messiah. These actions clearly confirmed not just man's unwillingness to accept God's will, but also a naked attempt to replace God's lordship by a rule of man. The parable of tenants mistreating the vineyard owner's servants and even killing his son (Mark 12:1–9) describes, in simple language, what happened, and the resulting consequences.

The birth, life, crucifixion, and resurrection of Jesus Christ marked the climax of God's historical dealing with mankind. In Jesus, the Old Testament's major prophecies and expectations about the Messiah as a man of God's choice, the appointed redeemer of Israel, and the judge of God's adversaries have been fulfilled. Facts in the life of Jesus Christ confirm that it has not been an accidental historical episode, but an event willed by God from the beginning as the culmination of His plan's strategy.

In the New Testament Gospels, Jesus' life and deeds are not just an intellectual entertaining spectacle on the level of Greek myths about gods visiting selected people for their own pleasure or personal advantage, but historical reports on God the Creator visiting man for man's own good. In Jesus, the quite abstract "God the Creator" became practically and directly comprehensible as a sinless human person. The world was lost in sin, but Christ was born and finished the work of salvation. Man's only reasonable response is "Hallelujah, praise the Lord."

The utmost importance of Christ's bodily death on the cross and His subsequent resurrection for man's salvation is stressed by the apostle Paul in his first letter to the Corinthian Christians: If Christ has not been raised, Christian faith is futile, and Christians should be pitied more than all men (1 Cor. 15:13–19). Without the triumph over death in resurrection, Jesus' kingdom and lordship are as illusory as other political ideologies or moral systems, Jesus was really forsaken by God the Father on the cross, and His ministry accomplished nothing.

The results of the crucifixion required a new universal covenant, this time sealed by Christ's own blood (Luke 22:20). That opened the door to free salvation (i.e., to restoration of a proper relation with God) to every individual human being by forgiveness of sin through God's grace, and available through faith in the resurrected Jesus Christ. This simplest tactic possible, supported by the presence and work of Holy Spirit, has proven very effective regarding the objectives of God's plan. Considering man's essentially sinful nature, and the depth of human depravity, it is actually the only way back to God.

This tactic of dealing directly with individuals reflects God's wisdom, and should be perceived as a warning to all who are considering or proposing solutions to spiritual, moral, social, or political problems on other levels, be it family, tribe, group, city, state, nation, or church. Their deviation from God's plan guarantees a failure, as experience from human history confirms. There are no society-wide solutions. As there is no collective guilt, there is no collective way to salvation either. The results of God's covenant with Israel clearly document that solutions at a national level do not work.

Despite a long sequence of man-caused disasters, God did not remain completely silent and hidden during any period of history. Before the Flood, He dealt with Cain, Enoch, and Noah, and after the Flood with Job and his friends, Abraham, and Lot, then during the time of Israel with Moses, judges, kings, and prophets and, finally, with all humanity through Jesus Christ—sometimes directly, in other times through human or angelic messengers. The Bible confirms that mankind now lives not only under the prince of this world, who governs through the rule of men, but also under God's grace, in a period before the promised Christ's second coming and establishment of His millennial kingdom.

ROLE OF ISRAEL

The call of Abram, whose name God later changed to Abraham, with its eight unconditional promises (Gen. 12:1–3), opened a new and unique chapter in God's intervention into human affairs.

The history of God's dealing with Israel in her critical periods through blessings, prophetic warnings, punishments, and forgiveness is well documented in the Old Testament. The timing of pivotal events, as well as of active lives of key personalities, is known with reasonable accuracy.[4] The Old Testament narrative ends in the time of Nehemiah around the year 410 B.C. Following periods of Macedonian, Egyptian, Seleucid, and Maccabean rules, and of Hasmodean and Roman dynasties, are also well described, but in documents outside the Bible, or by archeological findings. Many additional sources cover the history of Israel and Jews up to the current era,[5, 6] as well as Israel-related contemporary events.

Notwithstanding the amount of revealed information, the establishment, continued existence, and outlined future of Israel remain a mystery that surpasses all human understanding in many directions.[7] Jews themselves are aware that Israel is in her own way a highly unusual and unique phenomenon in human history, with suprahuman relationship to the rest of the world. Israel is in the world, but not of the world. Even though she suffers from the world, and is a subject to it, she is free from it through God's protection. She continues her mission, as the community of chosen people with promised and assured final reconciliation with Him but, most of the time, not being directly aware of it.

Israel is the community of earthly hope, awaiting God's kingdom here on the earth. She wants God's justice in time, in nature, in national community, and in the world's political and economic community, missing the key revelation that it is the Devil who is the current prince of the world. This makes her a close relative to the experiments of utopian thinkers of the Western world. Despite many prophecies and warnings, Israel stumbled many times against God, and was and still is caught in the trap of her own choices.

The most critical prophecies of Israel's failure are pointing to the rejection of her Messiah, and may be found in the book of Isaiah, e.g.:

- " . . . for both houses of Israel he [the Lord Almighty] will be a stone that causes men to stumble and a rock that makes them fall. And for the people of Jerusalem he will be a trap and snare. Many of them will stumble; they will fall and be broken, they will be snared and captured" (Isa. 8:14–15).

- "He [the Lord] was despised and rejected by men, a man of sorrows, and familiar with suffering. Like one from whom men hide their faces he was despised, and we esteemed him not" (Isa. 53:3).

These prophecies relate directly to the earlier warning and choice set before Israel by God in Deuteronomy 30:19–20, "This day I call heaven and earth as witnesses against you that I have set before you life and death, blessing and curses. Now choose life, so that you and your children may live and that you may love the LORD your God, listen to his voice, and hold fast to him. For the LORD is your life. . . ."

In the crucial moments of her history she had chosen the world instead, and became prisoner and victim of it. God's message was clear:

Leviticus 26:1–13—Rewards for obedience spelled out.

Leviticus 26:14–39—Punishments for disobedience outlined.

Leviticus 26:40–45—Repentance suggested and promoted as the way of dealing with sin.

But despite this clarity, a long list of examples of Israel's disobedience may be easily compiled from the Old Testament information, such as:

Exodus 15:22–24—Complaints about bitterness of water

Exodus 16:2–3—Complaints about lack of meat

Exodus 32:1–7—Worship of the golden calf

Numbers 14:1–4—People grumbling against Moses an Aaron

Deuteronomy 1:6–33—Rebellion against the Lord

Joshua 7:1–26—Achan's sin

Judges 3:7–8—Serving Baals and Asherahs

2 Samuel 11:2–27—David and Bathsheba

2 Samuel 24:1–17—David counts the fighting men

2 Kings 14:23–24—Evil king Jeroboam

2 Kings 17:7–23—Worshipping other gods.

Israel's rebellion had been predicted (Deut. 31:16–18) and led to God's overall assessment of Israel as stiff-necked people (Exod. 32:9, or 2 Kings 17:14). She preferred human kings over God's rule through judges (1 Sam. 8:7) and failed to recognize and accept her Messiah. The priests of Israel, with excellent reasons of political prudence, had chosen the Roman Caesar over their own Messiah and bound the whole people, with the exception of God's small remnant, to that choice against God.

It has been said that the tragedy of Israel is a localized and time-compressed image of the tragedy of the world, of the tragedy of man in his struggle against God's will and sovereignty.

From the biblical viewpoint, Israel plays a dual role in God's plan: A direct role, by giving the world the Savior, witnessing and documenting His life, deeds, and death, preserving the treasury of God's word in Scriptures, being a subject to God's promises, and bringing God's offer of salvation to the whole world through her fault. And indirectly by irritating the prince and powers of the world and, by that, stimulating thinking about God, His justice, love, and the mystery of forgiveness and grace.

The biblical metaphor of an unfaithful wife, long awaited by her loving husband, and with the original relationship finally restored, so well described in the poetical language of the Book of Hosea, is a perfect image of the relationship between Israel and God.

Since Christ's crucifixion and resurrection, the people of Israel live as the rest of the world under dispensation of grace. Presently, in the times of the Gentiles, from God's viewpoint there is no difference between Jew and Gentile (Rom. 10:12). As of the year 70 A.D., with the prophesied destruction of Jerusalem and dispersion of Jews fulfilled, the unique position of Israel in God's plan has been temporarily suspended. But these historical events do not cancel God's standing promises. All the major prophets documented God's plan to restore Israel to her planned special position: "Judah will be inhabited forever and Jerusalem through all generations. Their bloodguilt, which I [the LORD] have not pardoned, I will pardon" (Joel 3:20–21); "No longer will Jacob be ashamed; no longer will their faces grow pale" (Isa. 29:22); "No longer will I [the LORD] make you hear the taunts of the nations, and no longer will you suffer the scorn of the peoples" (Ezek. 36:15); or "At that time they will call Jerusalem The Throne of the LORD, and all nations will gather in Jerusalem to honor the name of the LORD" (Jer. 3:17). This restoration will take place after the "full number of Gentiles has come in" (Rom. 11:25) to salvation, and after the time of "Jacob's trouble"[8] at the end of the current era which will be marked by Christ's second coming. Reasons for this restoration of Israel may be found in God's covenant promises, as well as in the overall objective of God's plan

(Ezek. 36:22–23): "This is what the sovereign LORD says: It is not for your sake, O house of Israel, that I am going to do these things, but for the sake of my holy name, which you have profaned among the nations. . . . Then the nations will know that I am the LORD, declares the Sovereign LORD, when I show myself holy through you before their eyes."

The most optimistic assessment is Paul's statement that "all Israel will be saved" in Romans 11:26; quite frightening is the parable in Luke 16:19–31.

CHURCH IN HISTORY

There are a few observable similarities between Israel and the Christian church that caused some Christian thinkers to perceive her as the new Israel and heir of Israel's promises. The risk of this view rests with the fact that the majority of similarities relate mostly to the negative aspects of the institutionalized church's social conduct, and her similar position in respect to worldly political powers, including active involvement in wars and persecutions.

Institutionalized Christianity has, perhaps, proven more influential in shaping the history and culture of the West than any other organized ideology or philosophy. Therefore, there is a vast amount of research data and historical documents available to historians addressing the outline or notable episodes in history of Christianity and Christendom.[9, 10] Their work deals with Christianity's impact on power structures, philosophy, art, and general cultural environment. The Christian authors see here God's domination of history and His oversight of the Church, while the non-Christian authors perceive Christianity as only one of many social, political, or economic forces competing with, e.g., Hellenism, Enlightenment, Industrial Revolution, science, etc. In these studies the church does not come out as an admirable institution, and rightly so. When her well-documented internal conflicts and divisions, financial and moral corruption, sponsorship of violence, willingness to be misused for ideological propaganda purposes, and so on, are considered, not very much is left to be humanly proud of. Besides longevity, her historical outline has the form and contents similar to the history of any other worldly sociopolitical institution.

The intellectual history of the Christian church and of Christian thought[11] reflected in theology is mostly a story of application or rejection of ideas and reasoning processes originated at the outside, and put in agreement or conflict with biblical statements or Christian tradition. The results delivered over almost two millennia are not impressive and, in a way, similar to the paucity of worldly philosophies. The most significant accomplishment seems to be the demonstration of the rationality of the Christian mind, its ability to deal with all social or intellectual phenomena, and of the realism in its approach to the individual, society, and nature. But all the thousands of theological studies written do not add one single bit of new information to the essential knowledge revealed in the Bible.

The limited information about the church given in the New Testament clearly indicates, at least from God's point of view, the limited importance of the church organization, history, and tradition. This assessment is in line with Jesus' parable of the great banquet (Matt. 22:1–10, or Luke 14:15–24) where the invited but reluctant guests with a variety of excuses may well represent Israel, and the unorganized group of poor, crippled, blind, and lame accepting the invitation, the church;[12] with the parable of workers in the vineyard (Matt. 20:1–15) denying importance of seniority[13] or the amount of work delivered; Jesus' statement about the unimportance of the congregation size, or its hierarchical structure, for His spiritual presence (Matt. 18:20); and with the fact that the work of salvation has been finished by Jesus on the cross and, therefore, nothing important is missing or needs to be added.

This viewpoint is also consistent with the obvious need to recognize the work of the Holy Spirit and to give Him glory. Even though Christians are charged with spreading the Gospel, the actual growth of the church has nothing to do with the human credibility of Gospel interpretations, eloquence of preaching, communication media used, liturgical grandeur, social programs offered, etc., but is the result of the work of the Holy Spirit. It is God Himself who continually adds new believers to His flock (Acts 2:47; 5:14; 11:24).[14]

We may personally learn from the lives of past Christians, especially martyrs, witnesses, missionaries, and others. We may admire the work of the Holy Spirit in the sin-plagued world, His protection of the church against the gates of hell (Matt. 16:18), the fulfillment of prophecies, and the growth of the population of God's kingdom. But despite the numerical growth of the church's membership, the concept of progress does not apply. The contemporary Christian community is no better nor more dedicated than the past generations.

BIBLICAL VIEW OF HUMAN HISTORY

From its first book to the last, the Bible talks about both heaven and earth. To understand the meaning behind history, it is, therefore, necessary to consider events in both realms, especially the events presented as key milestones in God's plan. The Bible does not provide many details, but clearly indicates that (if the concept of time can be applied to the events in heaven) before man's fall, there had been in heaven rebellion by some angelic beings led by Lucifer and ending in their defeat (Rev. 12:7–9). Hints to these events are found in Isaiah 14:12–15 and, in a metaphoric form, in Ezekiel 28:12–19. By this information the Bible provides man with very important explanations:

- Sin and evil as such, originated with heavenly beings (Isa. 14:14, and Ezek. 28:17).
- Hell had been originally prepared as a place of punishment for the rebelling angels (Matt. 25:41).

- Satan, the rebellious Lucifer, has been permitted to influence individuals and events on earth since the time of the Garden of Eden (Ezek. 28:13), and, actually, given authority over all the kingdoms of the world (Luke 4:6). He is currently the temporary ruler (prince) of this world and era.

Behind all history there is God's spiritual conflict with the Devil and his fallen angels (Rev. 12:7–9). In Luke 10:18 Jesus talks about seeing Satan falling like lightning from heaven. This revelation is important because it points to the continuing spiritual warfare now taking place here on earth. There is purposefully evil personal authority behind the earthly historical power struggles, and behind the physical and intellectual disadvantage man has facing this personal evil. In his letter to the Ephesians (6:12), Paul also makes it clear that Christians' earthly struggle is not against flesh and blood, but against the rulers, authorities, and powers of the dark world, and against the spiritual forces of evil in the heavenly realm as well.

This also explains why published human history is not a story of ordinary people and good will, but a chronicle of deeds by the powerful, of betrayals, deceptions, trickery, lies, falsehood, murder, wars and disasters, thinly veiled by words of progress, liberation, and lately, peace process and defense of human rights.

Even though man lived in harmony with God and nature for some time in the Garden of Eden, the Bible indicates that the story of the human race actually begins with Satan's deception, leading to man's disobedience of God's commands, punishment by expulsion from paradise, and introduction of death to man. The following is mankind's history, which covers the major part of the "Seventh Day" and leads to the finale in God's White Throne judgment (Rev. 20:11–15). The Bible provides three different meanings and interpretations of this history depending on the perspective of the participating actor.

(1) From the Christian's perspective, human history documents the sin-distorted fulfillment of God's commands to be fruitful, increase in number, fill the earth and subdue it, and rule over the other earthly creatures (Gen. 1:28). It chronicles human efforts, both instinctive and purposeful, to minimize the impact of God's curse after Adam's fall (Gen. 3:14–19). There are many obvious examples:

- Medical sciences and the pharmaceutical industry search for ways to eliminate pain in childbearing.

- Suppression of woman's desire for her husband and his rule by many forms of no-fault divorce legislations and feminist ideology, trying to bring her to a complete independence.

- Man's continuing attempts to avoid toil by a variety of methods, from employment of slaves to high technology.

- Attempts to reduce sweat by deodorants and antiperspirants.

- Attempts to eliminate, or at least minimize the adverse consequences of human decisions and activity in general through, e.g., pollution control, environmental protection legislations, etc.

- A variety of strategies and efforts to prolong human life.

It also reflects man's continuing disobedience to God's will, his emulation of Satan's authority by repetitive attempts to rule over other human beings, an authority and role never given to man in general; and the variety and persistence of God's initiatives to save all mankind, or at least the desiring individuals, from the fatal consequences of sinful disobedience freely chosen by them.

(2) From Satan's perspective, it probably is a sequence of actions aiming to assure continuing human rebellion against God, to keep authority over earthly kingdoms and powers, and to sabotage and frustrate God's plan, with the overall goal of discrediting His omnipotence and omniscience and, by that, making himself equal to the Most High.

(3) For God, human history must be a frustrating story of painful and disappointing dealing with man's tragic rebellion and disobedience. God's interventions into human history, with the objective of destroying the works of Satan (1 John 3:8 and Heb. 2:14) and redeeming man, confirm the gravity of this revolt and of God's seriousness to resolve it in the framework of His plan.

The biblical view admits that man's participation in history is under a variety of limitations and liabilities over which he has no control, but it also understands that these do not eliminate the freedom he received from his Creator, do not minimize the responsibility for his decisions, or mitigate their consequences. Man lives a real life in an actual world, and participates in historical accidents, events, and ambiguities. This participation creates (intentionally or unknowingly) man's own personal history, his personal role in God's plan, and must be perceived in terms of individual, personal encounters with world events, and, in the framework of Christianity, encounters with the will of God made clear to man in Jesus Christ and the Bible.

The study of human history from the biblical perspective also provides a glimpse of God's greatness through the strategy of His plan implementation:

- God's justice will be satisfied by the judgment and punishment of the agents of personal evil and of unrepentant sinners.

- God's love is demonstrated through His patience with sinners, and through His offer of forgiveness, guaranteed by the death of Jesus Christ on the cross, and accepted by many.

- God's wisdom is reflected in His ability to achieve both, without compromising either.

• God's glory will be magnified by accomplishing His plan's objective in front of both heavenly and earthly audiences.

In summary, the Bible views human history as a dramatic implementation of God's plan through different strategies that account for man's continuing disobedience and limited response to God's goodwill, and for the devil's purposeful attempts to sabotage God's intents.

PANORAMA OF THE FUTURE

History, in human terms, is still in progress with the future unknown and final purpose undisclosed. Historians' assessments can, therefore, be oriented only toward the past and be no more than provisional. Biblical perspective, on the other hand, by accepting God's revelation in Jesus Christ, in prophecies, and in God's plan, is equipped by a true and permanent norm for evaluation of past and current events, and by a well-outlined picture of the world's future.

A general warning is now in order. When dealing with biblical prophecies it is a must to always rely on prayerfully requested guidance by the Holy Spirit, to use helpful suggestions of trusted experts, and always to acknowledge God's sovereignty and limitations of the human mind. In the world of interpretation of biblical prophecies related to the future, interpretation biases must be expected, and God's wise decision not to provide a complete knowledge before its time respected. Scriptural warning, such as, "If anyone adds anything to them [prophecies of the Book of Revelation], God will add to him the plagues described in this book. And if anyone takes words away from this book of prophecy, God will take away from him his share in the tree of life" (Rev. 22:18–19), must be taken with utmost seriousness. The perspective adopted in this study reflects a conviction that scenarios of the future are important, but not fundamental for Christian faith. They were revealed to provide hope, encouragement, and strength (2 Thess. 2:16–17). Christians know that the day of personal salvation is today, and rely on Jesus' promise to be with His own disciples always (Matt. 28:20).

The still unfinished part of general human history is characterized by political deception—"While people are saying, 'peace and safety,' destruction will come on them suddenly . . . and they will not escape" (1 Thess. 5:3), suffering of Israel (the Time of Jacob's Trouble mentioned in Jer. 30:7), followed by suffering of unbelievers under God's wrath (The Great Tribulation). This relatively short period will end with Christ's return to earth in glory, restoration of Israel to her originally intended role, and establishment of Christ's millennial kingdom.

The Christians' future is based on the fact of forgiveness of sins through personal belief in Jesus Christ and His redemptive work. His work of salvation takes Christians out of the unrighteous part of mankind, targeted for God's wrath and punishment. This fact is also the basis for arguments that Christians will not go through the times of great tribulation:

1. Presence of Christians is not in line with the two purposes of the great tribulation: to punish the Gentile world for sins and refusal of God's offer of forgiveness, and to bring Israel into an attitude of accepting Jesus Christ as their Messiah.

2. Presence of Christians does not fit the Israel-oriented character of Daniel's prophecy, nor the part of the book of Revelation that begins with its fourth chapter.

This hope makes Christians' interest in details of the great tribulation period secondary, only as the frightening part of God's message to the world. This hope is confirmed by Jesus' promise to receive His disciples for Himself (John 14:1–3), as well as by Paul in 1 Thessalonians 4:13–18, a message written to encourage believers there. There Paul talks about the rapture, about living Christians being taken away from the earth to heaven to be with Jesus forever.[15] The timing of the rapture is unknown (1 Thess. 5:1–2 and Matt. 24:36), which has led some thinkers to speculate about the time relationship between the rapture and beginning of the Millennium known to start three and a half years after the Antichrist's covenant with Israel is broken.[16] For biblical Christians listening to their Lord's demand to live every day as the last day of their individual life on the earth, or the day of His coming, the timing puzzle has been resolved by acknowledging that it may happen today.

Then the closure of human history will arrive at the end of the Millennium with the White Throne judgment. The age of new heaven and new earth will begin.

CONCLUSIONS

With the stage set by creation, history provides the time dimension in which God's dealing with man is unfolding. God's plan, then, forms a solid basis for interpretation of individual historical events consistent with the final objective still in the future. The biblical view of human history as the history of salvation related to events in heaven and the spiritual realm is in stark contrast to all constantly changing, humanistic interpretations. Most importantly, it points to three perspectives reflecting goals of the participants: believers, God, and the current ruler of this world with the unbelieving rest of humanity.

The particular history of Israel illustrates the tragedy of mankind pursuing autonomy from God's will, despite warnings of dire consequences. But even the most tragic moment in Israel's history, the rejection of her Messiah Jesus Christ, God in His wisdom has turned into victory over Satan, and into satisfaction of conditions for salvation opportunity for all mankind. The tragedies and turmoil of Israel, as a localized and time-compressed image of history of the whole world, document that mankind is not a "focus group" called by God to evaluate His thoughts and deeds or to suggest improvement ideas: "For My thoughts are not your thoughts," says the Lord (Isa. 55:8–9). Man's proper response is: "What do You want me to do, Lord?"

From the biblical point of view, now is the time for all Christians to preach the Gospel, to wait and be prepared for Jesus' return for His own, and not to worry too much about the chaos in the world and its future: "Let him who does wrong continue to do wrong; . . . let him who does right continue to do right; and let him who is holy continue to be holy" (Rev. 22:11).

Key personal conclusions from the biblical interpretation of history then are:

• The current generation is fortunate to live in the time of God's grace, which makes salvation as easy as accepting a valuable gift from a loving father.

• Because the era of grace will come to an end when the number of saved Christians is complete, the urgency of making a personal decision for God's offer of forgiveness is obvious, as well as the need to proclaim the good news about this offer to the yet unsaved.

• Considering the truth of God's word, documented in many already fulfilled prophecies and promises, it is prudent to watch for the signs of the expected end times, to be ready for Christ's second coming, and to live in hope that the current era of confusion, evil, and failure of worldly expectations of unlimited progress without God is just a temporary phenomenon soon to be replaced by God's own just rule over the world.

ANSWERS AT LAST

12

Our search for answers is finally coming to a definite closure. It has been quite an educational journey through the intellectual heritage of the brightest minds who lived and shared their findings, discoveries, doubts, difficulties, arguments, and conclusions. The current age of well-stocked libraries, reasonably priced books, innumerable professional magazines, electronic means of information processing and communication, as well as affordable advanced education, brings the benefit of an easy access to this wealth of knowledge to many, and in its popularized versions, almost to all members of Western society. There is no doubt that even a scant encounter with this heritage, e.g. as presented in this book, creates awe about its richness, respect to those who produced it, and justifiably high appraisal of the demonstrated human creative potential.

Nevertheless, a significant deficiency of this mass of information and knowledge comes to light with the recognition that to every proposed idea or stated opinion there is a contradictory idea and opposite opinion, and arguments or information inconsistent with their presuppositions or conclusions. It is discouraging to see the best and brightest who, while observing the same world and considering the same data, reach conflicting conclusions. It is also disheartening to learn that no credible single view of the world emerged from this overflowing world of ideas, nor a widely and well-accepted general system for the assessment of an individual idea's merit or utility or importance. The impression of paucity of unquestionable conclusions intensifies when personally important and for one's own life fundamental questions remain unanswered. There are no answers, just opinions—opinions almost always abandoned in the actual personal lives of their originators or subsequent holders, or projected as ideals into the faraway future. It is, therefore, not surprising that the notion of chaos emerges in one's mind when this abundance of man's mental products is viewed from a distance and without preconceptions. All this seems to confirm the postmodern perspective of incommensurability of different bodies of knowledge, and with it associated doubts about the reality of any other than quantitative progress, as reasonable and inescapable.

It is also important to notice that the enormity and complexity of the already accumulated human knowledge make it impossible for individual persons to discover and verify it by themselves. In fact, for most of us all the knowledge outside the direct personal experience has been actually revealed to us by parents, teachers, friends, communicators, and authors of published studies. Because there are at our disposal no valid objective criteria how to select what is right from this plethora of often conflicting ideas, opinions, and convictions, we are compelled either to accept them on their face value, or assess them as per the author's credibility, or their stability, popularity, or intuitive appeal. But there are no guarantees that the author of the views of the world accepted will stand by us and help in personal difficulties to apply them in daily life or reward our loyalty. Simply and clearly: we are on our own.

Considering that most of the knowledge we possess has been revealed to us by often distant and erring humans, why not accept revelation from the biblical God instead? Through the life of Jesus Christ and the Bible He shared with us parts of His omniscient knowledge and wisdom crucial for our stay on this earth and even beyond. He cannot lie (He is the Truth), His wisdom is complete and eternally solid (He is the creator of this world and man), and accepted by many today as it has been through past millennia. He also stands behind His disciples with His power and, at the end of their earthly life, promised to reward them with eternal life in His presence. Isn't this the best offer ever made to man?

Are there any risks, you may ask. Yes, but only social risks because in humanistic cultures biblical Christianity is destined to be perceived as foolishness. But let us not forget: accepting human ideas carries the same, if not bigger, risk.

Therefore, it seems prudent to check whether the biblical revelation contains the answers for our originally stated questions and what they are.

QUESTIONS ANSWERED

The Bible, being a written document revealing to sinful man the only way acceptable to God to escape from His wrath and damnation, is not focused on some narrow segment of readership, but is accessible and profitable to everyone: from the minimal familiarity with its Gospel of salvation offered through faith in Jesus Christ and, perhaps, a few parables and verses, up to extensive memorization and daily studies throughout man's whole life. Its style, therefore, cannot be uniform or similar to a rigorously organized textbook attempting to present a closed system of ideas; it is variable and flexible to accommodate all who seek the truth. This also means that answers to the question posed in the Introduction are only seldom formulated there in one precise sentence. They must be extracted from the spirit of the Bible and referred to pertinent verses or chapters for verification. This brings into the picture the delicate issue of biblical interpretation again. These four assumptions proved themselves vital for reaching a scriptural interpretation as correct as possible:

1. God is sovereign and directs His messages and actions toward reaching His objectives.

2. God is omniscient. He knows all things, so His revelations are not based on generalizations of past experience, but on His knowledge of the future as well. In other words, God's truth does not change with circumstances or time; it is eternal.

3. Biblical revelations are accurate, i.e., free from errors and always striking the essence of the concern.

4. God's revelation is understandable, especially when illuminated by the Holy Spirit, and valuable as guidance.

For the contemplation of the presented answers and related biblical quotations, it is prudent to repeat that the truth and power is not in this book or credibility of presented arguments, but in God's word proclaimed by the Bible and made visible in the life and works of Jesus Christ, God's word made flesh.

Q: *Who am I?*
A: Every single person is a unique, irreplaceable, by-God-created human being existing in irrevocable relation to his or her creator.

- "You made him [man] a little lower than the angels; you crowned him with glory and honor, and put everything under his feet" (Heb. 2:7).

- "I will praise You [LORD] because I am fearfully and wonderfully made; your works are wonderful, I know that full well" (Ps. 139:14).

- "Yet, O LORD, you are our Father. We are the clay, you are the potter; we are all the work of your hand" (Isa. 64:8).

Q: *What is the nature of my identity?*
A: Man's identity rests in being created in the image of God, albeit an image now distorted by sin and death.

- "Then God said, 'Let us make man in our image, in our likeness'" (Gen. 1:26).

- "[H]e [man] is the image and glory of God" (1 Cor. 11:7).

- "The LORD God formed man from the dust of the ground and breathed into his nostrils the breath of life, and man became a living being" (Gen. 2:7).

- "Man does not live on bread alone, but on every word that comes from the mouth of God" (Matt. 4:4).

- "Death came to all men, because all sinned" (Rom. 5:12).

Q: *Where did I come from?*

A: The physical body and soul come from one's physical parents under God's control. The spiritual birth comes from God as a gift for repentance and declared desire to reestablish the proper relation with God through Jesus Christ.

- "[F]rom my mother's womb you have been my God" (Ps. 22:10).

- "Who gave man his mouth? Who makes him deaf or dumb? Who gives him sight or makes him blind? Is it not I, the LORD? (Exod. 4:11).

- "For you created my inmost being; you knit me together in my mother's womb" (Ps. 139:13).

- ". . . unless a man is born again, he cannot see the kingdom of God" (John 3:3).

- "Flesh gives birth to flesh, but Spirit gives birth to spirit" (John 3:6).

Q: *Do I have a free will?*

A: Man, being created in God's image, has a free will up to the point of rejecting God's claim on him. This free will is recognized by God. But man does not have freedom to select consequences of his decisions and actions. Man's free will is also limited by the dynamics of nature, wills of other men, and the will of God. Full freedom is attainable only when living in full agreement with God's will.

- "Oh, that their hearts would be inclined to fear me [the LORD] and keep all my commandments always, so that it might go well with them and their children forever!" (Deut. 5:29).

- "'If you are willing and obedient, you will eat the best from the land; but if you resist and rebel, you will be devoured by the sword.' For the mouth of the LORD has spoken." (Isa. 1:19, 20).

- "Perhaps they will bring their petition before the LORD, and each will turn from his wicked ways" (Jer. 36:7).

- "If anyone chooses to do God's will, he will find out whether my [Jesus'] teaching comes from God or whether I speak on my own" (John 7:17).

Q: *Am I of any value?*

A: Man has a potential for supreme position in the universe. Not only is his creation the final work of God, but in man the previous creation finds its fulfillment and meaning. Man's ultimate value has been set by God's love in the sacrificial death of Jesus Christ, Son of God.

- "For God so loved the world that he gave his one and only Son, that whoever believes in him shall not perish but have eternal life" (John 3:16).
- He who forms the mountains [the LORD God Almighty] . . . reveals his thoughts to man . . ." (Amos 4:13).

Q: *Why was I born and what is the purpose or mission of my life?*
A: Physical birth is caused by the will of parents, spiritual birth by the will of God. The principal purposes of man's life are in loving, respectful, and trusting response to God's gracious love, in bringing glory to God through obedience, and by doing His will generally known through His commandments and the great commission given to believers.

- "Blessed are they who keep his [the LORD's] statutes and seek him with all their heart" (Ps. 119:2).
- "Teach me to do your will, for you are my God" (Ps. 143:10).
- "Fear God and keep his commandments, for this is the whole duty of man" (Eccl. 12:13).
- "If you love me, you will obey what I [Jesus] command. . . . He who loves me will be loved by my Father" (John 14:15, 21).
- "Blessed are those who hear the word of God and obey it" (Luke 11:28).
- "Therefore go and make disciples of all nations, baptizing them in the name of the Father and of the Son and of the Holy Spirit, and teaching them to obey everything I [Jesus] have commanded you" (Matt. 28:19, 20).

Q: *Who is the final arbiter about the success or failure of my life's mission?*
A: God in the person of Jesus Christ is the final judge. He suggested strategies leading to successful life.

- "God will bring every deed into judgment, including every hidden thing, whether it is good or evil" (Eccl. 12:14).
- "But I [Jesus] tell you that men will have to give account on the day of judgment for every careless word they have spoken. For by your words you will be acquitted, and by your words you will be condemned" (Matt. 12:36, 37).
- "[T]he Father judges no one, but has entrusted all judgment to the Son, that all may honor the Son just as they honor the Father" (John 5:22, 23).
- "What good is it for a man to gain the whole world, yet forfeit his soul?" (Mark 8:36).

- "Do not store up for yourselves treasures on earth . . . but . . . in heaven. For where your treasure is, there your heart will be also" (Matt. 6:19–21).

- "No one can serve two masters. You cannot serve both God and Money" (Matt. 6:24).

Q: *Must my knowledge and understanding stay within some fixed limits?*

A: Knowledge and understanding of nature and the world are limited by their complexity as well as by man's finite mental and cognitive faculties. Knowledge of the spiritual is limited to what God has chosen to reveal, and by man's sin-restricted spiritual discernment. All man's current knowledge is distorted by his sin.

- "The fear of the LORD is the beginning of knowledge" (Prov. 1:7).

- "I consider everything a loss compared to the surpassing greatness of knowing Christ Jesus my Lord" (Phil. 3:8).

- "None of the wicked will understand [prophecy] . . ." (Dan. 12:10).

- "The man without the Spirit does not accept the things that come from the Spirit of God, for they are foolishness to him, and he cannot understand them, because they are spiritually discerned" (1 Cor. 2:14).

- "For we know in part and we prophesy in part, but when perfection comes, the imperfect disappears" (1 Cor. 13:9–10).

- "Now we see but a poor reflection as in a mirror; then we shall see face to face. Now I know in part; then I shall know fully, even as I am fully known" (1 Cor. 13:12).

Q: *How can I find real inner peace in this turbulent world?*

A: For any sinful man the way to inner peace starts with making peace with God, with removal of sin's enmity through accepting the sacrifice of Jesus Christ. Then inward peace can follow, unhindered by the world's strife.

- "Peace I [Jesus] leave with you; my peace I give you. I do not give to you as the world gives. Do not let your hearts be troubled and do not be afraid" (John 14:27).

- "I [Jesus] have told you these things, so that you may have peace. In this world you will have trouble. But take heart! I have overcome the world" (John 16:33).

- "May the God of hope fill you with all joy and peace as you trust in him, so that you may overflow with hope by the power of the Holy Spirit. The God of peace be with you all. Amen" (Rom. 15:13, 33).

- "And the peace of God, which transcends all understanding, will guard your hearts and your minds in Christ Jesus" (Phil. 4:7).

Q: *Whom can I trust and rely upon?*

A: Trust in the LORD God is the essence of biblical faith. The Bible calls for abandoning all trust in one's own resources, and casting oneself unreservedly on the mercy of God, relying entirely on the finished work of Christ, on God's promises, and on the power of the Holy Spirit. Trust, in the Bible, implies obedience.

- "It is better to take refuge in the LORD than to trust in man" (Ps. 118:8).
- "Trust in the LORD with all your heart and lean not on your own understanding" (Prov. 3:5).
- "Whoever trusts in the LORD is kept safe" (Prov. 29:25).
- "'Have faith in God,' Jesus answered" (Mark 11:22).
- "Who shall separate us from the love of Christ? . . . [N]either death nor life, neither angels nor demons, neither the present nor the future, nor any powers, neither height nor depth, nor anything else in all creation, will be able to separate us from the love of God that is in Christ Jesus our Lord" (Romans 8:35, 38–39).

Q: *What are the right criteria for life's important decisions?*

A: Compliance with God's will, as revealed in the Gospel of Jesus Christ, brings glory to God, and therefore it is the only valid criterion for all decisions.

- "Judge for yourselves whether it is right in God's sight to obey you [rulers] rather than God" (Acts 4:19).
- "Our Father in heaven, . . . [Y]our will be done on earth as it is in heaven" (Matt. 6:9, 10).
- "For whoever does the will of my Father in heaven is my brother and sister and mother" (Matt. 12:50).
- "[W]hatever you do, do it all for the glory of God" (1 Cor. 10:31).

Q: *Are there any objective ethical truths?*

A: In sharp contrast to philosophical ethic, biblical ethic is God-centered. Moral teachings are phrased as commandments based on revelation. The basic ethical demand is to imitate God as He revealed Himself in Jesus Christ. This leads to the biblical concept of love, love that has no limits, and operates independently of any loveliness, or appeal, or charm, or beauty, because it is an action of will, not of emotion.

- "[T]he word of the LORD is right and true" (Ps. 33:4).

- "If you hold to my teaching, you are really my disciples. Then you will know the truth, and the truth will set you free" (John 8:31, 32).

- "Jesus replied, 'Love the Lord your God with all your heart and with all your soul and with all your mind.' This is the first and greatest commandment. And the second is like it: 'Love your neighbor as yourself.' All the Law and the Prophets hang on these two commandments" (Matt. 22:37–40).

- "If I speak in the tongues of . . . angels, . . . have the gift of prophecy and can fathom all mysteries and all knowledge . . . , . . . and have a faith that can move mountains, but have not love, I am nothing. . . . Love never fails. . . . And now these three remain: faith, hope, and love. But the greatest of these is love" (1 Cor. 13:1–13, selections).

Q: *Why is there affliction in this world?*

A: All calamities in the world are consequent upon man's sin and reflect God's justice. They are always less severe than man deserves because God's justice is tempered by His mercy. God is glorified in affliction of the wicked, that they may know that He is the Lord. Afflictions are beneficial also to the believers, and should be expected.

- "I am the LORD, and there is no other. . . . I bring prosperity and create disaster; I, the LORD, do all these things" (Isa. 45:6, 7).

- "You [LORD] laid burdens on our backs" (Ps. 66:11).

- "For hardship does not spring from the soil, nor does trouble sprout from the ground. Yet man is born to trouble as surely as sparks fly upward" (Job 5:6–7).

- "Christ suffered for you, leaving you an example, that you should follow in his steps" (1 Pet. 2:21).

- "If we endure, we will also reign with him" (2 Tim. 2:12).

Q: *Why is there something rather than nothing?*

A: Creation must be understood as a free act of God determined only by His sovereign will, and in no way as a necessary act. He chose to do so, and thus confirmed His independence of His creation, His self-existence and self-sufficiency. God created the world for the manifestation of the glory of His eternal power, wisdom, and goodness.

- "In the beginning God created the heaven and the earth" (Gen. 1:1).

- "[W]hen I [the LORD] laid the earth's foundation . . . the morning stars sang together and all the angels shouted for joy" (Job 38:4–7, selections).

- "For by him [the Lord Jesus Christ] all things were created: things in heaven and on earth, visible and invisible, whether thrones or powers or rulers or authorities; all things were created by him and for him" (Col. 1:16).

- "The LORD works out everything for his own ends—even the wicked for a day of disaster" (Prov. 16:4).

Q: *What about death?*

A: From man's point of view, death is the most natural of all things, and it seems to be a biological necessity. Physical decay and ultimate dissolution of the body seem inescapable. Yet the Bible speaks of man's death as the result of sin, as a divine penalty, not as something inherently natural. The most serious consequence of sin is "the second death" signifying eternal perdition.

- "[W]hen you eat of it [the tree of the knowledge of good and evil] you will surely die" (Gen. 2:17).

- "By the sweat of your brow you will eat your food until you return to the ground, since from it you were taken; for dust you are and to dust you will return" (Gen. 3:19).

- "Sin entered the world through one man, and death through sin, and in this way death came to all men, because all sinned" (Rom. 5:12).

- "There is . . . a time to be born, and a time to die" (Eccl. 3:2).

- "Even though I walk through the valley of the shadow of death, I will fear no evil, for you [LORD] are with me" (Ps. 23:4).

- "For the wages of sin is death, but the gift of God is eternal life in Christ Jesus our Lord" (Rom. 6:23).

- "Precious in the sight of the LORD is the death of his saints" (Ps. 116:15).

Q: *What comes after death?*

A: Despite its reality and apparent finality, the Bible does not consider death as the final end of man's existence, as humanists hope and the secular world is convinced, but as the beginning of a new, different existence, with God's judgment of resurrected individuals as its first major event. The character and quality of this new existence will depend on the verdict: if declared righteous, i.e., one's name has been found written in the Book of Life, eternal life in the presence of God will follow; otherwise, eternity will be spent in separation from God.[1]

- "[M]an is destined to die once, and after that to face judgment" (Heb. 9:27).

- "For he has set a day when he will judge the world" (Acts 17:31).

- "Multitudes who sleep in the dust of the earth will awake: some to everlasting life, others to shame and everlasting contempt" (Dan. 12:2).
- "[A] time is coming . . . when the dead will hear the voice of the Son of God . . . and come out—those who have done good will rise to live, and those who have done evil will rise to be condemned" (John 5:25, 29).
- "The sea gave up the dead that were in it, and death and Hades gave up the dead that were in them, and each person was judged according to what he had done. Then death and Hades were thrown into the lake of fire. The lake of fire is the second death. If anyone's name was not found written in the book of life, he was thrown into the lake of fire" (Rev. 20:13–15).
- "The last enemy to be destroyed is death" (1 Cor. 15:26).
- "Death has been swallowed up in victory" (1 Cor. 15:54).

The clear, definite, and authoritative answers the Bible provides to the stated and many other questions make dispensable a study of knowledge not based on the biblical text of God's revelation. They also stimulate in man two opposite responses. One, quite frequent, is the attitude of man putting himself into the role of examiner and referee determining what, if anything, God actually said. This attitude emulates the crafty serpent's of old powerful temptation to question God's truthfulness: "Did God really say . . . ?" (Gen. 3:1). Consequences of this position are well documented in chapters three to nine of the Book of Genesis and visible today around us in the violent and immoral state of human society and affairs, and in the ever-increasing number of improvement suggestions and self-appointed reformers.

The second and proper response is described in the episode of Saul's conversion on his journey to Damascus when he, trembling and astonished, blurted out the only meaningful set of words fitting his situation, "Lord, what do You want me to do?" (Acts 9:6 NKJV).

INVITATION

For those who feel closer to Saul, the later apostle Paul, than to Eve in the relaxed, safe, and peaceful setting of the Garden of Eden, it is beneficial to reconsider the overall flow of human life, its critical points, and life's own crucial decisions over which he or she has individually full control:

Conception—No

Abortion—No

Accepting God's Offer—Yes

Death—No

Final Judgment—No

Out of these five decisions critical for both earthly and eternal life only one is in man's own control: the reaction to God's free offer of reconciliation presented to man in the life, death on the cross, and subsequent resurrection of Jesus Christ, the only begotten Son of God. Even though no man has full control over the circumstances in which this decision is made, its consequences are well known and, therefore, the responsibility for it is unquestionably in the hands of each individual. There is an inevitable cause-effect relation between the crucial personal decision and its eternal consequences as established by God.

The rationality of the decision to accept God's offer has been described by one of the best minds—Blaise Pascal—in his wager:[2]

- If God does not exist, but we still live according to the Gospel, we will suffer small risks of human rejection but enjoy the benefits of a humanly satisfying life.

- If God does not exist, and we don't live according to the biblical Gospel, no harm to our lives will be done because our behavior is irrelevant.

- If God does exist, and we live according to the biblical Gospel, we will surely receive a major reward in eternal life with God in heaven.

- If God does exist, and we don't live according to the biblical Gospel, we will surely suffer a major loss in eternal life separated from God in hell.

This so-called "binary decision table" rationally identifies the acceptance of life under God's revealed will as the best strategy possible. Obedience to God's will based on fear, formal logic, or plain and simple shrewdness is unquestionably better in consequences than disobedience. The Bible confirms that sinners are actually closer to God than fools. It is the fool who says in his heart "There is no God" (Ps. 14:1) and will be held up to shame (Prov. 3:35), while a shrewd man may earn commendation (Luke 16:1–8). The limitation of this approach is in its inability to reach the full potential benefits of the new relationship with God, who prefers obedience based on trust and His demonstrated love.

Another argument rests with the temporal character of the era of God's grace, which makes man's salvation as easy as accepting a valuable gift from a loving father. The Bible's confirmation that the time of grace, the biblical time of the Gentiles, will come to an end when the predefined number of saved Christians will be achieved, as well as the uncertainty of man's time of death, make the personal decision not only critically important, but urgent as well.

What, then, does God want a man to do to show interest in His offer, and start a new life in accordance with His will? The simplicity of God's requirements is strikingly moving, and reflecting God's splendid tenderness and meekness toward His creation. Consider the few steps required:

- *Admit sin,* the rebellion against God, the refusal to respect His will and accept Him as the Lord, because all have sinned (Rom. 3:23).

- *Repent,* which means more than just to be sorry and apologize. The word "repent" covers also the meaning of "change"—change in attitude, change of mind, and change in the way of life. Repentance is the key first step to forgiveness of sin (Acts 3:19).

- *Believe in Jesus Christ;* this statement does not signify just an intellectual acceptance of some Christian doctrine, but a full trust in Jesus Christ, full confidence in His ability and willingness to lead His disciples through the rest of their lives from salvation to the eternal life in glory (John 11:25, 26).

- *Publicly and openly confess your faith,* "[I]f you confess with your mouth, 'Jesus is Lord,' and believe in your heart that God raised him from the dead, you will be saved" (Rom. 10:9). This is confirmed by Jesus' own warning: "[W]hoever acknowledges me before men, the Son of Man will also acknowledge him before the angels of God. But he who disowns me before men will be disowned before the angels of God" (Luke 12:8–9).

Published examples of simple confession statements are:

"O God, I am a sinner. I'm sorry for my sins. I'm willing to turn from my sins. I receive Jesus Christ as Savior. I confess Him as Lord. From this moment on I want to follow Him and serve Him in the fellowship of His church. In Christ's name. Amen."[3]

"I know the Lord knows my secret heart and wants me to know Him. As much as I know of me, I now trust to as much as I know Jesus Christ, my Lord and my Savior."[4]

The last required action of a public confession contains elements of a creed,[5] of a statement of faith that individuals, as well as Christian churches, prepare for use as authoritative declarations of certain articles of belief. The simplest confirmed version of a Christian creed is recorded in the Book of Acts (16:30, 31). As a reply to the Philippian jailer's question, "Sirs, what must I do to be saved?" Paul and Silas indicated that it is sufficient for his salvation if a man can truthfully say, I "believe in the Lord Jesus."[6] This single focus of the simplest confession on Jesus Christ demonstrates that He is the foundation of Christianity and plays the pivotal role in the implementation of God's plan, and in prophecies and revelations in both the Old and the New Testaments.

A simple review of the four required steps makes it clear that all is taking place in the spiritual realm. God does not require sacrifices, participation in religious ceremonies, fasting, some definite minimum amount of good deeds, etc., nothing from the visible material world. The whole affair of repentance and forgiveness is only between the Lord God and the repentant sinner simply because God is a Spirit, and because the visible price for the salvation has already been paid by Jesus Christ on the cross. Only later, the forgiven sinner returns to the world as the Lord's servant and brother with his own special mission.

This simplicity of the free offer is the crux of biblical Christianity. But it is also the stumbling block for religious Jews and even some tradition-bound Christians wanting to deserve God's salvation through a moral personal life, altruism demonstrated by good deeds, and religious piety. This simplicity—so contradictory to the views of many contemporary well-educated and noble people about ways to the top of the social ladder—demands a breakthrough in attitude and self-evaluation: from intellectual pride to the humility of a child (Matt. 18:2–4). To miss the importance of this change in personal disposition toward God's invitation will result in a serious error pointed to in the Book of Proverbs 14:12, "There is a way that seems right to a man, but in the end it leads to death."

CONSEQUENCES

The substantial difference between God's relationship with man and man's relation with the world's power holders is apparent in biblical messages about consequences. The world's reasoning rightly claims that the majority of consequences of human decisions and actions cannot be predicted due to the unknowns in the general dynamics of the world. Even in the domain of the human legal system, the adverse consequences of a committed crime for the guilty party are often unknown, or can be dismissed for some technicalities of the judicial process. But not with God! Because He, who has the future under His control and is just to man, revealed the established nonnegotiable consequences of both decision outcomes quite clearly in the Bible.

Consequences of Refusal

The only possible and permanent attitude of the holy and just God toward sin and related evil is summarized by the biblical term "wrath." Any tolerance of sin would defile God's holiness, devaluate His righteousness, and cause His love to turn into low-value sentimentality. Even though God's anger is tempered by His patience and mercy toward sinners, it is real, cannot be resisted, and has already been experienced by man in past terrors and afflictions. God's wrath is inevitably oriented toward unredeemed men, as seen in the destruction of the old world by the Flood (Gen. 7:21–23), dispersion of builders of the Tower of Babel (Gen. 11:8–9), destruction of Sodom and Gomorrah (Gen. 19:24–25), plagues of Egypt (Exod. 7:14–12:30), plague after the Israelites' worship of the golden calf (Exod. 32:33–35), death of Ananias and Sapphira for lying to the

Holy Spirit (Acts 5:1–11), etc. Looking to the future, the Bible is also full of warnings and woes oriented against, for example, Jerusalem and Judah (Isa. 3:1–9), the wicked (Isaiah 3:11), unrepentant cities (Matt. 11:20–24), teachers of the Law and Pharisees (Matt. 23:1–32), some churches (Rev. 2—3), and the whole unrepentant world (Rev. 8, 15, 16, and 18).

These warnings and woes are signs of the ultimate consequences of man's erroneous wish to justify himself and the world through even well-meant human effort, of his improper desire to attain power in the world through progress, revolutions, or the Pharisaic trend toward false religions or atheism. They must be taken as seriously as promises of God's love, established covenants, and blessings. Despite the frightening images these woes invoke, they are intended to play a positive role in the lives of individuals by installing fear of the Lord as one possible motivation for repentance. On this background of the coming wrath, the redeeming life, work, death, and resurrection of Jesus Christ shines in its absolute value for each and every member of the human race. He is the only deliverer from this coming wrath with eternal consequences, wrath that is to come in this age (1 Thess. 1:10).

Consequences of Accepting God's Grace

God's forgiveness, offered through Jesus Christ, makes God's amnesty for sinners accessible. When accepted, this grace (unlimited mercy) creates a new life situation as different from fear of wrath as the difference between heaven and hell, and, personally, between damnation and salvation.

The first positive result is in its contribution to God's glory. Jesus Himself confirms that "there is more rejoicing in heaven over one sinner who repents than over ninety-nine righteous persons" (Luke 15:7). This joy is illustrated in parables of the lost sheep and of the lost coin, in the same chapter.

A second benefit goes to the both known and anonymous witnesses who, under the guidance of the Holy Spirit, brought the good news of God's grace to the attention of the repenting individual. "Whoever turns a sinner away from his error will save him from death and cover over a multitude of sins" (James 5:20).

And then, of course, the overwhelming personal benefits traceable to God's love, such as forgiveness of sins (Acts 10:43), salvation (Rom. 3:24–25, 10:9), name written in heaven in the Book of Life (Luke 10:20), spiritual birth (John 3:5–7 and 2 Cor. 5:17), adoption into God's household (Eph. 2:19), guidance by the Holy Spirit (John 16:13), wisdom (James 1:5), protection (1 Cor. 10:13), peace of mind (John 14:27 and Phil. 4:6–7), joy (John 15:11), security (Phil. 4:19), eternal life with Jesus Christ (John 10:28), and many others.

The description of the abundance and quality of gifts made ready by God for His sons is summarized in 1 Corinthians 2:9: "No eye has seen, no ear has heard, no mind has conceived what God has prepared for those who love Him."

The New Testament is full of God's promises for many aspects of the Christian life.

The Cost of Discipleship

As already mentioned, there is no cost associated with the forgiveness of sins offered through God's grace. But in the consequent role of servants, some "cost" may be incurred. Jesus Himself indicated the possibility of discomfort; even the possibility of martyrdom is mentioned (Matt. 16:24), and later actually foretold (Matt. 24:9). The accuracy of Jesus' foresight is well documented in the church's history and reported upon in today's news as well. Christians are still being martyred. Consistently with God's love and promised care, these indications of potential suffering during earthly life in God's service are accompanied with encouragements and assurances that God will not allow Christians to be tested beyond what they can bear, that He will provide the support of personal strength needed, and that in all things God works for the good of those who love Him and have been called according to His purpose (Rom. 8:28). The apostle Paul, who himself endured many hardships, considered his own worldly suffering not worthy of much attention in comparison to the expected glory of the promised eternal life with Christ. He also pointed to the fact, to be always kept in Christians' mind, that God did not spare His own Son Jesus Christ from earthly suffering.

Throughout the Bible, it is possible to recognize the final purpose of hardship and suffering God allows to enter the lives of His people. From the unparalleled story of Job, to the wisdom reflected in Proverbs 3:12 ("the LORD disciplines those he loves, as a father the son he delights in") and confirmed in Hebrews 12:5–11, to Jesus' words in Revelation 3:19, the Bible always points to the affected individual's benefits, and to the eternal purpose of God's plan for His creation. Acknowledging God as the Lord means to accept with thanks both what our incomplete human understanding judges pleasant and troublesome (Job 2:10).

Another component of the cost of discipleship is the increased spiritual and cultural distance from the world. The change of the personal value system associated with accepting Jesus' advice and promise, "[S]eek first his [God's] kingdom and his righteousness, and all these [worldly] things will be given to you as well" (Matt. 6:33), will accelerate with increased knowledge of the Bible and God's revelation. This new knowledge will strongly influence understanding of the fact that man cannot serve two masters, and that man's possessions, and their character, are his principal motivator. This insight will turn man's preferences in favor of God versus world and money, and in favor of treasures in heaven versus those on earth.

Believers also experience the persistent conflict between remnants of the old sinful human nature and the influence of the in-dwelling Holy Spirit (Rom.

7:14–25) and will come to the recognition that it is the inner motivation to do the will of God that is the principal distinction separating a Christian from a culturally motivated moral man.

New spiritual perspective may require reassessment of the relationship to one's own family, and to political and social institutions as well. Topics such as participation in political activities, power structure, and secular organizations in general, must be now addressed with appropriate biblical messages in mind. Levels of patriotism, loyalty to family, to a visible church organization, to one's employer, and obedience to man-made legal systems are also set for reevaluation from the biblical perspective. These reevaluations must reflect biblical realism and God's focus on individuals, as well as the believer's understanding of God's will for the direction of his life, and be done in the spirit of humility. They also reflect realization that only individual human beings are real; mankind, society, race, nation, social class, company, etc., are abstractions.

All these consequences are signs of new life under the lordship of Jesus Christ. But in all this, focus on God's glory is most important. Christians are called by the pleasure of God's will, by His desire for close intimate relationships, by His love. These are the foundations for assurance of guidance and help in daily life, and for inner peace, peace transcending all human understanding (Phil. 4:7) promised by Jesus Christ Himself (John 14:27).

A FEW PRACTICAL SUGGESTIONS

Because spiritual birth is a real breakthrough in a life that started with a breakthrough in attitude toward God and His invitation to new relationship, breakthrough in knowledge of God's revelation must follow. That is where individual Bible reading, a group Bible study, Christian radio messages, and local church preaching play important roles.[7] Then, knowledge of God's will for one's own personal life needs to be sought.

Prayer is an important tool as well. There is no need for elaborate calls to God; simple sharing of one's own problems, thanks for gifts of daily life experiences, and petitions on behalf of others, in a way similar to communicating with a trusted friend or loving father, are best. The primary attitudes in prayer are in acknowledgment of God's lordship, in sincere thanks for His love visible in daily care, and "Your will be done" attitude in all petitions.

Christian behavior must also be practiced. A local church assembly may be the best training ground. It makes sense to look for a Bible-believing community with well-visible love for each other. See whether the church leader's life reflects the life of Christ, and whether salvation by grace through faith in Jesus, not by works, is proclaimed. Reliable Christian teachers and leaders will never point to themselves, but always to Jesus, the way, the truth, and the life (John 14:6). To find such a community may not be easy. The search for it may well become a test of endurance, practice of spiritual discernment, humility, and understanding that God's view of time is different from man's. There are many evangelistic organizations and fellow believers ready to help.

With the breakthrough in patterns of behavior will come the desired peace of mind, and the fruits of the work of the in-dwelling Holy Spirit: love, joy, peace, long-suffering, gentleness, goodness, faith, meekness, temperance (Gal. 5:22–23), and personal involvement in the great commission of spreading the Gospel. Here again, the key is in accepting God's will, His timing, His lordship, and His assignment, in full trust and knowledge that in all things God works for the benefits of those who love Him (Rom. 8:28).

BIBLICAL VIEW OF HUMAN KNOWLEDGE

The clarity of biblical view of the rebellious man who strives to replace God and put himself in the position of arbiter, authority, etc., brings proper insight into the earlier discussed intellectual chaos and vanity of man's intellectual efforts, and their causes as well.

The basis for this perspective may be found in biblical wisdom revealed in Ecclesiastes 1:9: "What has been will be again, what has been done will be done again; there is nothing new under the sun."

This insight verifies the postmodernist observation of incommensurability of human conceptual systems and perceives all human intellectual effort as nothing more than distortion of the truth revealed in the Bible. The whole history of ideas is, therefore, nothing else than history of heresy, history of opinions and doctrines, purposefully or incidentally, at variance with the teaching of the Bible. For example:

Biblical revelation/Substituted human ideas

- Personal God Yahweh/First cause, prime mover, the world is god, god as self-diversifying unity, god as final stage of cosmic process
- Knowledge through revelation/Knowledge through reason or through religious experience
- God's millennial kingdom/Utopian societies, communism, Hitler's one-thousand-year Reich, free market-based democracies under United Nations
- Creation out of nothing/Big Bang and other cosmogonies
- Heaven/Parallel universes
- Secondary creation/Evolutionary theories
- Man as image of God/Man as descendant of humanoids
- The Bible/Works of Marx, Mao, etc.
- God's wrath/Atomic war, environmental disaster

- History of salvation/Progress, invisible hand, objective economic forces
- Focus on the individual/Focus on classes, public, citizens, taxpayers, mankind, ethnic groups
- God's commandments/Ethical and moral systems
- God's laws/Man's legal systems
- Good and evil/Moral virtue and moral corruption, legal and illegal
- Sin/Crime, offense, transgression
- Grace/Tolerance
- Justice/Fairness, human rights
- Priests/Leaders
- Death as wages of sin/Death as biological necessity

Careful students of the Bible and human knowledge will undoubtedly discover biblical roots in every human idea, concept, opinion, etc., simply because man is incapable of suprahuman thoughts, and because all human thinking in the world of ideas starts with the often unrecognized, old temptation, "Did God really say . . . ?" known from the beginning. Man's false self-understanding, so prominent in our times, is based on humanistic illusions that praise man for his ideas of progress, freedom, privileged status, utopian social goals, etc., all claimed as achieved or achievable by humans themselves without any help from God. As a result, mankind perceives itself as an autonomous community with power to commission selected individuals with special leadership powers and put them in control over the destiny of others.

The main danger of false teaching is its tendency toward idolatry and dogmatism. Idolatry of one's own personal life or ambitions leads to hypocritical behavior, to play-acting in order to advance one's social position through deception of the observers. This manipulative and opportunistic abuse of situation is a real danger for persons in leadership, who may be tempted toward hiding personal doubts, or toward abuse of the granted authority.

Christian churches are not immune to false teaching and idolatry either. Legalistic deformation of Christianity idolizes observation of ethical or liturgical rules, and presents them as the primary objectives in the believer's life. The roots of leaning toward legalistic tendencies seem to be in human psyche ready to accept enjoyment of, and false reliance upon, ceremonies and rules as a way to lift the burden of responsibility for decisions and their consequences.

Because all forms of idolatry represent a common temptation to which all humans, including Christians, have an inclination to succumb, the biblical message advises how to deal with them as well. The key word in this message is repentance, which includes ideas of critical awareness of the Word of God and human reality, acknowledgment of them, and openness and willingness to change. Such conversion opens the door to the mystery of God, namely Christ, in whom are hidden all the treasures of wisdom and knowledge (Col. 2:2–3).

FUNDAMENTALS OF BIBLICAL CHRISTIANITY

The message underlying all previous discussions was that biblical Christianity, in its practicality, cannot be considered a systematic view of the world, a philosophical system, an ideology, a religion,[8] or a generalization of human discoveries, because they all carry a flavor of idolatry by absolutizing a product of the human mind, and also because God's revelation cannot be put in a straight-jacket of any human conceptual, ethical, or legal system.

Then, what is biblical Christianity? Taking into account the practical aspects of witnessing as described in the Bible and, later, documented in Christian literature by profiles of individual Christians, it is possible to think of biblical Christianity as a personal life lived in respect, trust, and love to the biblical God, in ultimate allegiance to Jesus Christ, and in love of other human beings; a life founded on beliefs[9] in:

- God the Creator and Lord over man's life

- God the Judge, whose holiness is offended by the fallen man's sinful nature and behavior, and whose justice demands punishment by death

- Jesus Christ, Son of God, who voluntarily accepted man's punishment in His death on the cross and, by that, satisfied demands of God's justice and opened the way to God's grace

- God's grace offering forgiveness of sin to all through repentance, faith in the resurrected Jesus Christ as personal Savior, and public declaration of this faith

- New life according to the will of God the Father, under the lordship of Jesus Christ, and the leadership of the Holy Spirit

- The Bible as the revealed word of God

This statement of beliefs reflects the rudimentary biblical advice, "If you confess with your mouth, 'Jesus is Lord,' and believe in your heart that God raised him from the dead, you will be saved" (Rom. 10:9). Classic expression of Christian belief is found in the Apostolic Creed,[10] which, as the Lord's Prayer is the Prayer of all prayers, and the Ten Commandments the Law of all laws, is the Creed of all creeds:

1. I believe in God the Father Almighty,
2. And in Jesus Christ, his only Son, our Lord;
3. Who was born by the Holy Ghost of the Virgin Mary;
4. Was crucified under Pontius Pilate and was buried;
5. The third day he rose from the dead;

6. He ascended into heaven; and sitteth on the right hand of the Father;
7. From thence he shall come to judge the quick and the dead;
8. And in the Holy Ghost;
9. The Holy Church;
10. The forgiveness of sins;
11. The resurrection of the body.

In the Protestant tradition, biblical Christianity can also be defined as man's acceptance of the originally intended relationship with his God based on the kernel of beliefs expressed in Martin Luther's words as life by:

sola fide . . . faith alone (i.e., faith in Jesus Christ),

sola gratia . . . grace alone (i.e., by grace of God the Father), and

sola Scriptura . . . the Bible alone (i.e., under the guidance of the Holy Spirit).

True biblical Christianity requires spiritual birth, literally to be born again, this time not of flesh but of the Spirit, not of the will of man but by the will of God (John 3:3–8). This birth, of course, involves the whole person: the intellect for recognizing and understanding of God's offer, will to accept it and turn away from sin, emotion of sorrow when admitting sin and of joy in having the burden lifted, consciousness when revising one's own value system to match it with the will of God and His definition of good and evil, and behavior in service to the Lord as witness to the Gospel. That is why the Bible describes the totality of the true conversion in relationship with God as new life. Christian God, in contrast to gods of other religions, does not require any work or sacrifice, just willingness on the part of man to seriously turn away from sin toward Him. Life in the framework of biblical Christianity is expected to result in spiritual peace, different from the one the world seeks (John 14:27), and reflect fruits of the Spirit such as kindness, meekness, forgiveness, humility, wisdom, and love (Col. 3:12–17). Being available by a simple request to God in the name of Jesus Christ (John 14:13–14), biblical Christianity is the best offer ever made to man.

God's messages and invitation to man to reestablish proper relationship with his Creator through Jesus Christ are clear in their confirmation of God's impartiality and of the universality of His love toward people. In a strong contrast to man's ideologies, God's love is not selectively aimed, does not bestow special favors, nor does it pay unique respect to any person. This leads to a self-evident conclusion that biblical Christianity, due to its generic nondenominational universality, is also pertinent to everybody without respect to any social categorization, and without respect to an individual's physical or mental abilities or disabilities.

The simplicity of the very few actions needed to be assured about this new relationship with God is His purposeful strategy making His offer available to everyone, the scholar and the illiterate, the old and wise as well as the young and inexperienced, the most pious person and the outlaw sentenced to death also.[11] If there is, or ever has been, a real situation of an "equal opportunity," an opportunity to which man can freely respond, not an equal inevitability such as of death and of taxes, biblical Christianity is it.

Biblical Christianity gratefully accepts God's grace and its benefits, but also recognizes the price Jesus paid on the cross to make them available (1 Cor. 6:20), and is willing to bear the temporary, in human perspective potentially "adverse," consequences of being a servant to Christ in this Gospel-unfriendly world. Accepting Jesus Christ as personal Lord is a full-time commitment with impact on all aspects of life and, therefore, its cost is not to be underestimated. Considerations of cost are a fitting response to God's openness and honesty; there is no hypocrisy, no false promises, no hidden agenda, only exciting challenge.[12]

Biblical Christianity does not impose any requirements to join or approve any aspect of the general or historical or traditional Christianity as projected in Christian politics, Christian economic thinking, Christian ethics, etc. It does not require acceptance of any institutionalized church authority, be it carried by a person or a dogma or a set of behavioral or liturgical rules. God's offer of salvation is also universal, not limited to a cultural sphere of historical Christendom. On the other hand, biblical Christianity responds to biblical commandments of meeting together (Heb. 10:25), loving one another (1 John 4:7–12), submitting to one another (Eph. 5:21), testing the spirits (1 John 4:1–6), and continually giving to God praises (Heb. 13:15) and thanks (Eph. 5:20), as well as to other commandments and admonitions found in the Bible, in the process of a believer growing toward spiritual maturity.

In contrast to traditional Christianity, which concerns itself with church organization and hierarchies, systematized teachings, role in human life, tradition, liturgy, moral conduct, social and political influence, etc., biblical Christianity, as the name suggests, focuses primarily on Jesus Christ as fulfillment of Old Testament prophecies, His life, words, death, resurrection, and aftermath as witnessed and documented in the New Testament. Biblical Christianity is the conscious personal fellowship with Jesus Christ, fellowship which turns the biblical message— initially second-hand information—into certainty of personal knowledge and experience. In other words, biblical Christianity stands in contrast to institutionalized Christianity, as the Old Testament's prophetic faith to priestly legalism and formalism.

CONCLUSIONS

It is satisfying that our review of the main bodies of knowledge available to man led not only to answers to stated questions, but also to the identification of

God's biblical revelation as the best source for making life's most important decision, the decision with eternal consequences. There is no more urgent and important decision in life than that of reestablishment of proper personal relation with God, man's Creator and final Judge.

It is amazing that achievement of this breakthrough in life and new relation is, thanks to God's love, so simple and with outcome guaranteed by God's word, by God who cannot lie. Only to turn to Jesus is what is needed to come to rest and peace in His salvation. He has done all the essential and necessary work on the cross where He died for our sins. Now all that must be done is to accept Him in trust as personal Savior and Lord.

"God has given us eternal life, and this life is in His Son. He who has the Son has life; he who does not have the Son of God does not have life. I write these things to you who believe in the name of the Son of God so *that you may know* that you have eternal life" (Emphasis added) (1 John 5:11–13).

God's invitation to accept His gift of salvation is not an invitation to a sweepstakes with some low numerical odds. Believers adopted into the family of God are assured about their new status, they know that they have eternal life, that there are unimaginable rewards prepared for them. For those who welcomed Christ into their lives and are faithfully living, heavenly rewards are guaranteed by God. It is the best offer ever made to man.

Comparing results of our study with findings of the seventeenth-century pilgrim on his journey through his world's society, as described by the earlier-introduced J. A. Comenius, confirms biblical wisdom that there is nothing new under the sun, and the truth that now, as then, the paradise of the heart rests in God's love, and is available just for asking through Jesus Christ.

Dear friend, may God help you to make the decision to ask Him for forgiveness, and to commit your life to Christ. You will be glad forever that you did. Amen.

NOTES AND REFERENCES

Introduction

[1]Dante Alighiery, *The Divine Comedy,* translated by Henry F. Cary (New York: P. F. Collier & Son Corporation, 1969 printing), 5.

[2]Goethe's *Faust,* translated by Walter Kaufman (New York: Doubleday, 1961), 107, vv. 562–564.

[3]John Comenius, *The Labyrinth of the World and the Paradise of the Heart,* translation by Howard Louthan and Andrea Sterk (Mahwah, N.J.: Paulist Press, 1998).

[4]John Amos Comenius (1592–1670) is widely acknowledged as one of the most important representatives of European pedagogy and often considered the father of modern education. Comenius was a pastor, spiritual leader, and the last bishop (elder) of the Bohemian Unity of Brethren (*Unitas Fratrum*), a Czech Protestant group inspired by the life and work of Jan Hus (1374–1415) who was burned at the stake during the session of the Council of Constance. Comenius had been forced into exile by the Habsburg's decree of 1627, and spent part of his life in Silesia, Poland, England, and Sweden. At the age of sixty-four he finally moved to Holland and, for the rest of his life, settled in Amsterdam. Comenius provided inspiration for trends in the Pietist movement (Francke and Zinzendorf) and influenced the thinking of Leibniz and Herder.

[5]There is an old comparison of the Bible-based Christian life to the one of a child securely living in his father's house, accepting sufficiency of only a superficial understanding of its construction and economics.

Chapter 1

[1]This doctrine claims that "general causes and principles" of philosophers are "higher" and "more ultimate" than those discovered, e.g., by science. Whether this is true is itself a difficult philosophical problem requiring resolution of the assumption that philosophy alone involves no presuppositions.

[2]Modern philosophy considers these seven key problems:
- Theology is the inquiry into the existence and nature of God
- Metaphysics is the inquiry into the nature of ultimate reality
- Epistemology is the inquiry into the nature of knowledge

- Ethics is the inquiry into the principles and presuppositions that are operative in our moral judgment
- Politics is the inquiry into the theory of the state
- History is the inquiry into its controlling patterns and regularities
- Aesthetics is the inquiry into the essence and nature of art as a special activity

Re.: Alburey Castell, *An Introduction to Modern Philosophy* (London: The Macmillan Company, 1963).

[3]The word "metaphysics" derives from Greek *meta ta physica* meaning, literally, "after the things of nature," and points to discussion topics removed from sense perception and, therefore, difficult to understand.

[4]A. N. Whitehead, *Process and Reality* (New York: Macmillan Company, 1941), 4.

[5]All the highly simplified descriptions of individual schools of thought, metaphysical systems, ideologies, theories, etc., used in this book, have been checked against definitions and information in these principal sources:

- Paul Edwards (ed. in chief), *The Encyclopedia of Philosophy* (New York: Macmillan Company, 1967).
- Philip P. Wiener (ed. in chief), *Dictionary of the History of Ideas* (New York: Charles Scribner's Sons, 1974).
- Alan Bullock and Oliver Stallybrass (eds.), *The Harper Dictionary of Modern Thought* (New York: Harper & Row, Publishers, 1977).
- Jess Stein (ed. in chief), *The Random House Dictionary of the English Language,* The Unabridged Edition (New York: Random House, Inc., 1969).
- *Encyclopaedia Britannica* (Chicago: William Benton Publisher, 1969).

[6]Huston Smith, *Beyond the Post-modern Mind,* part 1 (New York: Crossroad, 1982).

[7]A. J. Ayer, *Philosophy in the Twentieth Century,* chap. 1 (New York: Random House, 1982).

[8]Madan Sarup, *Post-Structuralism and Postmodernism,* 2nd ed. (Athens, Ga.: The University of Georgia Press, 1993).

[9]Rodollphe Gasché, "Infrastructures and Systemacity" in John Sallis (ed.), *Deconstruction and Philosophy* (Chicago: The University of Chicago Press, 1987).

[10]John Passmore, *Recent Philosophers* (La Salle, Ill.: Open Court Publishing Co., 1990).

[11]Among the most influential belong Thomas More's *Utopia,* Tommaso Campanella's *The City of the Sun,* and Francis Bacon's *New Atlantis.*

[12]Alan Ryan, "The L-word," in *The New York Review of Books,* Sept. 24, 1998, 50–54.

[13]Alan Brinkley, *Liberalism and Its Discontent* (Cambridge, Mass.: Harvard University Press, 1998).

[14]David Brooks, "What's Left of Liberalism, " in *Commentary,* May 1995, 63–65.

[15]This is, so called, complexity thesis, currently gaining importance even in natural sciences, such as physics of elementary particles and biology.

[16]Example of such metaphysical principle could be speculation-based new human rights with benefits not yet historically verified.

[17]Walter Laqueur (ed.), *Fascism, A Reader's Guide* (Los Angeles: University of California Press, 1976).

[18]Walter Laqueur, *Fascism: Past, Present, Future* (New York: Oxford University Press, 1996).

[19]*Encyclopaedia Britannica,* vol. 16 (Chicago: William Benton Publisher, 1969), 93–96.

[20]Louise M. Anthony and Charlotte Witt (eds.), *A Mind of One's Own: Feminist Essays on Reason and Objectivity* (Boulder, Colo.: Westview, 1994).

[21]Christina Hoff Sommers, *Who Stole Feminism? How Women Have Betrayed Women* (New York: Simon & Schuster, 1994).

[22]Nathan Perlmutter and Ruth Ann Perlmutter, *The Real Anti-Semitism in America* (New York: Arbor House, 1982).

[23]The perception of Jews as "Christ killers" and of the church as "New Israel" was common in the medieval institutionalized church, and may be found alive even in the present.

[24]Jean-Paul Sartre, *Anti-Semite and Jew* (New York: Schocken Books, 1946).

[25]Democrats' defense of a Jew as just another man equal with the rest of humanity strips him of his religion, family, ethnic community, culture, etc., with the goal to assimilate him with the other members of the society. This brings a result Jews don't like for its similarity with results of other strategies of extermination.

[26]John E. Smith, *Quasi-Religions: Humanism, Marxism, and Nationalism* (New York: St. Martin's Press, 1994).

[27]Allan Bloom, *The Closing of the American Mind* (New York: Simon and Schuster, 1987), or Bruce S. Thornton, *Plagues of the Mind* (Wilmington, DE: ISI Books, 1999).

[28]This cycle has been originally described in the *Third Book of Herodotus* in a report on an interesting conversation among seven Persian wise men discussing, in time of throne vacancy, what they would like to see in their country. Later this view has been also associated with Plato.

[29]Some of the observations of Hegel's philosophical thought are extremely well formulated by C. J. Friedrich in his introduction to Hegel's work.

[30]Georg Wilhelm Friedrich Hegel, *The Philosophy of Human History* (New York: Dover Publications, 1956).

[31]Hegel's notion of Germanic people includes the French, the English, and the rest of the Western world, i.e., the whole Western civilization. In the original work, Hegel distinguishes between *Germanisch* (= Germanic), and *Deutsch* (= German).

[32]Frederick Engels, *Herr Eugen Dühring's Revolution in Science* (Anti-Dühring) (New York: International Publishers, 1966).

[33]Karl Marx, "The Communist Manifesto" in Saxe Commins and Robert N. Linscott (eds.), *Man and State: The Political Philosophers* (New York: Random House, 1947).

[34]Robert L. Heilbroner, *The Worldly Philosophers,* 4th ed. (New York: Simon and Schuster, 1972).

[35]Karl Kautsky, *The Materialist Conception of History* (New Haven: Yale University Press, 1988).

[36]Oswald Spengler, *The Decline of the West* (New York: Alfred A. Knopf, 1962).

[37]Arnold Toynbee, *A Study of History* (revised and abridged edition) (Oxford, U.K.: Oxford University Press, 1972).

[38]Arnold Toynbee, *Mankind and Mother Earth* (New York: Oxford University Press, 1976).

[39]Arnold Toynbee confirms that all races are capable of civilization. Though differences among races are natural, the differences among civilizations cannot be traced solely to them.

[40]Eugene Webb, *Eric Voegelin* (Seattle: University of Washington Press, 1981).

[41]Karl R. Popper, *The Open Society and Its Enemies,* 5th ed. (Princeton: Princeton University Press, 1966).

[42]In his book *The Poverty of Historicism,* Karl Popper defines historicism as an approach to the social sciences that assumes that historical prediction is their principal aim, and which postulates that this aim is attainable by discovering the "rhythms" or "patterns" or "laws" or "trends" that underlie the evolution of history.

[43]The accidents of wars, the careers of rulers, etc., Karl Popper calls "That history of international crime and mass murder which has been advertised as the history of mankind" (see note 42, pp. 29, 30).

[44]Barbara W. Tuchman, *Practicing History* (New York: Ballantine Books, 1982).

[45]Arthur M. Schlesinger Jr., *The Disuniting of America* (New York: Norton & Company, 1992), chap. 2.

[46]Francis Fukuyama, *The End of History and the Last Man* (New York: Avon, 1992).

[47]Robert L. Heilbroner, *The Future as History* (New York: Grove Press, 1959).

[48]John Passmore, *Recent Philosophers* (La Salle, Ill.: Open Court Publishing Co., 1990).

[49]In our time, this conflict of interest is formally handled in mathematics by the Decision Theory under the name "Consultant's Dilemma."

[50]Alain Finkielkraut, *The Defeat of the Mind* (New York: Columbia University Press, 1995).

[51]Oliver Leaman (ed.), *The Future of Philosophy: Towards the Twenty-first Century* (London: Routledge, 1998).

[52]Dave Breese, *Seven Men Who Rule the World from the Grave* (Chicago: Moody Press, 1990).

Chapter 2

[1]"A fool sees not the same tree as a wise man sees" (Blake).

[2]Charles van Doren, *A History of Knowledge* (New York: Ballantine Books, 1991), chap. 8.

[3]For example, popular memory of Newton is based on his discovery of the law of falling bodies initiated by the observation of an apple falling from an apple tree.

[4]John Ziman, *Reliable Knowledge* (Cambridge, U.K.: Cambridge Univ. Press, 1978), chap. 3.

[5]Thomas S. Kuhn, *The Structure of Scientific Revolutions* (Chicago: University of Chicago Press, 1970).

[6]The most frequently cited historical examples are ether and phlogiston.

[7]See, for example, a series of three articles about revolution in cosmology, "New Observations Have Smashed the Old View of Our Universe: What Now?" in *Scientific American,* January 1999, 45–69.

[8]John D. Barrow and Frank J. Tipler, *The Anthropic Cosmological Principle* (Oxford, U.K.: Oxford University Press, 1988).

[9] *Ibid.,* 16.

[10]*Ibid.,* 21.

[11]*Ibid.,* 23.

[12]Richard Morris, *The Edges of Science* (New York: Prentice Hall Press, 1990), chap. 9.

[13]Refer to, e.g., David Berlinski, "Was There a Big Bang?" in *Commentary,* February 1998, 28–38, and following discussion in *Commentary,* May 1998, 5–13.

[14]John D. Barrow, *Theories of Everything* (Oxford, U.K.: Claredon Press, 1991), 10.

[15]This situation is similar to the one near the end of the nineteenth century when many also felt the work of science almost done. The Prussian patent office

was actually closed down because no more inventions were expected to be made.

[16]Stephen W. Hawking, *A Brief History of Time* (New York: Bantam Books, 1988), 168.

[17]The Uncertainty Principle of quantum mechanics was discovered by Werner Heisenberg, a German physicist, in 1927, and states that it is impossible to measure the position and momentum of a subatomic particle simultaneously with more than strictly limited precision.

[18]A frequently used example is the inability to find the exact solution of the motion of three bodies in Newton's theory of gravity. Solution difficulties grow with the increased number of bodies mutually impacting each other.

[19]An example for such an optimistic perspective may be found in Steven Weinberg, *Dreams of a Final Theory* (New York: Pantheon Books, 1992).

[20]History of the search for a Unified Theory—the Holy Grail of modern science—and a forceful argument that one will never be found, with related dangers of undermining the rules of doing good science, are presented in David Lindley, *The End of Physics* (New York: Basic Books, 1993).

[21]Leon Lederman and Dick Teresi, *The God Particle* (New York: Houghton Mifflin Company, 1993).

[22]Selected statements from the last chapter "Recapitulation and Conclusion" of Charles Darwin's *The Origin of Species* (1859; reprint, Philadelphia: University of Pennsylvania Press, 1959).

[23]A reasonably well-written and sufficiently accurate introduction may be found in David J. Depew and Bruce H. Weber, *Darwinism Evolving* (Cambridge: MIT Press, 1994).

[24]Discussion of the most controversial issues, altruism and cooperation, is presented in Matt Ridley, *The Origin of Virtue* (New York: Viking Press, 1997). Systematic defense is provided in many publications, e.g., Stephen Jay Gould, *Wonderful Life* (New York: Norton: 1989), and *Bully for Brontosaurus* (New York: Norton, 1991).

[25]David Stove, in his *Darwinian Fairytales,* in one way admires Darwin's propositions as overwhelmingly probable; on the other hand he points clearly that, when it comes to man, Darwinism is a mere festering of mass errors, and paints not a very nice picture of it. Interesting also is the Papal Encyclical pronouncing that Darwin's theory about the origin of life and Christianity were not in conflict, and the October 1996 letter of Pope John Paul II to the Pontifical Academy of Science stating that "fresh knowledge leads to the recognition of the theory of evolution as more than just a hypothesis."

[26]The strongest challenge to Darwinism comes from the proponents of concept of "Intelligent Design." Other conceptual challenges to continuous evolution are coming from the geological evidence of catastrophes having bigger impact than natural selection of the fittest, achieved human capability to

create man's own major catastrophes including destruction of most, if not all, life on Earth by atomic weapons, the still open and unexplained gap between chemistry and life, and the already mentioned difficulties of reductionism and limits in algorithmic compressibility.

[27]The concept of "irreducible complexity" needs to be contrasted with "cumulative complexity" describing a system of components which can be arranged sequentially so that successive removal of components will not lead to the complete loss of function; for example: system = city, components = people and services. Darwinian mechanisms can account for cumulative complexity.

[28]Representative studies from this movement are:

Phillip E. Johnson, *Darwin on Trial* (Downers Grove, Ill.: InterVarsity Press, 1993).

Michael J. Behe, *The Biochemical Challenge to Evolution* (New York: Free Press, 1995).

J. P. Moreland (ed.), *The Creation Hypothesis* (Downers Grove, Ill.: InterVarsity Press, 1994).

[29]James Lovelock, *The Ages of Gaia: A Biography of Our Living Earth* (London: Norton and Company, 1988).

[30]Gregory Stock, *Metaman* (New York: Simon & Schuster, 1993).

[31]Tom Sorell, *Scientism* (London: Routledge, 1991).

[32]Richard Morris, *The Edges of Science, Crossing the Boundary from Physics to Metaphysics* (New York: Prentice Hall Press, 1990).

[33]In his book *Frontiers of Illusion* (Philadelphia: Temple University Press, 1996), 10, Daniel Sarewitz suggested a comparable set of myths:

- The myth of infinite benefits: More science and more technology will lead to more public good.
- The myth of unfettered research: Any scientifically reasonable line of research into fundamental natural processes is as likely to yield societal benefits as any other.
- The myth of accountability: Peer review, reproducibility of results, and other controls of the quality of scientific research embody the principal ethical responsibilities of the research system.
- The myth of authoritativeness: Scientific information provides an objective basis for resolving political disputes.
- The myth of endless frontier: New knowledge generated at the frontiers of science is autonomous from its moral and practical consequences in society.

[34]John Morgan, "The Worst Enemy of Science," in *Scientific American,* May 1993, 36–37.

[35]Robert Bell, *Impure Science* (New York: John Wiley & Sons, 1992), or Daniel J. Kevles, *The Baltimore Case: A Trial of Politics, Science, and Character* (New York: Norton, 1998), or Alexander Kohn, *False Prophets:*

Fraud and Error in Science and Medicine (New York: Barnes & Noble, revised edition, 1997).

[36]From among the many examples of government "junk science" it is worthwhile to mention at least earth warming research and AIDS research. There is no doubt about the fact of atmospheric warming, which has been taking place for circa ten thousand years, since the last Ice Age. It is also observable to everyone who visited Alaska over a period of couple of decades, or compared today's Alaskan glaciers with those observed and described by John Muir during his visits there more than a hundred years ago. The suspicious aspect of the research is that without knowing the causes of the past long-term warming, dogmatic statements are made about the current era and future significant impact of a few industrial pollutants that were completely absent in the past. Another example is the AIDS research commented upon, for example, by Richard Horton in his article "Truth and Heresy About AIDS" published in *The New York Review of Books,* May 23, 1996, 14–20, in which he reviewed three AIDS related books by Peter H. Duesberg. In such situations, the highest risks are associated with the frequent jettisoning of sound judgment and sound research methods because such neglects affect, among other things, the medicines we take, the bridges we drive on, the buildings we live in, the costly regulations imposed on some industries, and the weapons that are supposed to defend us.

[37]Benno Müller-Hill, *Murderous Science* (New York: Oxford University Press, 1988).

[38]Nikolai Krementsov, *Stalinist Science* (Princeton, N.J.: Princeton University Press, 1997).

[39]Brian Appleyard, *Understanding the Present: Science and the Soul of Modern Man* (New York: Doubleday, 1992).

[40]Ilya Prigodine, *The End of Certainty: Time, Chaos, and the New Laws of Nature* (New York: Free Press, 1997).

Chapter 3

[1]F. A. Hayek, *The Counter-Revolution of Science,* 2nd ed. (Indianapolis: Liberty Press, 1979).

[2]Norbert Elias, *What Is Sociology* (New York: Columbia University Press, 1978).

[3]For example, students of anthropology at the University of Chicago reported that before World War II they were taught that "everyone is different" but, after the war, that "there is absolutely no difference between anybody." See Kurt Vonnegut, *Slaughterhouse Five,* (New York: Dell, 1991), 8.

[4]Robert C. Bannister, *Social Darwinism: Science and Myth in Anglo-American Social Thought* (Philadelphia: Temple University Press, 1979).

[5]Craig Calhoun, *Critical Social Theory* (Oxford, U.K.: Blackwell Publishers, 1995), xi, xii.

[6]Alvin W. Gouldner, *The Coming Crisis in Western Sociology* (New York: Basic Books, 1970).

[7]The quote is from the founding statement of the "Student Nonviolent Coordinating Committee" in Judith C. Albert and Steward E. Albert (eds.), *The Sixties Papers* (New York: Praeger, 1984), 113.

[8]Charles Lembert, *Sociology After Crisis* (Boulder, Colo.: Westview Press, 1995), chap. 9.

[9]Samuel P. Huntington, *The Clash of Civilizations and the Remaking of World Order* (New York: Simon & Schuster, 1996).

[10]Francis Fukuyama, *The End of History and the Last Man* (New York: Avon Books, 1992).

[11]Two widely read books representing this view are:
- Daniel Patrick Moynihan, *Pandaemonium: Ethnicity in International Politics* (Oxford: Oxford University Press, 1993).
- Zbigniew Brzezinski, *Out of Control: Global Turmoil on the Eve of the Twenty-first Century* (New York: Scribner, 1993).

[12]Kenneth Clark, *Civilization: A Personal View* (New York: Harper & Row, Publishers, 1969), 346–347.

[13]A. L. Kroeber and Clyde Kluckhohn, *Culture: A Critical Review of Concepts and Definitions* (New York: Vintage Books, 1963).

[14]Martin J. Gannon and Associates, *Understanding Global Cultures* (Thousand Oaks, Calif.: SAGE Publications, 1994).

[15]Here are some examples of books belonging to this opportunistic class:
- Daniel Bell, *The Cultural Contradictions of Capitalism* (New York: Basic Books, 1976).
- Christopher Lasch, *The Culture of Narcissism* (New York: W. W. Norton & Co., 1978).
- John Kenneth Galbraith, *The Culture of Contentment* (Boston: Houghton Mifflin Company, 1992).
- Stephen L. Carter, *The Culture of Disbelief* (New York: Doubleday, 1994).

[16]Paul A. Samuelson and William D. Nordhaus, *Economics,* 13th ed. (New York: McGraw-Hill Book Company, 1989), chap. 1.

[17]Lester C. Thurow, *The Zero-Sum Solution* (New York, Simon & Schuster, 1985).

[18]Patrick J. Buchanan, *The Great Betrayal: How American Sovereignty and Social Justice Are Being Sacrificed to the Gods of the Global Economy* (New York: Little, Brown, 1998).

[19]Andrew Carnegie can be selected as one of the best and most successful practitioners of *laissez-faire* capitalism in the U.S. A recent, well-known theorist and ideologist of this form of capitalism is Ayn Rand with her books:

- *Capitalism: The Unknown Ideal* (New York: New American Library, 1967), and
- *The Virtue of Selfishness* (New York: New American Library, 1974).

[20]Robert Kuttner, *Everything for Sale: The Virtues and Limits of Markets* (New York: Alfred A. Knopf, 1997).

[21]Charles Lewis and the Center for Public Integrity, *The Buying of Congress: How Special Interests Have Stolen Your Right to Life, Liberty, and the Pursuit of Happiness* (New York: AVON, 1998).

[22]Lester Thurow, *Head to Head* (New York: William Morrow and Company, Inc., 1992).

[23]Hill Gates, *China's Motor: A Thousand Years of Petty Capitalism* (Ithaca, N.Y.: Cornell University Press, 1996).

[24]Franky Schaeffer (ed.), *Is Capitalism Christian?* (Westchester, Ill.: Crossway Books, 1985).

[25]Charles R. Strain (ed.), *Prophetic Visions and Economic Realities* (Grand Rapids, Mich.: Wm. B. Eerdmans Publishing Co., 1989), or Mary E. Hobgood, *Catholic Social Teaching and Economic Theory* (Philadelphia: Temple University Press, 1991).

[26]Charles Hampden-Turner and Alfons Trompenaars, *The Seven Cultures of Capitalism* (New York: Doubleday, 1993).

[27]Francis Fukuyama, *Trust* (New York: Free Press, 1995).

[28]David S. Landes, *The Wealth and Poverty of Nations: Why Some Are So Rich and Some So Poor* (New York: Norton, 1997).

[29]Subroto Roy, *Philosophy of Economics* (London and New York: Routledge, 1989).

[30]Robert Heilbroner and William Milberg, *The Crisis of Vision in Modern Economic Thought* (New York: Cambridge University Press, 1996).

[31]The associated lack of understanding is highly visible in well-publicized misjudgments of the economic reality or trends by the prominent personalities.

- For example, in November 1997 President Clinton dismissed the financial tumult in Asia Pacific as "a few glitches on the road," but in the summer 1998 he declared it "the biggest financial challenge facing the world in fifty years" and, then, the world financial community did very little.
- Another example may be seen in the IMF and World Bank reports declaring financial health of economies in Thailand and South Korea a few months before their currencies collapsed.
- Still another irony stemming from the dismal science: In 1997, Myron Scholes and Robert Merton received their Nobel prize for option-pricing theories. In 1998, the Long-Term Capital Management hedge fund they helped found using their prize-winning theories slid toward insolvency.

The confused thinking about global financial markets is, in narrative form, described in George Soros, *The Crisis of Global Capitalism* (New York:

Public Affairs, 1998). The ever increasing velocity and volume of capital flows, and of exchange rates, are already so overwhelming that they are beyond the control of major financial institutions and governments. Because this trend will continue, misjudgments of the world's economic reality may become more frequent, and their consequences more severe.

[32]A. L. Kroeber, *The Nature of Culture* (Chicago: The University of Chicago Press, 1952), Introduction to Part I.

[33]Tom Sorell, *Scientism* (London, Routledge, 1991).

Chapter 4

[1]It is important to note that some results of the studies of comparative anatomy, which deals with the similarities and differences among animal morphological structures, can be interpreted in terms of a variety of speculative hypotheses, e.g., to support Darwinian theory of evolution.

[2]Leslie Stevenson, *Seven Theories of Human Nature*, 2nd ed. (New York: Oxford University Press, 1987).

[3]Plato, *Republic* (London: Penguin, 1955).

[4]T. B. Bottomore and M. Rubel (eds.), *Karl Marx: Selected Writings in Sociology and Social Philosophy* (London: Penguin, 1963).

[5]While reviewing this secular Marxian mythology involving the struggle between the greedy blood-sucking werewolf, the Lord Capital, and the creative but suffering proletariat, let us quickly refresh the concept of "myth." A myth is usually perceived as a "sacred" narrative used to justify existing institutions, laws, rights, authorities, theories, etc. There are numerous explanations of myths and several theories of their origin, all revolving around these principles:
- Science creates myths as the outcome of a desire to explain natural phenomena.
- Personification of causes behind observed natural phenomena.
- Inanimate objects are endowed with humanlike personality.
- Allegorical inventions aimed at teaching ethical precepts by illustration.
- Distortion of actual historical events.
- Misinterpretation of metaphors.

As explanations, all these principles are untrue, but the tendencies that they recognize do exist. The multiplicity of causative forces refutes any explanation that uses, or allows, only one of them. This means that myths have no identifiable origin. Like all arts and all institutions, myths are as old as man. The history of myth is at least as long as the history of mankind. Of course, the original myths did not remain unaltered.

[6]R. Wollheim and J. Hopkins (eds.), *Philosophical Essays on Freud* (New York: Cambridge University Press, 1982).

[7]Sigmund Freud, *Civilization and Its Discontent* (New York: W. W. Norton & Co., 1961), 92.

[8]Jean-Paul Sartre, *Being and Nothingness*, special abridged edition (Secaucus, N.J.: The Citadel Press, 1974).

[9]B. F. Skinner, *Science and Human Behavior* (New York: Macmillan, 1953).

[10]Konrad Lorenz, *On Aggression* (New York: Bantam Books, 1974).

[11]Jacob Bronowski, *The Ascent of Man* (Boston: Little, Brown and Company, 1973).

[12]Martin Heidegger, *What Is Metaphysics?* (New York: Harper & Row, 1977).

[13]Hannah Arendt, *The Human Condition* (New York: Doubleday, 1959).

[14]Robert Nozick, *Philosophical Explanations* (Cambridge, Mass.: Harvard University Press, 1981), 578.

[15]Hubert L. Dreyfus and Paul Rabinow, *Michel Foucalt: Beyond Structuralism and Hermeneutics,* 2nd ed. (Chicago: University of Chicago Press, 1983).

[16]Howard Moody, *The Fourth Man* (New York: The Macmillan Co., 1964).

[17]Arthur Kroker, *The Possessed Individual* (New York: St. Martin's Press, 1992).

[18]Louis Renou (ed.), *Hinduism* (New York: George Braziller, 1962).

[19]Richard A. Gard (ed.), *Buddhism* (New York: George Braziller, 1962).

[20]John Alden Williams (ed.), *Islam* (New York: George Braziller, 1962).

[21]The information introduced in this section of the chapter dealing with studies of man has been extracted from the book: Martin J. Gannon and Associates, *Understanding Global Cultures* (Thousand Oaks, Calif.: SAGE Publications, 1994).

[22]Catherine McCall, *Concepts of Person* (London: Glasgow University Press, 1990).

[23]David Hume, *On Human Nature and the Understanding* (New York: Macmillan Publishing Co., 1962).

[24]John Searle, *The Rediscovery of the Mind* (Cambridge, Mass.: MIT Press, 1992).

[25]Thomas Nagel, "The Mind Wins!" in *The New York Review of Books,* March 4, 1993, 37–41.

[26]Roger Penrose, *The Emperor's New Mind* (Oxford, U.K.: Oxford University Press, 1989), chap. 10.

[27]John Horgan, "Can Science Explain Consciousness?" in *Scientific American,* July 1994, 88–94.

[28]Ray Kurzweil, *The Age of Spiritual Machines* (New York: The Viking Press, 1999).

Chapter 5

[1]Plato, *Republic,* 352 D, in Edith Hamilton and Huntington Cairns (eds.), *The Collected Dialogues of Plato* (Princeton, N.J.: Princeton University Press, 1961), 603.

[2]Elizabeth Anderson, *Value in Ethics and Economics* (London: Harvard University Press, 1993)

[3]John Laird, *The Idea of Value* (Cambridge, U.K.: Cambridge University Press, 1929), 24.

[4]Abraham Edel, "The Concept of Value and Its Travels in Twentieth-Century America," in Murray G. Murphey and Ivar Berg (eds.), *Value and Value Theory in Twentieth-Century America* (Philadelphia: Temple University Press, 1988).

[5]Mortimer J. Adler, *Desires, Right and Wrong* (New York: Macmillan Publishing Co., 1991).

[6]Kitarô Nishida, *An Inquiry into the Good* (London: Yale University Press, 1990).

[7]Adam Smith, *The Theory of Moral Sentiment* (Indianapolis: Liberty Fund, Inc., 1984 reprint).

[8]Alfred Jules Ayer, *Language, Truth, and Logic* (New York: Dover Publications, 1952).

[9]Bernard Williams, *Ethics and the Limits of Philosophy* (Cambridge, Mass.: Harvard University Press, 1985).

[10]Tom L. Beauchamp and Norman E. Bowie, *Ethical Theory and Business,* 2nd ed., (Englewood Cliffs, N.J.: Prentice-Hall, Inc., 1983), chap. 1.

[11]Immanuel Kant, *Fundamental Principles of the Metaphysics of Morals* (Buffalo, N.Y.: Prometheus Books, 1987).

[12]Here are a few examples of such principles:
- To each an equal share
- To each according to individual needs
- To each according to merit
- To each according to delivered effort
- To each according to value of societal contribution

[13]John Rawls, *A Theory of Justice* (Cambridge, Mass.: Harvard University Press, 1971).

[14]Bertrand De Jouvenel, *The Ethics of Redistribution* (Indianapolis: Liberty Press, 1990).

[15]Robert Nozick, *Anarchy, State, and Utopia* (New York: Basic Books, 1974).

[16]Ramsey Colloquium, "On Human Rights, The Universal Declaration of Human Rights Fifty Years Later," in *First Things,* April 1998, 18–30.

[17]Alasdair MacIntyre, *A Short History of Ethics* (New York: Macmillan Publishing Company, 1966).

[18]James Sellers, *Public Ethics* (New York: Harper & Row, 1970).

[19]Aristotle, "Nicomachean Ethics," in Richard McKeon (ed.), *The Basic Works of Aristotle* (New York: Random House, 1941).

[20]Helmut Schoeck, *Envy* (Indianapolis: Liberty Fund, Inc., 1987).

[21]Norvin Richards, *Humility* (Philadelphia: Temple University Press, 1992).

[22]Raziel Abelson and Marie-Louise Friquegnon (eds.), *Ethics for Modern Life* (New York: St. Martin's Press, 1982).

[23]Ronald Dworkin et al., "Assisted Suicide: The Philosophers' Brief," in *The New York Review of Books,* March 27, 1998, 41–47.

[24]"Roe: Twenty-Five Years Later," in *First Things,* January 1998, 9–11.

[25]A Symposium: "Is Affirmative Action on the Way Out? Should It Be?" in *Commentary,* March 1998, 18–57.

[26]August B. Mundel, *Ethics of Quality* (New York: Marcel Dekker, Inc., 1991).

[27]For example: Samuel Soothard, *Ethics for Executives* (New York: Thomas Nelson, Inc., Publishers, 1975), or Kenneth R. Andrews (ed.), *Ethics in Practice: Managing the Moral Corporation* (Boston: Harvard Business School Press, 1989).

[28]Philip K. Howard, *The Death of Common Sense: How Law Is Suffocating America* (New York: Random House, 1994).

[29]Lyall Watson, *Dark Nature: A Natural History of Evil* (New York: Harper Collins, 1995).

[30]Plato, "Theaetetus," 176, in Edith Hamilton and Huntington Cairns (eds.), *The Collected Dialogues of Plato* (Princeton, N.J.: Princeton University Press, 1961), 880–881.

[31]Lionel Tiger, *The Manufacture of Evil* (New York: Harper & Row, 1987).

[32]Robert C. Solomon and Mark C. Murphy, *What Is Justice? Classic and Contemporary Readings* (New York: Oxford University Press, 1990).

[33]Marvin Henberg, *Retribution* (Philadelphia: Temple University Press, 1990).

[34]Susan Jacoby, *Wild Justice* (New York: Harper & Row, Publishers, 1983).

[35]Arthur R. Hogue, *Origins of the Common Law* (Indianapolis: Liberty Fund, 1986).

[36]Heinrich A. Rommen, *The Natural Law* (Indianapolis: Liberty Fund, 1998).

[37]Gertrude Himmelfarb, *The De-Moralization of Society* (New York: Knopf, 1993), or William J. Bennett, *The Devaluing of America* (Colorado Springs, Colo.: Focus on the Family Publishing, 1992), or William J. Bennett, *The Book of Virtues* (New York: Simon & Schuster, 1993).

[38]Heta Häyry and Matti Häyry, "Applied Philosophy at the Turn of the Century," in Oliver Leaman (ed.), *The Future of Philosophy* (London: Routledge, 1998), 90.

Chapter 6

[1]Niccolò Machiavelli, *Prince* (New York: St. Martin's Press, 1964).

[2]Friedrich Nietzsche, *The Will to Power* (New York: Random House, 1967). It should be noted that despite Nietzsche's presentation of this concept only as a hypothesis, which he never claimed proven even in the limited realm of psychology, its influence has been enormous: from poets and writers to philosophers and sociologist, to politicians and ideologues.

[3]Adolf A. Berle, *Power* (New York: Harcourt, Brace & World, Inc., 1969).

[4]Bertrand de Jouvenel, *On Power: The Natural History of Its Growth* (Indianapolis: Liberty Fund, 1993).

[5]Political power is the right to make laws and establish the death penalty and, consequently, lesser penalties for the preservation and regulation of properties; and also the right to employ force in enforcement of such laws, and in defense of the commonwealth from external injury. All aspects of the political power are aimed at the public good. John Locke: *An Essay Concerning the True Origin, Extent and End of Civil Government* (New York: Barnes & Noble, 1996).

[6]Symposium: "The End of Democracy?" in *First Things,* November 1996, 18–42, and follow-up discussions in January 1997, 2–8, 19–28, and February 1997, 2–10.

[7]Václav Havel et al., *The Power of the Powerless* (Armong, N.Y.: M. E. Sharpe, Inc., 1985).

[8]Erik H. Erikson, *Gandhi's Truth* (New York: W. W. Norton & Co., Inc., 1969).

[9]Robert Payne, *The Life and Death of Mahatma Gandhi* (New York: E. P. Dutton & Co., Inc., 1969).

[10]The issue of "Civil Disobedience" has been raised before Gandhi, e.g., by Henry David Thoreau in his book of the same title. His key idea is expressed in the motto, "That government is best which governs least" which, of course, contains an underlying assumption that men are well prepared for self-government and self-discipline.

[11]See, for example, Anthony de Jasay, *The State* (Indianapolis: Liberty Fund, 1998).

[12]Vilfredo Pareto, *The Mind and Society,* new edition (New York: Harcourt, Brace, 1935).

[13]C. Wright Mills, *The Power Elite* (London: Oxford University Press, 1958).

[14]Thorstein Veblen, *The Theory of the Leisure Class* (New York: Book-of-the-Month Club, 1981).

[15]E. H. Carr, *The New Society* (London: Macmillan, 1951), or Gustave Le Bon, *The Crowd* (London: Ernest Benn, Ltd., 1952 edition).

[16] Jacob Burckhard, *Force and Freedom* (New York: Pantheon Books, 1943).

[17] Stanley Aronowitz, "On Intellectuals," in Bruce Robbins (ed.), *Intellectuals* (Minneapolis: University of Minnesota Press, 1990).

[18] It is worthy to refresh here the already mentioned reluctance of science to submit to public control, contrasting with its willingness to be subordinated to state and corporate institutions providing research resources.

[19] Alvin Gouldner, *The Future of Intellectuals* (Los Angeles: SAGE, 1979).

[20] Russell Jacoby, *The Last Intellectuals* (New York: The Noonday Press, 1987).

[21] Julien Benda, *The Treason of the Intellectuals* (New York: William Morrow & Co., 1928).

[22] Owen Harries, "The Cold War and the Intellectuals," in *Commentary,* October 1991, 13–20.

[23] A few names, such as, George Orwell, Hannah Ardent, Whittaker Chambers, and Jean-Francois Revel, may serve as an illustration of intellectuals subjected to such fearful visions.

[24] Christopher Lasch, *The Revolt of Elites and the Betrayal of Democracy* (New York: Norton, 1995).

[25] Daniel Bell, *The End of Ideology* (New York: Collier Books, 1961).

[26] *Ibid.*, chap. 7.

[27] Examples of studies of lives of well-known intellectuals are, e.g.,

• David W. Breese, *Seven Men Who Rule the World from the Grave* (Chicago: Moody Press, 1990).

• Paul Johnson, *Intellectuals* (New York: Harper & Row, Publishers, 1988).

• Ian Gibson, *The Shameful Life of Salvador Dalí* (New York: Norton, 1998).

• E. Michael Jones, *Degenerate Moderns* (San Francisco: Ignatius Press, 1993).

Chapter 7

[1] Ludwig Wittgenstein, *Philosophical Investigations* (Oxford, U.K.: Oxford University Press, 1953).

[2] Colin McGinn, *Problems in Philosophy* (Cambridge, Mass.: Blackwell Publishers, 1993).

[3] James V. Schall, *At the Limits of Political Philosophy* (Washington, D.C.: The Catholic University of America Press, 1996).

[4] Robert Nozick, *Philosophical Explanations* (Cambridge, Mass.: The Belknap Press, 1981), 645–647.

[5] Charles Lemert, *Sociology After the Crisis* (Boulder, Colo.: Westview Press, 1995), chap. 4.

[6]"In ideology men and their circumstances appear upside-down." Statement by Karl Marx in his "The German Ideology." See Robert Tucker (ed.), *The Marx-Engels Reader* (New York: W. W. Norton, 1978), 154.

[7]Hannah Arendt, *The Origin of Totalitarianism* (New York: Harcourt Brace Jovanovich, Inc., 1973).

[8]One of the early examples, known to the author from his native country, is traceable to the nineteenth century. "Ancient" Czech manuscripts, supposedly discovered in 1817 and 1820, were actually later-day forgeries inspired by the desire to strengthen Czech nationalism suffering since 1620 under the Habsburg's Germanization drive. Critique by Thomas Garrigue Masaryk, the first president of Czechoslovakia established in 1918 after the World War I, forced contemporary scholars to admit the influence of nationalism on the budding social sciences through, e.g., the deeply rooted national myths. See, e.g., H. Gordon Skilling, *T. G. Masaryk: Against the Current: 1882–1914* (University Park, Penn.: The Pennsylvania State University Press, 1994), chap. 1. Similar attitudes toward truth were demonstrated in Central and Eastern Europe by revisionist historians on payroll of communist governments ("Truth is what supports the power and leadership of the Communist Party").

[9]Pietre Geyl, *Napoleon: For and Against* (Peregrine Paperback, 1965), 18.

[10]Gunnar Myrdal, "The Case Against Romantic Ethnicity," in *Dialogue Discussion Paper* of The Center for The Study of Democratic Institutions, May 13, 1974, 9–17.

[11]Alexander Stille, "The Betrayal of History" in *The New York Review of Books,* June 11, 1998, 15–20, or Michel Rolph Trouillot, *Silencing the Past: Power and the Production of History* (Boston: Beacon Press, 1995).

[12]Burleigh Taylor Wilkins, *Has History Any Meaning?* (Ithaca, N.Y.: Cornell University Press, 1978).

[13]As an example, let us consider the physical event of light propagation. Physicists have precisely measured the velocity of light in a vacuum and found it to be 299,748±15 kilometers per second, as per U.S. National Bureau of Standards. But they are unable to explain "<u>why</u> this particular speed and not some other." To answer this question, if the answer can be found, requires using concepts from the outside of physics' domain, e.g., from cosmogony.

[14]Madan Sarup, *An Introductory Guide to Post-structuralism and Postmodernism* (Athens, Ga.: The University of Georgia Press, 1993), chap. 6.

[15]Steven Weinberg, "Sokal's Hoax," in *The New York Review of Books,* Aug. 8, 1996, 11–15, with follow-up in Oct. 3, 1996, 54–56.

[16]Alan D. Sokal, "Transgressing the Boundaries: Toward a Transformative Hermeneutics of Quantum Gravity," in *Social Text,* Spring/Summer 1996, 217–252.

[17]Carlos Castaneda, *The Teachings of Don Juan: A Yaqui Way of Knowledge* (New York: Pocket Books, 1974).

[18]Charles Lemert, *Sociology After the Crisis* (Boulder, Colo.: Westview Press, 1995), Introduction.

[19]Robert Nozick, *Philosophical Explanations* (Cambridge, Mass.: The Belknap Press, 1995), chap. 1.

[20]Margaret Mead's book *Coming of Age in Samoa,* first celebrated as an anthropological breakthrough, has been rejected in 1983 as an example of wholesale deception in the history of behavioral sciences. See Derek Freeman, *Margaret Mead and Samoa: The Making and Unmaking of an Anthropological Myth* (Cambridge, Mass.: Harvard University Press, 1983).

[21]Carl N. Degler, *In Search of Human Nature: The Decline and Revival of Darwinism in American Social Thought* (New York: Oxford University Press, 1991).

[22]John Horgan, *The End of Science: Facing the Limits of Knowledge in the Twilight of the Scientific Age* (New York: Addison-Wesley, 1996).

[23]See, for example, Edward O. Wilson, *Consilience: The Unity of Knowledge* (New York: Knopf, 1998).

[24]Frederic Jameson, *Postmodernism, or The Cultural Logic of Late Capitalism* (Durham, N.C.: Duke University Press, 1997).

[25]Matt Ridley, *The Origins of Virtue: Human Instincts and the Evolution of Cooperation* (New York: Viking, 1997).

[26]Antonin Scalia, *A Matter of Interpretation: Federal Courts and the Law* (Princeton, N.J.: Princeton University Press, 1997).

[27]Nicholas Lobkowitz, "Christianity and Culture" in *Review of Politics* 53 (Spring 1991), 188.

[28]T. S. Eliot, *Little Gidding* (London: Faber and Faber, 1942).

Chapter 8

[1]Robert Alter and Frank Kermore (eds.), *The Literary Guide to the Bible* (Cambridge, Mass.: The Belknap Press of Harvard University Press, 1987).

[2]Introduction to the story of Dead Sea Scrolls is provided by Hershel Shanks et al., *The Dead Sea Scrolls After Forty Years* (Washington, D.C.: Biblical Archeological Society, 1991). A complete treatment may be found in Randall Price, *Secrets of the Dead Sea Scrolls* (Eugene, Oreg.: Harvest House Publishers, 1996).

[3]An overview of history of the Bible and its spread may be found in encyclopedias and dictionaries, e.g., Pat Alexandra (ed.), *The Lion Encyclopedia of the Bible* (Batavia, Ill.: Lion Publishing, 1987).

[4]Doron Witztum, Eliyahu Rips, and Yoav Rosenberg, "Equidistant Letter Sequences in the Book of Genesis," *Journal of the Royal Statistical Society,* 151/1 (1988), 177–178.

[5]Jeffrey B. Statinover, "Divine Authorship?" in *Bible Review,* October 1995, 28–45, and follow-up discussion, February 1996, 7–45, and Michael Drosnin, *The Bible Code* (New York: Simon & Schuster, 1997).

[6]Duane Christensen, "The Lost Books of the Bible," *Bible Review,* October 1998, 24–31.

[7]Introduction with a few selected books is in Rutherford H. Platt, Jr. (ed.), *The Forgotten Books of Eden* (New York: Bell Publishing Co., 1980); full text in James H. Charlesworth (ed.), *Pseudoepigrapha,* vols. 1 and 2 (Garden City, N.Y.: Doubleday and Company, Inc., 1985).

[8]Philip R. Davies: *Whose Bible Is It Anyway?* (Sheffield, England: Sheffield Academic Press, 1995), chap. 3.

[9]Current examples may be found in the "genderless" and "politically correct" editions such as *The New Testament and Psalms: An Inclusive Version* (Oxford), while the *Thomas Jefferson's World Bible* may serve as an example from U.S. history. For more detailed familiarization with the extremes of what is being done to the Bible, or how far mistranslating may go, refer to a collection of post-structuralist, narratological, and womanist essays published under the title *The Postmodern Bible* by Yale in 1995.

[10]Mark G. Brett: "The Political Ethics in Postmodern Allegory," in: M. Daniel Carroll, R. David, J. A. Clines, and Philip R. Davies (eds.): *The Bible in Human Society* (Sheffield, England: Sheffield Academic Press, 1995), 67–86).

[11]For anybody who is in touch with the contemporary book market, it is impossible not to notice the many works of actual and pseudoscholarship supposedly questing for the true historical Jesus, and discovering the freedom-fighting Jesus, erotic Jesus, proletarian or revolutionary Jesus, etc., all of them actually images of the "researchers." Then the many new translations of the Bible profitable only to the publishers, containing words, phrases, and paraphrases that may well be called revisionist, whereby the original and essential message of man's sin, risk of eternal punishment, and of access to God's free forgiveness and saving grace is either modified or completely changed. To complete this picture of deceit it is necessary to add the accomplishments of the entertaining industry. To be fair to the secularist treatment of Jesus and the Bible, the cornerstones of Christianity, the work of Freudian priests and counselors, and theologians celebrating the death of God, seem to be even more unethical and damaging.

[12]Sometimes the advocates of academic secularity presuppose that all disciplines pursued by modern universities are just different ways in quest for the same single all-encompassing truth. This presupposition then implies conclusion equating secular beliefs with truth and Christian belief with dogma (an authoritative set of principles laid down by the church) automatically assumed to be false.

[13]A similar claim, but on the Old Testament only, have the communities of Judaism which, of course, read it differently than the church.

[14]Among the most visible people representing this view belong Saint Augustine, Martin Luther, John Calvin, and Blaise Pascal.

[15]A concise review of the difference between the current Catholic and Protestant views and trends in theologians' view of the Bible may be found in Avery Dulles, S. J.: "Scripture: Recent Protestant and Catholic Views," in *Theology Today,* XXXVII/1 (April 1980), 7–26.

[16]To be complete, it is necessary to admit that there also were people associated with Christianity (e.g., Dante Alighieri, William Blake, T. S. Eliot) whose approach was outside the three perspectives indicated. Their position vis-à-vis the Bible illustrates that nonecclesiastical perspectives do not always deprive readers of the sense of right and wrong, nor do they necessarily diminish the joy of reading it.

[17]Harold Lindsell: *The Battle for the Bible* (Zondervan, 1976), and his sequel: *The Bible in the Balance* (Zondervan, 1979).

[18]Personal disappointments with the image of the institutionalized church and many individual Christians are frequent and based on actual data from history and present-time observations as well. What is needed is understanding that these observations are again confirming the truth of the biblical message. Part of the disappointment is a simple offense to personal pride and desire (themselves a sign of man's sin) demanding, or at least longing for a direct, immediate, and rewarding association with some well-recognized and admired social group. This is humanly natural, but contrary to the biblical witness of Jesus' willingness to be seen with, and caring for, society's outcasts (Matt. 11:18), or of the human characteristics of the early church as well. Another part relates to man's constant readiness to judge others according to some high and stringent standards without considering his own weaknesses (Matt. 7:1–5). Yet another reason for this disappointment is based on the reality of the fulfillment of Jesus' prophecy about false teachers appearing at the end of the age (Matt. 24:11, 24). In general, everywhere one looks, one can see confirmation of apostle Paul's statement that no one is righteous (Rom. 3:10–18), and of the facts that without Christ's sacrificial death on the cross all would perish (Rom. 3:22–26). The Bible admonishes believers to be perfect as their God is perfect, but provides no indication that this perfection will be achieved by the individual Christians or the Church. Jesus' messages to the seven churches (Revelation 2—3) make their weaknesses quite explicit. Local churches, even today, should be viewed more as hospitals for ailing souls than clubs for display and entertainment of perfect saints.

[19]The question whether or not Jesus said these things is answered through the availability of thousands of early manuscripts of the New Testament books and letters providing significantly better confirmation of biblical accuracy than

the handful of much later manuscripts does for other ancient classical texts. In fact, there is no similar quality and quantity of evidence for any other ancient book.

[20]Kenneth S. Kantzer: "Problems Inerrancy Doesn't Solve," *Christianity Today,* Feb. 20, 1987, 14–15.

Chapter 9

[1]This name, usually translated as "I am who I am," has always been considered too sacred by the people of Israel, that its tetragrammaton YHWH was not even vocalized, but substituted by titles such as Lord, The Most High God, The Holy of Israel, Ancient of Days, The Lord of Host, God Almighty, etc.

[2]What makes our inability to know things absolute is that they are simple in themselves, while we are composed of two opposing natures of different kinds, soul and body. This explanation was proposed by Blaise Pascal in his *Pensées,* #199 (Baltimore, Md.: Penguin Books, 1975).

[3]The word "transcendence" describes God's existence over and above His created universe. God's transcendence is apparent, e.g., from the Lord's Prayer, which addresses "Our father in heaven" (Matt. 6:9). A complementary term "immanence" means God's all-pervading presence and power within His creation, i.e., He is not a mere disinterested spectator observing His created world.

[4]Some Christians speculate that people, who have never heard about Jesus, may be judged according to the "Golden Rule" known, at least in negative formulation, to all cultures. See also Matt. 12:36, 37.

[5]Consider this in contrast to the legal system of the U.S., perceived to be one of the best in the world, as described, e.g., by Mortimer B. Zuckerman, editor-in-chief, in *U.S. News & World Report,* May 9, 1994, 72:

• Fewer than 10 percent of burglaries result in an arrest, barely 1.2 percent in imprisonment.

• Convicted criminals serve only about a third of the sentence.

• About 3 million criminals are on the streets without serious probation or police supervision.

• Homicide arrest level is about 50 percent today (1994), down from 95 percent in the early 1980s.

Even though statistics are only a part of the picture, it is clear that in America there is crime without punishment, or without open and legally valid forgiveness.

[6]It is a weakness of contemporary Christianity that it allowed itself to be influenced by this worldly attitude. The topics of modern Christian preaching and writing indicate that this fundamental aspect of God's revelation is being highly neglected, with the obvious result of a lack of moral responsibility.

[7]The worst case scenario seems to have been put forward by Paul in his first letter to the Corinthians 3:12–15. It indicates the possibility that a person's work will be found worthless, lost in the cleansing fire, but he or she will still be saved. Christians, whose work is built on the foundation which is Jesus Christ, will receive their rewards.

[8]Ian Wilson, *Jesus: The Evidence* (New York: HarperCollins Publishers, 1996), or Gerd Theissen and Annette Merz, *The Historical Jesus: A Comprehensive Guide* (Minneapolis: Fortress Press, 1996)

[9]Michael Grant, *Jesus, An Historian's View of the Gospels* (New York: Charles Scribner's Sons, 1977).

[10]Albert Schweitzer, *The Quest for the Historical Jesus* (Baltimore: The Johns Hopkins University Press, 1998).

[11]Malachi Martin, *Jesus Now* (Part I and II) (New York: E. P. Dutton & Co., 1973).

[12]See, e.g., report on the Jesus Seminar by Luke T. Johnson, "The (Wrong) Search for Jesus" in *Bible Review,* December 1995, 20–44.

[13]Malcolm Muggeridge, *Jesus, the Man Who Lives* (New York: Harper & Row, Publishers, 1975).

[14]Jaroslav Pelikan, *Jesus Through the Centuries* (New Haven, Conn.: Yale University Press, 1985).

[15]*Prophecy Bible Edition* (Akron, Ohio: Rex Humbard Ministries, 1985), 35–41

[16]Parables, as well as allegories, are means of teaching that present interesting illustrations from which moral or religious conclusions can be drawn. The value of this teaching method is obvious, because it allows people to see common experience in a new way. Parables are also means to bring the hearers to a point of decision, especially about their attitude toward the discussed subject. The key problem is interpretation of parables coming from a different cultural environment. Exposition of Jesus parables for today must be based on careful understanding of the original message in the original environment.

[17]The word "Messiah" is related to the idea of anointing, as well as anointed person. Because redemption of the Old Testament chosen people has been achieved also in the "secular" domain (so to speak), we see its use also in relation to a few earthly kings, such as Cyrus (Isa. 45:13). Consider Jesus' direct claim of being anointed in His reading Isaiah's prophecy in synagogue at Nazareth, and confirming: "Today this scripture is fulfilled in your hearing" (Luke 4:16–20).

[18]The messianic portrait of the suffering servant of God is introduced in Isaiah 40—55.

[19]Description of this conqueror by Isaiah, in chapters 1 through 37, hardly differs from the description of king (Isa. 11:2–4) and the servant.

[20]See Jeremiah 23:5–6 and 33:14–17.

[21]This prophecy, going far back to the tragedy of man's fall (Gen. 3:15), is stressing the humanity of the Messiah, and the promise that this calamity will be reversed.

[22]Jesus' own preferred title (Mark 8:29–33), traceable to, e.g., Daniel 7:13.

[23]In antediluvial times, e.g., Enoch (Gen. 5:24) and Noah (Gen. 6:8), and after the Flood, Job (Job 1:8) and Abraham (Gen. 22:16–18).

[24]It is interesting to note the primary linguistic characteristics of this name:

• Jesus is a Greek form of the common Jewish name Joshua, meaning "Yahweh is salvation."

• Christ is an English form the Greek *Christos* meaning "The anointed one," which corresponds to transliterated Hebrew word "Messiah."

Note: In the fact that Peter, in his confession (Luke 9:20), called Jesus *Christos,* not "Messiah," some interpreters see the revealed and recognized universality of Jesus' mission, a mission reaching beyond the Jewish nation.

[25]The role of Jesus as the Savior is His from the beginning. It is found, e.g., in the angelic announcement to the shepherds in the Christmas story (Luke 2:11).

[26]Cynthia Pearl Maus, *Christ and the Fine Arts* (New York: Harper & Row, Publishers, 1977).

[27]Leonard C. Yaseen, *The Jesus Connection* (New York: Crossroad, 1985).

[28]Malcolm Muggeridge, *Christ and the Media* (Grand Rapids: William B. Eerdmans Publishing Co., 1977).

[29]Malcolm Muggeridge, *Jesus Rediscovered* (Garden City, N.Y.: Doubleday & Company, Inc., 1969).

[30]An interesting collection of contemporary views of Trinity has been published in *Theology Today,* 54/3 (October 1997), 293–380.

[31]J. D. Douglas (ed.), *The Illustrated Bible Dictionary* (Wheaton, Ill.: Tyndale House Publishers, 1980), part 3, 1597–1599).

[32]Billy Graham, *The Holy Spirit* (Waco, TX: Word Books, 1978).

[33]As an example of such a treatment, see Eberhard Jüngel's book *The Doctrine of Trinity* (Grand Rapids: William B. Eerdmans Publishing Co., 1976) where he talks about God's self-interpretation, self-relatedness, God being-as-object, God being-as-act, etc. These intellectual curiosities have questionable value from the practical perspective of the Great Commission.

[34]A story is told of the Roman general Pompey who, while entering Jerusalem in the first century B.C., insisted on being shown the sachet, the inner chamber of the synagogue, desiring to see the Jewish representation of their God. He found, of course, no graven image. His anger and disbelief reflected the difference of spiritual Yahweh from all other, by human hands and minds created, gods.

Chapter 10

[1]*Creatio ex nihilo* is a Latin expression indicating that the world (universe) was not made out of any preexisting material, but out of nothing. It is necessary to understand that this idea is not an exhaustive formula for biblical teaching about creation. For example, man was not created *ex nihilo,* but out of the dust of the ground (Gen. 2:19). This is technically called the secondary creation.

[2]See discussion in chap. 2, "Anti-Darwinism."

[3]See, e.g., Dean Kenyon and Percival Davis, *Of Pandas and People* (Richardson, Tex.: Foundation for Thought and Ethics, 1989).

[4]For an example see Kenneth R. Miller's article "Life's Grand Design," in *Technology Review* 97/2 (February/March 1994), 25–32.

[5]The most visible examples of disregard for accurate chronology may be found in Matthew 4:1–11 vs. Luke 4:1–13, both describing Christ's temptations but in different order, and in Psalm 78:15 and 24, which place the manna incident after the smiting of the rock by Moses, contrary to the description in Exodus 16:13 and 17:6.

[6]Donald E. Chittick, *The Controversy* (Portland, Oreg.: Multnomah Press, 1984).

[7]Examples are Psalm 90:4 ("For a thousand years in your sight are like a day that has just gone by, or like a watch in the night"), 2 Peter 3:8 ("With the Lord a day is like a thousand years, and a thousand years are like a day"), and Luke 4:19, where the mentioned "year" of the Lord's favor now actually lasts almost two thousand solar years. In the rank of Bible-believing creationists this interpretation is called "day-age theory." Two additional interpretations have been also proposed, namely the "gap theory" placing a long geological age between Genesis 1:1 and 1:2, and "literal-historical theory" that regards the six days of creation as twenty-four hour periods followed in immediate succession. A complete treatment of all three views may be found in Henry M. Morris, *Scientific Creationism* (San Diego: Creation-Life Publishers, 1976). It is also important to consider timing difficulties the theory of evolution has due to data from geology, paleontology, and anthropology as well. See, e.g., Scott M. Huse, *The Collapse of Evolution* (Grand Rapids: Baker Book House, 1990).

[8]Confirmation that absolute perfection (in human terms) is not the proper viewpoint is confirmed in Gen. 2:18 when the Lord God Himself declared, "It is not good that man should be alone."

[9]Jesus Christ is called "the last Adam," because He restored the state of man to what it was before the fall (1 Cor. 15:45).

[10]The apostle Paul recognized the positive influence of unbelievers on him also: "I am a debtor both to Greeks and Barbarians, both wise and unwise" (Rom. 1:14, NKJV). We, as the first Christians, in many aspects of our daily lives depend on non-Christian's skills, tolerance, morality, etc., both here in the U.S. and in distant lands, even on different continents.

NOTES AND REFERENCES ✢ 243

[11]Billy Graham, *Angels: God's Secret Agents* (Garden City, N.Y.: Doubleday & Company, 1975).

[12]J. Oswald Sanders, *Satan Is No Myth* (Chicago: Moody Press, 1975).

[13]Jacques Ellul, *What I Believe* (Grand Rapids: William B. Eerdmans Publishing Co., 1989).

[14]Physical models of the universe proposed during modern times also contemplate ways how it may end. Among the better known theories belong the thermal death of universe and collapsing universe (Big Crunch in opposition to Big Bang). Other theories have been addressing the possibility of the end of the earth, e.g., as a result of the expansion of sun's outer atmosphere after exhaustion of its hydrogen nuclear fuel, as well as through a variety of catastrophes such as collision with another large space object, human-caused nuclear war, or disastrous environmental degradation. The main problem of all these theories remains the same: they seem to be driven by some random event and do not suggest any clue what they mean in the bigger framework of man's life, life in the universe in general, and of existence of the universe as a whole.

[15]Hades, and other words (Sheol, Gehenna, Abyss, the underworld) with a similar meaning, in most situations denote the place where the dead are assembled and awaiting resurrection. It is also used as name for the place of demons, sometimes even for hell. The parable of Lazarus (Luke 16:20–31) provides a good illustration.

Chapter 11

[1]For the "scientifically minded," God's cursing the ground may be imaginatively interpreted as a poetical representation of God initiating the Second Law of Thermodynamics, which may not have been in force before the curse.

[2]Another confirmation how great must be God's love for men when, despite the experience with the antediluvial wickedness, God makes human life sacred. Previously there was no death penalty for murder, see, e.g., protection of Cain by a mark (Gen. 4:15), or threat of avenging for hurting the murderous Lamech (Gen. 4:23–24).

[3]Stephen W. Hawking, *A Brief History of Time* (New York: Bantam Books, 1988), 175.

[4]Leon Wood, *A Survey of Israel's History* (Grand Rapids: Zondervan Publishing House, 1970).

[5]Paul Johnson, *A History of the Jews* (New York: Harper & Row, Publishers, 1987).

[6]H. H. Ben-Sasson (ed.), *A History of the Jewish People* (Cambridge, Mass.: Harvard University Press, 1976).

[7]Jacques Maritain, *Ransoming the Time* (New York: Gordian Press, 1972), chap. VI.

[8]The term "Time of Jacob's trouble" is found in Jeremiah 30:7, and refers to Israel's future persecution, a relatively short period just before Jesus Christ will assume His rightful lordship over her and the whole earth.

[9]Paul Johnson, *A History of Christianity* (New York: Atheneum, 1977).

[10]John McManners (ed.), *The Oxford Illustrated History of Christianity* (New York: Oxford University Press, 1990).

[11]Paul Tillich, *A History of Christian Thought* (New York: Simon and Schuster, 1968).

[12]This parable also indicates God's unwillingness to force the acceptance of His invitation, continuing search for replacement by willing guests, limitation on the total number of guests, and God's anger and some level of punishment for the invitees who refused to come. All of these interpretations are important for the people who did not yet accept God's offer of free forgiveness of sins, as well as for Israel.

[13]Jesus' closing statement in the following verse 16, "So the last will be first, and the first will be last," may be interpreted also as an indication of the unimportance of earthly hierarchies and pecking orders, even those in the Christian church.

[14]The living church, the whole body of true believers, is different from any religious organization. It is an organism with the living Christ as its head. The Holy Spirit plays a major role in it:
• Church was brought into being by Him.
• By Him, Christians are baptized into one body having many members.
• He builds the church and dwells in her members.
• He gives special gifts to specific people to equip them for God's service.
Billy Graham, *The Holy Spirit* (Waco, Tex.: Word Books, 1978), 35–36.

[15]The actual text is: "Brothers, we do not want you to be ignorant about those who fall asleep, or to grieve like the rest of men, who have no hope. We believe that Jesus died and rose again and so we believe that God will bring with Jesus those who have fallen asleep in Him. According to the Lord's own word, we tell you that we who are still alive, who are left till the coming of the Lord, will certainly not precede those who have fallen asleep. For the Lord Himself will come down from heaven, with a loud command, with the voice of the archangel and with the trumpet call of God, and the dead in Christ will rise first. After that, we who are still alive and are left will be caught up with them in the clouds to meet the Lord in the air. And so we will be with the Lord forever." Paul also confirms that God did not appoint Christians to wrath, but to receive salvation in Jesus Christ (1 Thess. 5:9–11).

[16]Arguments have been presented for three opinions: pretribulation, midtribulation, and posttribulation rapture. An overview of these three interpretations is available, e.g., in R. Ludwigson, *The Bible and Future Events,* published by Zondervan in 1974. The currently most accepted view is pretribu-

lationist, but Robert Van Kampen, in his book *The Sign* (Wheaton, Ill.: Crossway Books, 1994), presented an argument for prewrath (midtribulation) rapture to be taken seriously also.

Chapter 12

[1]Billy Graham, *Facing Death and the Life After* (Minneapolis: Grason, 1987).

[2]Blaise Pascal, *Pensées,* #418 (Baltimore: Penguin Books, Inc., 1975 reprint), 149–153.

[3]Billy Graham, *Approaching Hoofbeats* (Waco, Tex.: Word Books, 1983), 236. Note: If you prayed this prayer, you may write for help to: Billy Graham Evangelistic Association, Minneapolis, MN 55403.

[4]Proposed by the Ben Haden Evangelistic Association, Inc., P.O. Box 100, Chattanooga, TN 37041. Additional spiritual help is also available without charge at the address above when requested by a letter (not a postcard) and accompanied by the suggested statement.

[5]"Creed" is an English derivative from the first word Credo (= I believe) in the Latin version of the Apostle's Creed. A creed may cover the whole Christian doctrine and practice, or it may be brief and expressed in a simple popular language. It never precedes faith, but presupposes it. Because creeds are subordinate to the Bible, their value depends on the measure of agreement with it. Despite their independence of external situations, they may be a subject of interpretation and controversy.

[6]The first confession is contained in Peter's answer, "You are the Christ, the Son of the living God" to Jesus' question "Who do you say I am?" in Matthew 16:15 and 16.

[7]Following are a few titles that may further clarify the benefits of accepting God's invitation and what is to be done to receive them:

- Billy Graham, *Peace with God* (Minneapolis: World Wide Publications, 1984).
- C. S. Lewis, *Mere Christianity* (New York: Simon & Schuster, 1996).
- Billy Graham, *Hope for the Troubled Heart* (Minneapolis: Grason, 1991).
- Malcolm Muggeridge, *Jesus—The Man Who Lives* (New York: Harper & Row, Publishers, 1975).
- Thomas V. Morris (ed.), *God and the Philosophers* (New York: Oxford University Press, 1994).
- Arthur Trace, *Christianity and the Intellectuals* (La Salle, Ill.: Sherwood Sugden & Company, Publishers, 1983).

[8]There are many definitions of religion. According to Paul Edwards (ed.): *The Encyclopedia of Philosophy,* vol. 7 (New York: Maxmillan Publishing Co., Inc. & The Free Press, 1972 reprint), 140–145, religion is:

- a recognition that all things are manifestation of a Power which transcends our knowledge (Herbert Spencer)
- a propitiation of powers superior to man which are believed to direct and control the course of Nature and of human life (J. G. Frazer)
- an attempt to express the complete reality of goodness through every aspect of our being (F. H. Bradley)
- ethics heightened, enkindled, lit up by feeling (Matthew Arnold)
- emotion resting on a conviction of a harmony between ourselves and the universe at large (J. M. E. McTaggart)
- a pure and reverential disposition of frame of mind, which we call piety (C. P. Thiele)
- an expression of man's ultimate attitude toward the universe, the summed-up meaning and purport of his whole consciousness of things (Edward Caird)
- a belief in the persistency of value in the world (Harold Høffding)
- a feeling of an absolute dependence (Friedrich Schleiermacher)
- an outreach of man, the social animal, for the values of the satisfying life (A. E. Haydon)
- a dealing with human solitariness expressed externally through ritual, emotion, rationalization, and belief (Alfred North Whitehead)

[9]Most people perceive a difference between what they do believe in and what they don't. What one does not believe is very clear and precise. What one does believe is complex, diffuse, and often almost unconscious. One can distance himself from what is not believed, but what one believes makes him totally implicated personally. This applies to a society as well; a society without collective beliefs would soon fall into lawlessness and enter a process of dissolution. Beliefs may well be considered the *raison d'être* of society. This is easy to verify just by a look on the international scene at the close of the twentieth century: decomposition of the former Soviet Union, separatist movement in Canada, Rwanda, Afghanistan, etc. In biblical Christianity, beliefs are part of the overall faith, i.e., trust, in God and in His word revealed in the Bible. Because of the incomprehensibility of the biblical God who revealed Himself to man only partially, faith in Him cannot be verbalized completely through statements of belief. In summary, a belief that enables society to maintain itself is necessarily collective, while faith is a personal relation that may actually turn into a force causing breaks in social ties. Biblical faith receives transcendent God, who discloses Himself to man through Jesus Christ, the Bible, and the person of the Holy Spirit, on the level of a child wishing to join his or her parent. Re: Jacques Ellul, *What I Believe* (Grand Rapids: William B. Eerdmans Publishing. Co., 1989), 1–9.

[10]The Apostles' Creed contains all the fundamental articles of the Christian faith necessary for salvation in the form of biblical facts, in simple biblical

language, and in most natural order—the order of revelation—from God and the creation forward to the resurrection, and life everlasting. It is not a logical statement of abstract doctrines, but a profession of living facts and saving truths. It is intelligible and edifying to a child, and fresh and rich to the most profound Christian scholar, who, as he matures in life with God, delights in the simplicity of this new life's foundations and in God's wisdom reflected in it. Philip Schaff (ed.), *The Creeds of Christendom,* vol. I (Grand Rapids, Baker Book House, 1983 reprint), 14–23.

[11]For those who in their lives were affected by a failure of human relations, either in the family or in the public, social, or industrial area, and by the immense difficulties or outright impossibility associated with attempts for their restoration, this amazing simplicity reflects God's wisdom and love, and opens the door to joyful life to everyone willing to accept this gift. Compare the requirements of a postgraduate degree to be accepted by scholars; the thousand-dollar-a-plate dinners to be allowed to shake the hand of, or exchange a few words with, a politician; the résumé, application forms, and interviews needed for a job or unemployment benefits; the physical exam as a condition for acceptance by some health insurance company; the fee for joining a golf club, etc.—all prerequisites for achievement of some temporary and limited benefits—with the most valuable free offer from man's Creator, an offer guaranteed by His omnipotence, omniscience, and love of man demonstrated through the blood of the crucified Jesus Christ, and verified throughout history by millions of dedicated disciples, which makes its rejection quite unreasonable if not outright foolish.

[12]To understand the gravity of the Lord's demand of total life, of full commitment, it is proper to review Jesus' answers to some of the would-be followers (Luke 9:57–62), His promise of help (1 Cor. 10:13), and of the purpose of trouble in the believer's life as well (Rom. 8:28).